Don't Look Back

Don't Look Back

Olympic Skiing Competitor
and Coach Shares His Story
and Training Program

John Morton

STACKPOLE
BOOKS

Published by
STACKPOLE BOOKS
Cameron and Kelker Streets
P.O. Box 1831
Harrisburg, PA 17105

Printed in the United States of America

10   9   8   7   6   5   4   3   2   1

First edition

Line drawings by Peter Gallenz,
U.S. Biathlon Team
Cover design by Mark Olszewski
Cover photo by John Morton
Interior design by Marcia Lee Dobbs
Interior photos by John Morton unless otherwise credited

Library of Congress Cataloging-in-Publication Data

Morton, John, 1946–
    Don't look back : Olympic skiing competitor and coach shares his
story and training program / John Morton.
        p.   cm.
    Includes bibliographical references and index.
    ISBN 0-8117-2434-4
    1. Cross-country skiing.   I. Title.
GV855.3.M66   1992
796.93′2 — dc20   91-34326
                                                              CIP

This book is dedicated to

Shirley Morton, who introduced me to skiing;

Mimi and Julie Morton, who have endured with patience and support the highs and lows, as well as the extended absences, that are part of the career of coaching;

and more than a decade of Dartmouth Ski Team Members, from 1978 through 1989: Olympians and World Champions, as well as nonracers from Palo Alto to New York City; young student athletes whose enthusiasm, energy, and commitment made coaching them both challenging and infinitely rewarding.

Contents

Acknowledgments

THIS BOOK IS really a group project. Scores of people have encouraged, brainstormed, proofread, edited, typed, and offered constructive criticism. My special thanks to Bruce Adams, Dave Bradley, John Caldwell, Dave Chioffi, Marge and Reuben Cole, Jay Davis, Dennis Donahue, John Donovan, Peter Dorsen, M.D., Eric Evans, Elizabeth and Ted Fay, Peter Gallenz, Win Griffith, Peter Hale, Alex Kahan, Bob Kean, Tom Kelly, Don Mattersdorf, Joe Medlicott, Sally Metz, Ruff Patterson, Jeff Robbins, and Rob Sleamaker. Without their support this book would never have been completed.

I am also indebted to three genuine professionals at Stackpole Books. Mary McGinnis, Judith Schnell, and Joyce Spitzer transformed my original idea (and clumsy manuscript) into the finished product.

Finally, I am grateful to coaches and mentors that have taught me the joys of Nordic skiing: John Caldwell, Ted Garland, Marty Hall, Sven Johanson, Jim Mahaffey, Al Merrill, Dick Mize, Lynn Roumagoux, and Bobo Sheehan. Without the inspiration and example they provided, this book would never have been written.

Preface

CROSS-COUNTRY SKIING is not an exact science. Even though the sport has been influenced dramatically by recent technological changes, there are still countless variables that make consistent top performance all but impossible. This observation is borne out at the World Cup or Olympic level of international competition, where year after year different individuals from various nations emerge as champions.

During my eight years of international racing and fifteen years of coaching, I have tried to figure out why the Europeans and Soviets are so strong in Nordic skiing and what we Americans must do individually and as a nation to compete successfully with them. We have had fleeting moments of brilliance: John Bower's Nordic Combined victory at the 1968 Holmenkollen, Bill Koch's 1976 Olympic 30K silver medal and 1982 World Cup, Josh Thompson's 1987 Biathlon World Championship silver medal, and Anna Sonnerup's 1990 silver medal in a World Cup Biathlon Competition. These successes have not been representative of a strong national effort in Nordic skiing, but rather the determination, perseverance, and talent of individual athletes.

There are five major areas of concentration that must be recognized and addressed if an athlete is to succeed in Nordic skiing. Victory results from skillfully keeping these areas in balance.

Conditioning. Anyone who has entered a cross-country ski race realizes almost immediately the rewards of being fit. World-class Nordic racers are aerobically the best-conditioned athletes on earth. Scores of books, hundreds of articles, and countless hours of brainstorming have been dedicated to training for the Nordic racer.

Technique. Technique, along with conditioning, probably commands 90 percent of the attention of cross-country athletes and coaches. No matter how impressive a skier's conditioning, proper technique is essential to transmit the athlete's power efficiently to the snow. The focus on technique has been intensified by the relatively recent emergence of skating, or freestyle.

Nutrition and Health. Not long ago, when asked to analyze his team's impressive international results, prominent Swedish ski coach Kjell Kratz listed nutrition as an important factor. He said, in effect, that we could not demand such a high level of performance, both in training and in competition, without giving careful attention to the fuel used to generate that performance.

Although Nordic skiers are often regarded as "health freaks," in actuality a dedicated racer on a comprehensive training program is constantly flirting with illness. More cross-country races are lost because of the common cold than any other cause, perhaps than all other causes combined.

Equipment and Waxing. Technological changes have revolutionized our sport. Skis are lighter, faster, and more durable than ever before. Poles are lighter and stiffer. Significant advances in waxing seem to be made monthly. I used to take great pains to convince my high school ski team that "the skis don't win races, the competitor on the skis wins races!" Some of the recent technological advances in our sport (for better or worse) have challenged that remark. Today there are frequent instances where ski or wax selection have provided the winning edge.

Psychology. This category may, for the elite racer, be the least understood and yet the most important. All world-class competitors train hard, have excellent technique, eat well, and have access to good equipment. What separate true champions from everyone else are vague characteristics like determination, self-confidence, commitment, positive self-talk, and visualization. Since physical conditioning for cross-country skiing is so extensive, a racer's mental preparation is not limited to race day or even the competitive season; it becomes a matter of lifestyle.

Through years of coaching and competition I found these five components to be essential for victory. When an athlete appeared to be extremely successful, I usually found these areas in balance, but if a racer was having difficulty, it often reflected a weakness in one area or more. To help my athletes focus and remember each area, I began depicting them in the Olympic rings (which symbolize the five major continents).

The interlocking rings reinforce the concept that these five ingredients for success are interrelated — a skier's technique is directly affected by conditioning and wax, proper training requires a good diet and a positive mental attitude, and so forth. In fact, to be truly accurate, the rings should *all* interlock with one another.

The diagram can also serve as a reminder of the ultimate goal for many young skiers. Little League baseball players may dream of hitting a home run in the World Series, while high school football players fantasize about making the game-winning touchdown in the Super Bowl. For cross-country skiers the ultimate dream is to compete in the Winter Olympics.

In actuality, there is a sixth component to international success. I have not included it along with the others because, to put it simply, there is absolutely nothing we can do about it. This mysterious sixth category could be labeled

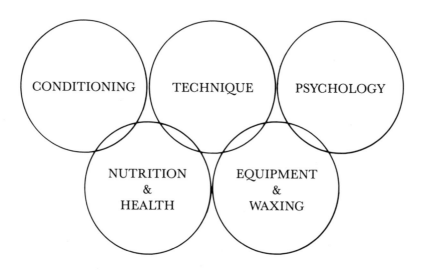

Natural Talent or even *Heredity*. Despite what Thomas Jefferson wrote in the Declaration of Independence, we are *not* all created equal. In terms of athletic success, an essential ingredient is natural talent. The truly exceptional champions — Ingmar Stenmark in Alpine skiing, Edwin Moses in the hurdles, Eric Heiden in speed skating, Alexander Tichonov in biathlon, and Gunde Svan in cross-country skiing — all have it. But natural talent is very difficult to define, and it is impossible to instill in anyone, short of carefully choosing one's parents (and even that is no guarantee). Those of us who are not especially "gifted" can take heart, because often our opponents with abundant natural talent seem to have a glaring weakness in one of the other five areas. In some sports those athletes who are naturally gifted do rise to the top (sprinters in track and basketball players, for example), but in cross-country skiing a lack of natural talent can often be compensated for by careful attention to the other components.

So this will be my first and last reference to the sixth component for success in cross-country skiing. We were all endowed with a varying degree of natural talent, but this is totally beyond our control. Our task is to concentrate on the other five areas, which are within our control and will enhance whatever natural talent we do have.

In June 1989, after eleven years as head coach of men's skiing at Dartmouth College, I decided it was time for a change. I didn't regard it as a "mid-life crisis," although at forty-three years old with no firm plans for my next "career move," I suppose I displayed some of the classic symptoms. As I weighed various options, it became obvious that I had a strong desire to ski race again, after fifteen years of coaching. Since the 1976 Winter Olympics, my last major international competition, I don't know how many times I had thought, "If I only knew then what I know now!"

In a blaze of enlightenment I came up with the concept of this book: What if I trained and raced, incorporating my coaching experience, and wrote a book about the whole adventure? I could use myself as an example and a guinea pig, in the process giving the reader some tried and true methods for improving cross-country skiing performance. Of course, I might discover that much of what I had been preaching as a coach was out of date, inappropriate, or simply didn't work. So be it. I might as well find out and honestly present the results. Naturally it would be wonderful if, by using my own methods, I won the National Championships or even the World Championships, but in cross-country skiing *nothing* is a sure bet. In September 1989 my success in any of those events was pure fantasy.

So here it is, the story of a forty-three-year-old former Winter Olympian who made a realistic commitment to get back in competitive condition, master new techniques, and once again experience the thrill and excitement of cross-country ski racing. The narrative, roughly chronological, is interspersed with informative chapters on each of the above five components for success.

Perhaps the most challenging aspect of the entire project turned out to be selecting a title. After months of brainstorming, telephone conferences, and seeking the advice of various people, we settled on *Don't Look Back*. That phrase suggests an important rule of racing strategy—and it's a good guideline for those of us over-forty Masters competitors who may have been "hot shots" a couple of decades ago. Unlike many sports, cross-country skiing is something you can enjoy all your life, something you can look *forward* to. But, as you will see, much of the book consists of reflections and anecdotes that are in fact glances back over thirty years of Nordic skiing. I'm admitting this in advance, so please don't tell me the title is a contradiction.

I sincerely hope that the book provides reading enjoyment, helps you derive more pleasure from cross-country skiing, and perhaps even contributes to improved results for American athletes both nationally and internationally. I look forward to seeing you on the trails.

John Morton
Thetford, Vermont

1: Ancient History

NORDIC SKIING HAS been a major facet of my life for almost thirty years. I grew up in the small town of Walpole, in southwestern New Hampshire. When I was about ten, my mother bought me some rummage-sale ski equipment, bundled me up in warm clothes, and pushed me out the door saying, "It's a disgrace that we live in the heart of ski country and you kids spend all winter in front of the television." Our house was high on a hill surrounded by cow pastures, so I could ski in any direction.

In those days I specialized in two events: slalom and jumping (using the terms very loosely). I would take a run down a pasture, then sidestep back up. If the snow was dry and cold, I would pack out a zigzag slalom course, sometimes using my ski poles for the most strategic gates. If the snow was wet and could be worked, I would build a jump, packing a straight inrun leading to the mounded-snow takeoff and a wide landing hill. I'd use my poles to generate speed down the inrun and drop them at the last instant. Sidestepping back up the landing hill, I would inspect my ruts. If they were far enough down the hill to warrant measurement, I would take off my skis, place them end to end, and measure my flight. A good ride was five or six ski lengths, thirty to thirty-five feet. I always did pretty well at the Ramsey Hill Road Ski Flying Tournaments. There are advantages to being chief of hill, announcer, jumping judge, and sole competitor.

When I was an eighth-grader, a fellow in our town asked my mother if I had ever considered going away to prep school. He was a graduate of Tilton School in central New Hampshire, which had just established a scholarship program for deserving northern New England students. At the time, Walpole had a graduating class of slightly more than twenty, mostly girls since many of the boys quit school at sixteen to work on the farms. There were three varsity sports: basketball, baseball, and soccer (in its infancy and still struggling).

Tilton intrigued me because it had a wide range of varsity sports, including cross-country running, football, tennis, track, and skiing. I asked my mother if I could apply for a scholarship, take the tests, and see what might happen. I was awarded a scholarship amounting to 50 percent of the school's tuition and decided to accept.

It wasn't all smooth sailing that first year at Tilton. As a scholarship student, I felt obligated to work hard, compete in sports, and live up to the school's expectations. On the other hand, the ski team had a small rope tow a few miles south of town. I was thrilled to actually be part of a ski team with the luxury of a rope tow after all my days of sidestepping up cow pastures.

Home for Thanksgiving, I talked my mother into taking me to the Army/ Navy store in Brattleboro, Vermont, to buy new ski equipment. I picked out midpriced West German skis, wooden of course, but with metal edges and plastic-coated bottoms. I got what the salesman recommended for bindings and a pair of leather boots with inner and outer lacings (a big step up for me). I was thrilled with my new gear, ready to take on the world.

After the 1960 Winter Olympics in Squaw Valley, Egon Zimmerman, the Austrian Olympic downhill ace, married Penny Pitou and the couple went to work at the nearby Gunstock Ski Area. Tilton arranged for Egon to coach our ski team one day a week at our little rope tow. He looked like an Olympian — tall and thin, deeply tanned face, with a broad smile and quick, sharp eyes. He had wavy brown hair and never wore a hat — an earband maybe — on the coldest days. His English was rough, and we strained to make out the words. He talked about hard work, about learning to ski before we could race. He asked names, shook hands, patted shoulders down the line. When he got to me, he stared at my skis, then asked, "Where you get this skis? You can't race on this shit!" Egon didn't beat around the bush.

I did race on "that shit" for at least a year because it was all I had. I know Egon's remark influenced my own coaching almost fifteen years later. I've always emphasized to my athletes that proper maintenance and care of your equipment is important, but the specific brand you ski on is almost irrelevant. Great racers can win on almost anything, and do.

Tilton provided me with two significant opportunities: it introduced me to cross-country and it directed me toward college. Every year the prep school ski season culminated in the Eastern Prep School Championships. These four-event competitions were usually hosted by a college and included all the major prep school teams in the East. My sophomore year at Tilton the championships were hosted by Middlebury College in Vermont. I remember being impressed by the campus and the college-owned ski facilities, but most of all I remember being approached in the dining hall by college students who asked us how we had done and what we thought of their Snow Bowl. There was genuine interest in our Prep School Championships, a wholesome appreciation of skiing — and girls! After more than a year and a half of the puritanical discipline of a traditional all-male prep school, sharing the Middlebury dining hall with beautiful college women created a strong impression.

The fall of my senior year at Tilton, I announced confidently to the college guidance counselor that I was going to apply "early decision" to Middlebury. He suggested a couple of backup schools, to which I responded, "It's Middlebury or nowhere." In retrospect, I'm embarrassed by my naiveté. I wasn't a straight A student, and I certainly wasn't a superstar ski racer. But I made clear my desire to attend Middlebury, and fortunately I was accepted.

The first meeting of the Middlebury Ski Team in the fall of 1964 took place the evening of the opening day of classes. The head coach, Bobo Sheehan, was a legendary character with a red face, a husky voice, and a free-wheeling attitude. As a World War II carrier pilot in the Pacific, Bobo had seen it all and wasn't bothered much by bureaucratic procedures or academic protocol. The ski team at Middlebury was the elite athletic group on campus and Bobo had a pretty free rein with budgets, class absences, and equipment procurement.

In the opening meeting Bobo introduced the returning upperclassmen — superstars of International Ski Federation (FIS) or National Championship fame like Gordi Eaton, John Clough, Peter Ruschp, and Roger Buchika. Then he introduced the promising incoming freshmen (I was not mentioned). He wrapped up the meeting with the following comments: "Now look you guys, good Alpine skiers around here are a dime a dozen." (There were self-conscious smirks around the room.) "If you want to make this ski team, you'd better get in shape and you'd better plan to race cross-country!"

Was that music to my ears! My junior year at Tilton I had filled in for an injured teammate in a cross-country race. Not only did I outscore our regular cross-country skiers, but I actually enjoyed the race (something any decent Alpine racer would never admit). By senior year at Tilton I was a capable four-event skier (downhill, slalom, jumping, and cross-country), but I was beginning to have my best results in cross-country.

So I tried to tag along unobtrusively with the upperclassmen I knew made up Middlebury's cross-country team as they informally trained through the fall. One afternoon as I checked behind the field house for a pickup soccer game, Gordi Eaton yelled to me from his car: "Hey, freshman, we're headed to the Bowl for a hike. Ya wanna go?" By coincidence, there were three Alpine skiers, Eaton, Buchika, and Clough, and three Nordic "apes," Dennis Donahue, "Zippy" Wells, and me. After a hair-raising ride through Ripton (Alpine racers never take their time going anywhere), we arrived at the Snow Bowl. It was a crisp, crystal-clear autumn day, the brilliant reds and golds of the foliage just about at peak.

After a few minutes of stretching, Gordi jogged toward the base station of the lift with the rest of us in tow. As the hill became steeper, I expected him to slip into a strong hiking pace, but he just kept jogging from one rock or hummock to the next. It became a contest to see who would drop off first. My thighs burned, but as the only freshman I was determined to keep up. The steady jog continued right up the lift line to the summit station. With sweat pouring and pulses pounding, we stretched and admired the magnificence of the Adirondacks beyond Lake Champlain.

Then Gordi was off, with some challenge shouted over his shoulder, blasting full tilt down the ski trail. Back at the base, with knees like rubber, we staggered toward the car.

"That was great!" said Gordi with conviction.

"Yeah, let's do it again," responded Buchika.

Gordi whipped around with fire in his eyes and a tight smile on his face. Without a word, he jogged back toward the mountain! The rest of us looked at each other in disbelief. He had to be bluffing! But he reached the base of the lift and kept jogging, never looking back. We ran to catch up. I don't remember much of that second trip up the mountain, except that my thighs and calves burned till they cramped, but I didn't get left behind. When we finally staggered to the car, nobody said a thing.

As we unloaded at the field house, Gordi called casually, "Hey, John, you can go with us any time we have room." I walked back to my freshman dorm feeling like I had just won an Olympic medal.

Middlebury was great to me. I worked hard academically but I lived for skiing. My best friends were the members of the ski team, which amounted to an informal fraternity.

Middlebury also had required ROTC (Reserve Officer Training Corps) for all freshman and sophomore males. It was a pain in the butt — regulation haircuts (embarrassingly short by Beatles-era standards), Thursday afternoon drill sessions in full uniform, and a rinky-dink academic course that you couldn't fail even if you slept through all the classes and skipped the exams. But the army paid us forty dollars a month, and in 1964–65, with the Vietnam War seeming very distant and unreal, the military uniform still had a certain fascination for many of us.

At the start of the ski season my sophomore year, we traveled to Lyndonville, Vermont, for the traditional opening race of the Eastern Cross-Country schedule. Before the event I saw several guys in USA uniforms, none of whom I recognized. Since I had attended U.S. Cross-Country Team training camps in nearby Putney and knew most of the national team members by name, these impostors baffled me. After the race I learned they were members of the newly formed U.S. Biathlon Team, specializing in skiing and shooting. I also learned that most members of the team were active-duty military, assigned to Fort

Richardson, Alaska, fulfilling their military service by training for and competing in international biathlon races every winter in Europe. It didn't sound like bad duty to me!

After a few letters to Sven Johanson, the coach of the team, and George Wilson, secretary of the Army Sports Branch, I elected to stay in ROTC for my final two years at Middlebury. I was offered an ROTC scholarship, covering all tuition, books, and lab fees, plus my forty dollars per month cadet pay. The down side of the offer was a four-year (rather than two-year) active-duty obligation. After more letters to Alaska and Washington and more assurances that the four-year commitment would help my chances of assignment to the Biathlon Unit, I signed on the line, accepting the scholarship and the four-year commitment. The next decision was which branch of the army to select. At the time, there were ten options: the three combat arms (infantry, armor, and artillery) and seven support branches (such as finance, personnel, and transportation). Mr. Wilson advised that the infantry, the army's largest branch, could easily give up an officer to a special assignment like Biathlon. With a distinct uneasiness, I signed up for the infantry.

My final year at Middlebury was filled to the brim. I was a reasonably strong contender for the 1968 Winter Olympic Team, although most of the guys who made the team were either finished with college or had taken the year off to train. I commuted between first-semester final exams in Middlebury and the Olympic tryout races in Putney and failed to make the team. The Olympic ambition and conscientious fall training did serve me well on the college racing circuit, however. I won all the collegiate cross-country races in the East and finished three seconds out of first place in the NCAA Championships in Steamboat Springs, Colorado.

Late in May 1968, just before graduation, I was faced with still another military decision. As a result of the scholarship, my athletic and academic performance, and my competence in the final two years of ROTC, I was designated a Distinguished Military Graduate. If that had meant a certificate or a plaque, it would have been fine, but the designation of Distinguished Military Graduate carried with it the promise of a regular army commission. For someone planning a military career, the RA commission is a godsend. It means that the military cannot "rift" you out against your wishes. You can count on the job security of a minimum twenty-year hitch whether it is peacetime or wartime. My intentions, on the other hand, were to get to the Biathlon Training Center in Alaska as fast as possible after I went on active duty and to stay there for my four-year obligation. If all worked according to plan, I would serve my military hitch training and competing in biathlon and cap the four years off at the 1972 Olympics in Sapporo.

The down side of the RA commission was that the military did not have to let you out. In other words, an RA officer could not be released from service against his will, but he could be retained in the army against his will if "the needs of the service" dictated his retention. This dilemma prompted yet another conference with George Wilson. He enthusiastically congratulated me on my selection as DMG and wholeheartedly endorsed the RA commission. It virtually assured my assignment to Alaska, he said; since the army had me indefinitely, they wouldn't mind letting me ski for a few years. I tried to remind him that I wasn't interested in a military career. He suggested I might change my mind after I'd been in for a while. I came away from the conversation more uncertain than ever, but Mr. Wilson was the man who controlled the assignments to the Biathlon Training Center, so I figured I should follow his recommendations. The day I graduated from Middlebury, I loaded my car and drove to Indiantown Gap, Pennsylvania, for ROTC Summer Camp.

In retrospect, I think there were two purposes to the nine-week training session. The first was to give us "smart assed" college kids (soon to be officers) a crash course on the military. Our weekly drills and classroom stuff back on campus hadn't even scratched the surface. But more important, as ROTC cadets we were among the lowest grubs on the military totem pole. Privates in the mess hall ordered us around, referring to us as "whaleshits" (nothing on earth sinks lower than that). In nine memorable weeks we learned firsthand what it was like to be an enlisted man in the army, a feeling no officer (even a general) should ever forget.

My ski training served me well. We jogged double time in formation from one training site to another; we did hundreds of push-ups; we did chin-ups on a bar outside the mess hall before every meal. For the nonathletes this amounted to torture. Captain Meade, our cadre platoon leader, was big on physical training (PT) and made it clear our goal was to win the company PT test. This test totaled each unit's combined score on five different events: the grenade throw; the overhead bars; the low crawl; the run, dodge, and jump; and the mile run. When Captain Meade saw that I was in decent shape, he asked to see me in his office. He relieved me from the drudgery of KP and guard duty in exchange for my promise that I would train for and win the mile run. Weeks later I plodded in combat boots around the cinder track, finishing ahead of the other cadets in our battalion. From the look on Meade's face, I had made him very happy, and maybe even a little richer.

From Indiantown Gap it was on to Fort Benning, Georgia, and the Infantry Officers' Basic Course. I had been commissioned at the completion of summer camp and put immediately on active duty, which suited me fine. The sooner I completed Infantry Officers' Basic, the sooner I would be in Alaska training for biathlon. I arrived at Fort Benning about a third of the way through the basic course cycle, too late to join the course in progress. I was assigned a comfortable room and instructed to stay out of trouble for a few weeks until the next cycle began.

I quickly searched out the Advanced Marksmanship Training Center and timidly introduced myself to Colonel Pullum, the unit's commanding officer, explaining my intention to compete for the Biathlon Team upon completion of the Officers' Basic Course. I mentioned my current "snowbird" status until the next cycle began.

"Goddam, that's great!" he shouted. "For once we'll get the chance to teach a ski-shooter how to hit the target before they screw you all up in Alaska!"

Under the guidance of my personal coach, Lt. Nels Nelson, I learned all the basics of position shooting, practiced several hours a day, and met a few of the world's best marksmen. One of the most colorful was Lt. Jack Writer, an intense, high-strung guy who would go on to win Olympic, Pan-American, and World Championship medals, in the process setting new world records. If three rounds out of fifty missed the bull's-eye (slightly larger than the diameter of a bullet), Writer was furious. One day on the fifty-meter range we were working on offhand (standing) shooting. Jack broke everyone's concentration by excitedly yelling, "Look at target fifteen. Hey, everybody, watch fifteen!" We obediently swung our scopes to fifteen to see the telltale hole dead center of the bull. A second glance revealed a large horsefly walking deliberately across the top of the white paper target. The fly was barely visible to the naked eye.

"All right you guys, watch this," said Writer. We heard the bolt close smoothly on a round. Then silence as we stared through the scopes. At the sound of the shot the fly disappeared, replaced by a bullet hole on the paper flanked on either side by the fly's wings.

Finally my snowbirding days came to an end as the next IOBC cycle began, and I became immersed in the world of the infantry officer. It was pretty unsettling for a couple of reasons. First of all, everyone else in my course was RA, most of them from West Point, Virginia Military Institute, or The Citadel. These guys were the real McCoy—they cherished that RA commission, and they were all on the first step of the ladder they were sure would ultimately lead them to the Joint Chiefs of Staff. Boy, did I feel out of place! Second, all of the problems and exercises we studied and rehearsed at Benning were oriented specifically to Vietnam. Our instructors were all Vietnam returnees who added impact to their classroom presentations with firsthand experiences. My classmates ate this up. The sooner they got their "tickets punched" with a combat tour, the sooner they would move up the ladder. It motivated me to fill out a 1049 (a form used to request personnel action such as a change of assignment) asking to be assigned to the Biathlon Training Center, Fort Richardson, Alaska, upon completion of IOBC.

Several weeks later, as our course was winding down, a friend who had pulled CQ (charge of quarters) duty the previous night casually mentioned that my 1049 was in the first sergeant's desk drawer! When I confronted the first sergeant about it, he smiled good-naturedly and said, "Lieutenant, you're not going to Alaska. This whole cycle of RA officers is going to ranger school, then to Fort Polk, Louisiana, then to the 'Garden Spot of Southeast Asia.'" Within minutes I was on the phone to George Wilson in Washington, explaining in detail the first sergeant's attempts to block my assignment to Alaska. Mr. Wilson listened patiently, then, to my horror, confirmed everything the first sergeant had said.

"It's much more important for your career that you get ranger school and that first combat tour out of the way now. Who knows how long this Vietnam thing will last? You may not get another chance for combat experience."

"But I don't want combat experience!" I pleaded. "I'm not interested in a military career! I'm interested in the Sapporo Olympics and I've leveled with you about that from the start!"

"Sorry about that Lieutenant," he answered dryly. "The needs of the service come first. Contact me about Biathlon when you return stateside."

Panic set in. The prospect of the Olympics in Sapporo became very remote, while a tour in Vietnam seemed very real. Within a week I was a graduate of IOBC signed into the ranger company, doing push-ups in the gravel outside ranger headquarters for some hard-core, badass airborne ranger NCO who was going to whip me into shape before they shipped me to Vietnam. Before our ranger cycle began there were a couple of days of slack time. I lied about my mother being seriously ill, signed out on four days' emergency leave, hopped in my car, and headed north. Almost twenty-four hours later, having driven straight through the night, I was at the Office of Personnel, Infantry Branch, outside Washington, D.C. I found the major who controlled the assignments of all infantry second lieutenants. He was a huge man who could have played defensive tackle for any NFL team in the country. I explained my situation, skipping any mention of George Wilson or the Army Sports Branch. I expected this major to toss me out on my ear. When I had finished, he leaned back in his chair, put his hands behind his head, and said, "Sheeit, Lieutenant, Arthur Ashe is one of my boys. I send him a telegram every time he wins a big match for Uncle Sam! These guys in Alaska want you?"

"Yes sir," I responded enthusiastically. "Give them a call on the AUTOVON [military telephone system]."

We talked a while and he agreed to call Alaska later in the day (they were five hours behind the East Coast). When I returned in the afternoon, the Major was all smiles. "Yep, they want you all right," he said. "I'll have your orders out in a couple of days and sent to the Ranger Company at Benning."

By noon the following day I was on my way back to Fort Benning with orders releasing me from ranger school. Nobody at Fort Benning could change those orders, but they certainly made it difficult for me to leave. I had to sign out of places on that post I had never seen before. At the dispensary they gave me about a dozen inoculations (some of which I had already received a few weeks earlier). I've been nervous about needles ever since. It took me five days to clear post, which is normally accomplished in one or two.

I arrived in Anchorage on November 7, 1968, and by Christmas had earned a spot on the twelve-man contingent traveling to Putney, Vermont, for the Biathlon National Championships and tryouts for the World Championships scheduled for Zakopane, Poland. The races in Putney went well, and I was one of six headed for Europe in early February. Our first stop was Chamonix, France, and a large international biathlon competition. I was the top American, in eighth place. Then it was on to Switzerland for their national championships, where I again placed among the top Americans. We settled into the beautiful alpine village of Klosters for several days of training before heading to Poland and the World Championships.

None of us offered much of a challenge to the Scandinavians, the East Germans, or the Russians in Zakopane, and we didn't win any medals in Andermatt at the Military Championships either, but we learned a lot and returned to Alaska determined to train harder for the 1970 season.

In April I took a month's leave to drive my car from the East to Alaska since it looked like I would be in the frozen North for a while. Mimi Seemann, a friend I had dated a couple of times at Middlebury, had never seen the West Coast and agreed to accompany me as far as Seattle. By the time we reached the Pacific we were in love, and a week after arriving in Anchorage we were married. I moved out of bachelor officers' quarters and into married officers' quarters with my new bride and began to concentrate on training for the winter.

The 1970 Biathlon World Championships were held in Östersund, Sweden, and biathlon team coach Sven Johanson couldn't have been more proud. It was bitterly cold, hovering around −20°F, so we used all of our Alaskan tricks to stay warm; socks over our ski boots and more socks stuffed in the fronts of our knickers.

Östersund held mixed memories for me. I skied my brains out in the 20K race and finished totally exhausted, only to discover I had placed third from

Sven Johanson, coach of the U.S. Biathlon Training Center at Fort Richardson, Alaska. He coached all of America's biathletes from 1960 to 1974. Peter Hale

last. I still can't figure that one out. Sloppy shooting didn't help, but I think I wanted so badly to do well that I tightened up and beat myself to a pulp in the skiing. I felt humiliated.

In spite of my dismal 20K result, I was selected to ski the relay and resolved to redeem myself. I shot clean (hit all the targets) and skied fast, turning in the eleventh-fastest leg of the day. Although a couple of the other fellows on the relay team had trouble and we finished a disappointing tenth overall, I came away confidant that I could ski and shoot with the best of them.

When we returned from Europe and checked in at the Biathlon Office at Fort Richardson, a bitter, disillusioned NCO, who shuffled our paperwork and counted the days until his retirement, announced casually, "Oh, Lieutenant Morton, your orders came in."

I was mystified.

"What orders?" I asked.

With a long pause for effect and a sense of drama he must have rehearsed for weeks, he reached into his desk drawer and responded brightly, "Why your orders for Vietnam, sir," delight beaming from his face. As he handed me the thick packet of mimeographed orders, it was as if I had been hit in the chest with a sledgehammer. It was all I could do to maintain some semblance of composure, if for no other reason than to deny the sergeant the pleasure of seeing me suffer.

Over the next weeks and months I contacted everyone I could think of who might have the clout to get the orders changed. I pointed out that since I was an RA officer, the army had me for as long as it wanted me. I asked only that the Vietnam tour be postponed until after the 1972 Winter Olympics. The responses were all the same: "Due to equity in infantry officer assignments and career development programming, it is essential . . ."

Naively, I sought help from George Wilson.

"Sorry, Lieutenant, nothing I can do. If you'd gone when I advised you, you'd be back by now," was his comment. It wasn't until then that it occurred to me he might have "pulled my card" on purpose to admonish me for having previously gone over his head.

In August 1970 I boarded a stretched DC-8 at Elmendorf Air Force Base in Anchorage. Several hours later I walked off the plane into an oven at Tan Son Nhut airport in Saigon. I gasped for air in the stifling heat as I descended the stairs. As I hit the pavement, I heard jeering and catcalls from a large group of men behind a chain-link fence. I stared in disbelief. Many had shoulder-length hair and Fu Manchu mustaches. Their clothes were faded, bleached almost white by the sun. They wore necklaces and bracelets woven from bootlaces and grenade safety pins. A wave of understanding crashed over me. "Jesus," I thought, "they're Americans! They're our guys!" As the troops sauntered toward the empty plane, they still taunted us by singing, "You're going home in a body bag, doo da, doo da; you're going home in a body bag, yea doo da day."

It is one of my most vivid memories from Vietnam, and I wondered for a long time whether, if I was lucky and survived my tour, I would look like them when I rotated home.

Soon I was off to the Mekong Delta to "win the hearts and minds of the people." It was the land of canals and rice paddies, not much suitable terrain for ski training. My one foot-running workout during five months in the delta consisted of jogging several miles up Route 4 closely followed by a jeep driven by our team medic, Sergeant Boone, with Sergeant Smith riding shotgun, his M-16 across his knees. It was a one-shot deal. My district senior advisor, a tough, no-nonsense West Pointer, called me in for a little chat soon after my workout.

Major Haushill (in a loud, irritated voice): "Just what the hell were you doing?"

Captain Morton (sheepishly): "Going for a run, sir."

Major Haushill: "Well, that's the last goddam run you're going for in my district! First of all, you pull that stunt more than twice and the VC will take care of you *and* the jeep right in broad daylight. Second, what the hell are the locals supposed to think? You look more like some goddam criminal being punished than a mobile advisory team leader!"

Captain Morton (voice dripping with repentance): "I see your point, sir. It won't happen again . . . Sir!"

Major Haushill (mumbling): "You're goddam right it won't."

After several months I learned that GIs had occasionally received up to sixty days' "curtailment" of their 365-day assignment in Vietnam and still retained full credit. I approached my commanding officer about the possibility of a curtailment to train for the Olympics. He went to bat for me in a big way. Within a few days he had arranged a fifty-seven-day "drop" and a reassignment to the Biathlon Training Center in Alaska. Motivated by the reassignment orders and a transfer within Vietnam to the Advisor school as an instructor, I resumed training on a daily basis.

My readjustment to the team was a little rocky. First of all, the countdown to the tryouts and the Olympics was heating up. At least a dozen guys, many of whom had been training intensively for the past several years, had a reasonable shot at the six Olympic team slots. An informal pecking order had developed and I wasn't part of it. My return and unanticipated level of fitness had thrown some of the guys for a loop. Adding to the state of confusion, in a blatantly political move, Sven Johanson had been replaced as Olympic coach. Among the athletes feelings ran strong either in support of Sven or his adversaries.

The tryouts in Jackson, Wyoming, in January were a disaster. If they had been held in 1988 rather than 1972, the lawyers would have had a field day with suits and countersuits ad infinitum. Races were canceled or postponed, results of completed races were thrown out, and a race that was held in a blizzard of heavy wet snow and should have been canceled counted. But the Olympic Team was named (amid much grumbling and ill will), and I was on it.

A second set of tryouts in Sapporo went well, and I looked forward to racing at least the Olympic 20K event. But when a starting list was posted in the press center, my name was not among the American entries. How was this possible, considering my results in Jackson and in Sapporo? Then it occurred to me that our best chance for success was the relay. Jay Bowerman had earned a spot on the relay team with a good race in Jackson, but his shooting had been inconsistent. Perhaps the coaches were planning to race Jay in the twenty and put me in the relay?

A week or so later the relay teams were posted. I was not on the relay team either! I came unglued. Barely able to contain my emotion, I asked to see the coach and team leader alone in the wax room. I asked, as calmly as I could, how they had selected their racers, on what results they had based their decisions, and why I was not among those chosen to race.

The team leader hung his head and wouldn't look at me, but the coach who had replaced Sven lashed out with a fury that caught me off guard: "You don't *deserve* any explanation at all. In fact, you don't *deserve* anything! You came back from Vietnam thinking you *deserved* a spot on this team and you *deserved* to race in the Olympics! Well, Morton, *we* decide who races here and who doesn't, and you don't *deserve* anything. Does that answer your questions?"

I left the room confused and completely spent. My wife, Mimi, who was at the Olympics as a spectator, probably saved me from a mental breakdown or at least the potentially serious consequences of beating the shit out of the coach.

I survived the 1972 Olympics like you survive a death in the family: little by little the pain fades away and you remember the bright spots. Back in Alaska at the end of the winter, my wife and I had a family conference. I had planned to resign my commission, the four-year ROTC commitment having been fulfilled, and retire from biathlon competition. I was still eager to be a civilian, but Sapporo had left a very sour taste in my mouth concerning biathlon. Mimi encouraged me to hang in there for four more years and try for the Innsbruck Olympics.

The winter of 1973 I raced with a vengeance and finished twenty-fourth in the World Championships. Friendships flourished with athletes from other countries, especially Norwegians and Soviets. I earned credible results in 1974 in the Soviet Union and in 1975 in Italy, even though by that time I was a full-time high school teacher (on a leave of absence for the World Championships).

The 1976 Olympic biathlon team was divided between promising young newcomers and seasoned veterans. Dennis Donahue and I were the old men of the team. Before setting up shop in Seefeld, the alpine village in the mountains above Innsbruck where the Olympic Nordic events would be held, we raced in Chamonix, France, and in Italy. Through these preliminary races I had earned the opportunity to race the Olympic 20K individual event, but the relay team would be selected based on Olympic results. As we trained through the opening days of the Olympics, inspired by Bill Koch's phenomenal silver-medal performance in the 30K cross-country, several of my teammates were struck down by a stomach virus. I sympathized, but I was intensely focused on the upcoming 20K. Before dawn on the morning of the event, I awoke sweating with an ominous churning in my stomach. For a couple of minutes I tried to convince myself it was just nerves, but when the waves of nausea forced me to dash down the hall, there was no question I had succumbed to the virus.

My starting number must have been jinxed. Less than five minutes into the race, Peter Dascoulias, who had taken my place, fell on a tricky section of track, broke his rifle stock in half, and was forced to abandon the race. A disappointing day for American ski-shooters.

The fallout from the 20K was that the coaches were in a real pickle in terms of choosing a relay team. Dennis Donahue, with his consistently strong shooting, was an automatic selection. Lyle Nelson and Martin Hagen had both finished the 20K, but their results were not spectacular. Lyle was named to the relay team along with Dennis, and the remaining four of us were to ski a mock relay two days before the Olympic event to determine who would fill the final two slots.

On a beautiful, bright Austrian morning two days before the Olympic biathlon relay, four of us skied our brains out to determine who would represent the United States two days later. I hit all my targets, beat my closest teammates by almost thirty seconds, and finally, after twelve years of trying, earned the right to compete in the Olympics.

The Olympic relay was anticlimactic. Although I turned in our team's second-fastest leg (behind Lyle's spectacular leadoff effort), I was physically and emotionally spent from the virus and the time trial. I missed a target and skied half a minute slower in the real thing than I had in the rehearsal.

Back home in Alaska I settled into the rewarding routine of teaching and coaching at Dimond High School. No longer concerned about my own training schedule, I devoted myself to coaching the high school team. Under the expert guidance of Lynn Roumagoux, who had in the preceding years developed a skiing dynasty at Dimond, I learned fast.

In August 1977 our daughter, Julie, was born, and I figured we were Alaskans for good. Within a year, however, former biathlon friends in the East told me Dartmouth College was looking for a men's ski coach. Initially I wasn't interested. First of all, Dartmouth was the enemy; I could never work for them. Second, I wasn't sure I had had enough coaching experience to take on a big-name ski team like Dartmouth. Nevertheless, I was encouraged to apply, and when the dust settled, I had been offered the job! I felt honored to have been selected, and the thought of being closer to our families back East was appealing, so Mimi and I agreed to try it for a year. We leased our Alaskan home and headed to Hanover in the autumn of 1978, hitting town at exactly the same time as about a thousand wide-eyed freshmen.

It was the start of an eleven-year tenure as head coach of men's skiing — the most rewarding and at times the most frustrating years of my life. The athletes who were drawn to the Dartmouth Ski Team were intelligent, highly motivated, multifaceted young people who generated energy and excitement. They soon came to be, and still remain, my best friends. But to my amazement, I discovered that Dartmouth's historic prominence in skiing was regarded with complacency in Hanover. And the school's "tradition" had its bad side, tending to hamper innovation and creativity.

I wasn't bursting with optimism that autumn. But I figured I had three ace cards up my sleeve: Dave Thomas, Tim Moerlein, and Scott Taylor, all fine Nordic skiers I had coached in Alaska. But, in their senior year, Dave was focusing on academics and Tim's interest in racing had waned. (I couldn't blame Tim; I had seen many top Alaskan junior racers pushed too hard too early only to burn out before they reached their peaks.) Scott was a tough, scrappy Alaskan who, as a freshman, had finished seventh in the NCAA Championships (top American in the race). But in the fall of 1978 he was diagnosed with Hodgkin's disease.

The 1980 season brought a new challenge: the weather. With the Winter Olympics scheduled for Lake Placid, the eastern United States suffered its

Al Merrill pulled off a miracle and became a legend at the Lake Placid Olympics
by covering twenty-five kilometers of barren cross-country trails with man-made snow.
Dartmouth College Archives

worst snow year in decades. Al Merrill, on leave from Dartmouth to oversee the Nordic events, took a bold, innovative step. Rather than move the events north to Canada or cancel them altogether, Al announced that the Nordic races would go off on schedule at Lake Placid—on man-made snow! More than twenty-five kilometers of trail, mostly in dense woods, were covered with snow, one truckload at a time. The Nordic events at Lake Placid were a big success, and Al Merrill became an overnight legend in the international skiing community.

Back in Hanover, the mood was despondent. The Dartmouth Outing Club was faced with canceling the skiing events of the Winter Carnival, a yearly student extravaganza dating back to 1911. I suggested that we might attempt on a smaller scale what Al had done at the Olympics. Within a few days an army of volunteers was plowing, hauling, shoveling, and raking a two-foot-wide track that snaked for almost three kilometers over the brown grass of the golf course. We even covered the ski jump!

The carnival events went off without a hitch and drew more wildly cheering spectators than any other college skiing event in recent history.

But the warm glow of success didn't last long. Monday morning I was back on the golf course with the dean of the college, the business manager, the

The skiing was great at the 1980 Dartmouth Winter Carnival—as long as you didn't step off the track. Dartmouth College Archives

director of the Outing Club, the golf pro, the head greenskeeper, and other dignitaries, who took turns chewing me out because I hadn't gone through the proper channels to secure approval for our solution to the snowless winter, and driving the truck over the links had done several thousand dollars worth of damage to the grass, for which the ski team would be held responsible. Not one had a positive word to say about the students' effort and cooperation in conducting a very successful event under seemingly hopeless circumstances. (Nor did I hear anyone admit he might have overreacted when, in May, the golf course opened as green and lush as ever!)

The 1985 season was an emotional roller coaster, and the NCAA Championships in Bozeman, Montana, symbolized the entire year. Through a combination of successful recruiting, hard work, and excellent coaching by Mark Ford, our Alpine team was the best in the East. With our captain, Jory Macomber, leading a talented squad through the Eastern Winter Carnival season, Dartmouth's Alpine men emerged as the dominant team in the East and headed to Montana confident of strong results at the National Championships. In the opening event, the giant slalom, the men were superb, placing first as a team. But the real fireworks came from sophomore Tom Foote, a feisty, five-foot-six spark plug, who carved his way to the individual gold medal. At the finish line the Dartmouth guys were ecstatic: Both individual and team honors were a great way to begin!

Amid the excitement and laughter at the finish line, however, I noticed a pained look on Tom's face and I asked if he was okay.

"Yeah," he groaned, "I'm okay, just a wicked pain in my stomach. Probably just nerves. I was really up for this one." When the excitement had abated and the van was loaded for the drive back to the motel, "Footie" lost his lunch in the parking lot. Amid the ongoing teasing about his victory and his "case of nerves," Mark and I watched him carefully.

By morning it was clear Tom should see a doctor. Since it was a race day for cross-country and a training day for Alpine, Mark said he would take care of Tom. Around noon, as the cross-country race was winding down, an announcement over the loudspeaker called me to the race headquarters.

"Morty," said one of the race officials, steering me away from spectators and press, "you've got a problem! Tom Foote is in the hospital with acute appendicitis but will not allow the doctors to operate! They say his condition is serious. You'd better get right down there."

At the hospital the corridor outside Footie's room was filled with scowling nurses and doctors. The biggest of the group, in green operating scrubs with mask hanging below his chin, could have played defensive tackle for any NFL team. He grabbed me as I headed into the room.

"You his coach?" he demanded.

"Yes, I am," I answered surprised by the viselike grip on my arm.

"Well let me tell you something, Buster—that's one very sick kid in there. That appendix could burst any minute, and when it does, it will be one hell of a mess! I'm going to give you about two minutes to talk some sense into him before I wash my hands of the whole situation. You got that, coach?"

"Yes, doctor!" I headed into the room.

Footie didn't look too bad. He was sitting up in bed reading contentedly. He assured me he had had these types of stomach pains before and they had always gone away. He wasn't eager to go under the knife, as a recent knee operation had resulted in a slow and painful recovery.

I tactfully suggested a second opinion and ran the gamut of doctors and nurses in the hallway to find the doctor who had been recommended by Dartmouth alums living in Bozeman. I quickly found the doc and he graciously agreed to follow me back to Footie's room for a diagnosis.

As we walked the long, sparkling halls together, he smiled reassuringly. "You know, coach, there is one very reliable method of diagnosing appendicitis. If you press your hand gently and firmly on the patient's right abdomen, then release the pressure suddenly, the pain of appendicitis will launch the patient through the roof."

This doc was smooth! He chatted with Tom about the race, skiing in the West, and his college major, all the time conducting a general examination. Only after a few minutes of easygoing conversation and superficial inspection did he begin to gently palpate Tom's abdomen. The doc casually glanced at me as he steadily increased pressure on the right side of Tom's stomach. When he released his hand, Tom's yell could be heard halfway to Bridger Bowl! The doc put his hand on Tom's shoulder and in a matter-of-fact tone said, "Tom, you have acute appendicitis, no question about it! The best thing for us to do is get it out right away.

Tom, still recoiling from the pain, mumbled, "Okay, okay, okay." Ten minutes later his appendix was out; in a few days he had completely recovered.

The third day of competition at Bridger Bowl was the slalom, and the Dartmouth skiers were riding high. We had individual and team event champions in the giant slalom, and everyone was relieved that Footie was going to be okay.

Jory Macomber was primed. In his senior year he was Alpine co-captain and had had one of the strongest slalom seasons in the East. His first run was blistering—the fastest of the morning. But the slalom consists of two runs, and at the NCAAs everyone goes for broke; there would be no "cooling it" second run to protect his lead. The heavy, wet spring snow was tricky for the easterners, but Jory was the epitome of quiet confidence and determination. He blasted the second run with the same assurance and power that had led to his first-run victory. As the entire Dartmouth contingent watched, silently chanting, "He's gonna do it, he's gonna do it," Jory rocketed his way through the bottom half of the course. He was as good as home when, two gates from the finish, he hooked a tip on a pole and fell. It was devastating! To have skied so brilliantly for more than 140 gates and lose it two gates from the finish! None of us could quite believe it was over.

It took me several minutes to recover from the disbelief and a horrible, gut-wrenching empty feeling. Then I saw Jory standing alone several hundred yards below the finish. He wasn't whacking his poles in the snow in frustration (as is often the case in similar situations); he was just standing by himself, his back to the course and the finish line, looking at the magnificent skyline of Bridger Bowl. This is one of the most difficult and delicate moments in coaching — helping an athlete through the intense disappointment of a bitter defeat. Usually, in our own insecurity, we tend to say too much. I just skied up to him, put an arm around his shoulders, and gave a squeeze. Jory nodded a silent acknowledgment, and I could see the tears streaming down his face.

In my mind we had two national champions in 1985. Tom Foote skied one of the most dramatic giant slalom races of his impressive career and "blew the socks off" his competition. Jory Macomber, through his quiet leadership and inspiring Winter Carnival results, convinced his teammates they could win in Bozeman. And what took the most maturity and discipline was ignoring his personal disappointment in the slalom to celebrate the overall team success.

Certainly my worst nightmares during the eleven years at Dartmouth involved vans loaded with skiers on icy New England roads. Although we had our share of near misses, we were never involved in an accident. But one close call made me believe *someone* was looking out for us. We were heading home after a few days of training in northern New York, and it began to snow. I was tired, the van was heavily loaded, and snow was accumulating on the road — normal winter driving conditions for a ski coach. A glance in the rearview mirror revealed a van full of exhausted, snoring athletes.

We were descending a long, gradual hill somewhere near Lake George when the road fell away to the left. I turned the wheel but the van kept going straight toward the snowbank and guardrail. I pumped the brakes gently to no effect. I said calmly to my sleeping passengers, "Hold on, boys, we're going in!" and braced myself for the imminent crunch of the guardrail on our right side. Like some master magician's trick, we just disappeared into a "poof" of snow as we bashed through the roadside bank. No crunch of metal! We just seemed to float gently through the snow. Then I realized we were plowing through a roadside rest area blanketed by about a foot of new snow.

Before we came to a stop, I turned the wheel back toward the highway and accelerated. Without skidding or spinning wheels, we bulldozed our way back to the road, bashing through the snowbank onto the pavement. I resumed breathing several minutes down the road. I stole another glance at my passengers in the rearview mirror. This time they were awake, sitting up straight, eyes wide. I tried to sound casual: "I just thought you guys might need to stop to pee. Didn't notice till we pulled in that it was closed for the season."

Someone deadpanned, "We didn't need to go *that* bad!"

One aspect of fall training that was a constant headache was roller skiing. In fact, many of our roller-ski workouts had a pretty high stress level, and a few were downright terrifying. Falls on the pavement always produced serious abrasions, or "road rashes," as we called them. It wasn't uncommon in the autumn for several team members to have scabs on their elbows, knees, or butts the size of doughnuts.

Among the many traditions I had inherited from Jim Page, my predecessor at Dartmouth, was a fifty-kilometer roller-ski time trial that took place just before Thanksgiving vacation. It was a long, three-hour test that involved some very serious downhills, two with sharp turns into covered bridges. It had become a rite of passage for the freshmen, and since it was a time trial, there was motivation to "go for it" on the downhills.

After starting my dozen charges in Norwich at one-minute intervals, I leapfrogged along the route in the van providing water stations. By the time I reached the common on Thetford Hill, my skiers were spread out over forty-five minutes. I ran alongside as each athlete charged past, handing over a cup of water and cautioning about the steep, turning downhill into the Union Village covered bridge. It soon became decision time. I wanted to be on the turn above the covered bridge to warn the guys (especially the freshmen), but I knew I wouldn't make it if I waited for all the stragglers. I left some cups of water on the roadside and roared to the last pitch before the covered bridge. I thought I had caught and passed almost everyone, but I couldn't be sure. As I pulled the van off the road on the steepest section of the hill, my heart stopped. There was a ghastly smear of congealed blood across the road!

"Oh, God," I thought, imagining one of my skiers plowing into the hood of an oncoming car, the panicked driver throwing the broken body in the backseat for a fruitless trip to the hospital. At that instant a skier thundered around the corner. He was crouched low with legs spread and skis vibrating wildly on the rough pavement. Sparks were flying from his pole tips as he dragged them in a futile effort to slow down. His eyes widened with panic as he took in the steep, twisting approach to the quaint covered bridge.

I sprinted full bore down the road behind the skier and grabbed his waistband. As I slowed to a jog and then a walk, the panic left the skier's face. From a standing start, a hundred yards above the bridge, the turn was negotiable, so I released my grip and watched the skier roll smoothly into the covered bridge. Then, still terrified about whom I had missed, I sprinted back up the hill to intercept the next skier. One by one they roared into sight. I sprinted to catch them, slowed them to a stop, then raced back up the hill for the next.

It was such a scene that Joe Cook, a local celebrity whose house guards the entrance to the bridge, pulled a lawn chair to the edge of his porch and sat down to enjoy the show. As I sprinted up and down the hill in front of the house, Joe watched with the detached amusement of a world-class figure-skating judge. I half expected him to hold up the card "5.9" after I made an especially good save. I was still trying to remember who had been in the lead and was by now dying on the operating table back in Hanover. I was also trying to remember which of the less-experienced freshmen might have fallen behind and might still be coming. After several minutes of no skier traffic and several checks of the start list, I was pretty sure everyone had passed the bloody corner.

As I hiked up the hill for the last time, Joe Cook stood up from his lawn chair and began to clap. "Crisalmighty, that was great! You fellas gonna do this every Sunday morning?"

"Nope," I responded, "this is the last time as long as I'm involved." Then with a sense of dread, I asked, "Was there an accident here earlier, one of my guys hit by a car?"

"Huh?" Joe looked confused.

"All that blood on the road—did one of my guys get hit?"

Joe's face resolved itself into a broad smile. "Oh, that. Hell no. One of the Barker boys got hisself a nice little buck down by the river 'bout sunrise this mornin', had to drag it up the bank an' crost the road to 'is pickup. That's deer blood ya see there!"

The success of the Development Team skiers was one of the truly rewarding aspects of coaching at Dartmouth. Of course, it was exciting to recruit nationally prominent high school racers, help them adjust to the challenges of college life, and see them succeed in Winter Carnivals and the NCAA Championships. But there was something truly heartwarming about a kid from Palo Alto, California; Little Rock, Arkansas; or New York City with an intense desire to be part of this famous Dartmouth tradition and to become a respected member of the team. The dedicated ones would hang around Robinson Hall hoping for a vacant seat in the varsity van to the Skiway, or furtively eaves-dropping on a cross-country workout at the golf course in hopes of picking up a pointer or two. These guys referred to themselves (with a perverse kind of pride) as "The Gerb Squad."

Over the course of several years we legitimized the Gerb Squad with a van, a part-time coach, a competitive schedule, uniforms, and most impor-tant, the assurance that if and when one of their members challenged a mem-ber of the varsity, they would be promoted to the varsity. Spirit and pride blossomed, and without an ultimatum from me, "Gerb Squad" disappeared from our vocabularies.

It was, in fact, the success of the Development Team that, among other things, led to my departure from Dartmouth. We were mobbed with Dart-mouth students who wanted to be part of the team. Budget and coaching support was always a year or more behind demand, so we were stressed to the limit. The Alpine coaches felt the pressure the most as they jockeyed for training space on the limited terrain at the Skiway. I hadn't realized the extent of their frustration until, at a typical staff meeting, they railroaded through a proposal to drastically limit the size of the Development Team. As head coach of the Men's Team, I refused to support the plan. I was later overruled. It became increasingly clear to me that the head coach of men's skiing no longer directed the course nor interpreted the philosophy of the oldest collegiate ski team in the nation. I had become a caretaker following the dictates of adminis-trators who had no experience in skiing.

In March 1989 I stuck my neck out and wrote a comprehensive proposal outlining how the ski team's administration could be streamlined and modern-ized. After several weeks without a response, I learned that my proposal had been reviewed by the appropriate administrators and no further action would be forthcoming. With an overwhelming feeling of frustration, I composed a letter of resignation, indicating the lack of administrative interest in my pro-posal as the major reason.

I had felt that my drastic action would shake the administrators out of their apathy, but days passed without even an acknowledgment of my resigna-tion. Then it hit home. I had resigned effective June 1, 1989, and no one was going to stop me. Maybe I had been too demanding on behalf of my skiers. Maybe I knew too much about how the admissions process worked (or didn't work). At any rate, someone in the administration felt the ski team would run more smoothly without me. After initial anger, I resolved to concentrate on the future and have my office cleaned out by June 1.

It was a tough spring. It was hard for me to imagine not coaching at Dartmouth and impossible to imagine coaching anywhere else. In fact, I had no idea what I wanted to do. Coaching had flowed naturally from my love of skiing, but I hadn't grown up planning to be a ski coach. A gnawing fear grew in my stomach that I had just thrown away the most coveted ski-coaching job in the country, and I didn't even have a clue as to what I wanted to do next.

When the news started to filter through the skiing community, there were a couple of intriguing offers. But my wife and daughter made it clear that they were not excited by the prospect of a move. We had worked hard on our place in Thetford and none of us wanted to leave it.

As the summer progressed, a plan began to emerge. What had gotten me into coaching in the first place was racing. I loved to compete on skis. What if I considered the year a sort of unpaid sabbatical and, after fifteen years of coaching, put my knowledge and experience to the test by racing the Masters circuit? I'd spent the last fifteen years watching skiers, evaluating technique, developing training plans, waxing skis, and trying to motivate my racers. Why not find out firsthand if everything I had been advocating for the past decade made sense? I could also use the time to sort out what my next career move should be. By late September I had resolved to "go for it." I studied the competitive schedule, sent in entry forms, and bought nonrefundable, low-cost airline tickets. I was committed. I also began training daily for the first time since the 1976 Winter Olympics.

2: Going for It

MY PLAN TO train and race through the winter had emerged over several months. I had not planned to leave Dartmouth and, in fact, had given no thought to what I would do next. The prospect of being unemployed at age forty-three was both exciting and terrifying. Not too long into the summer I began to feel significant relief at the prospect of not returning to Dartmouth in September. Although working with the athletes was tremendously rewarding, I had not been aware of the stress that had gradually been increasing from my being out of step with the administration.

It was exciting to consider that the possibilities were wide open; nothing said I had to remain in ski coaching, or even skiing, for that matter. It occurred to me that since 1968 most of my career decisions had been made for me (in the army) or had been the logical outgrowth of my desire to compete in skiing. Now, with the opportunity to do *anything*, it seemed to make sense to take a breather while I sorted out the options.

Of course, there was another side to it. Although confident I could provide for my family one way or another, I had heard horror stories about talented, qualified professionals who were laid off in their forties and were unable to find decent employment. Like it or not, in the job market I was a ski coach and there were relatively few openings. I was afraid my "shelf life" in the coaching world would be short. If I intended to coach again, I couldn't stay out too long before I would become obsolete.

The plan to train and race seemed perfect. It would allow me to do something I truly enjoyed; would keep me in the sport (perhaps even enhance my coaching knowledge); would allow me to remain at home, causing minimal disruption to my family; and would give me time to plan my next career move. Despite the fact that it was late September and I hadn't had much summer training, I was ready to get after it.

Current Reality

My first step was to evaluate where I was in terms of training and competition. Earlier in the year, after the skiers had returned from spring vacation, Whit Mitchell had tested several of my top athletes in Dartmouth's physiology lab. Cross-country skiers are aerobically the finest athletes in the world. In terms of the amount of oxygen inhaled and transported to the muscles, cross-country skiers (and biathletes) routinely record the highest test scores. The test involves running on a treadmill and breathing through large tubes connected to a sophisticated machine that measures the mixture of gases exhaled and determines how much oxygen the athlete is able to consume and how much carbon dioxide is given off.

Although no Nordic coach would pick a team based solely on the results of an oxygen uptake test, it does provide valuable information about the level of an athlete's fitness. An athlete's "VO_2 max" (or maximal volume of oxygen consumption) is largely due to heredity but can be improved to some degree by endurance training. When an athlete reaches the midtwenties, VO_2 max scores cease to improve regardless of how conscientiously the athlete trains. In a team situation it is not productive to compare athletes' scores, but it is very valuable to study successive tests by the same individual to evaluate the training and racing schedule from year to year. Whit and the others in the lab were generous and supportive of the ski team, usually testing my athletes three times a year.

World-class cross-country skiers, those who win medals at the Olympics, all have VO_2 max scores in the 80s. This means they can inhale and transport to their muscles, per kilogram of body weight, more than eighty milliliters of oxygen per minute. Most college skiers have test scores in the high 60s to low 70s. We tried to use the tests as motivation for the skiers, especially the October one, which served to evaluate their summer training.

Whit and his staff offered to test Dartmouth coaches free of charge, and I was one of the first to sign up. Back in my U.S. Ski Team days (1974–76) I had been tested at the University of Colorado, and I had supervised the testing of dozens of my Dartmouth skiers, so I knew the protocol well.

The first step was to be weighed, as the athlete's result must be divided by body weight. At the height of my biathlon career I weighed 150 pounds, but coaching had added another 10 (most of it in the form of a "spare tire").

The next step was even more intimidating: the fat calipers. Using a pair of spring-loaded pliers, of sorts, the lab assistant pinched a fold of skin and measured its thickness. She repeated the procedure on five or six specific locations on my chest, arms, and back. From those measurements, my weight, and height, she could determine with fairly good accuracy my percent of body fat. It has been determined that among male elite endurance athletes 4 to 12 percent body fat is desirable, and among women, 10 to 18 percent (a reading below 10 percent for a female endurance athlete is considered dangerously low).

As the technician opened the calipers' jaws wide to encompass my left "love handle," I imagined a final tally of about 35 percent. I was pleasantly surprised to learn that my score was 17 percent—nothing for an elite Nordic skier to be proud of, but not hopelessly out of it for a forty-three-year-old who had spent the past eleven years holding down a desk and driving a van. If I could lose ten pounds, the results of my next caliper test and treadmill run would both improve dramatically.

Next, spots on my chest were shaved and lubricated with electronically conductive jelly, and a half-dozen electrodes were stuck in place. A wiring harness was plugged into a small, battery-operated transmitter strapped around my waist. Plastic headgear—a halo-like contraption that held an awkward mouthpiece in place during the run—was adjusted to fit snugly. Then a flexible air tube was attached to the mouthpiece.

Once I was wired and attached to the machine by the hose, the treadmill was started. I walked slowly to get the feel of it and warm up. After a couple minutes the revolving mat was moving fast enough to require a comfortable jog; then it speeded up to a steady run. I tried to ignore the hoses and wires and concentrate on the spring scenery outside the window, mentally reassuring myself that I felt great and was running smoothly. The computerized analysis machine kept clicking away, spitting out a long paper tape with my results.

Then Whit increased the slope of the treadmill. I focused more intently, reminding myself that as a racer I had loved the uphills. My breathing became more labored and my pulse pounded in my ears. Whit increased the pitch again. By now the lab assistants were all shouting encouragement, and Whit was begging: "Thirty seconds more, Morty, just give me another thirty seconds!" I'd seen the drill too many times to be taken in: he'd cajole an athlete to the next printout, which were at thirty-second intervals, only to report, "Great, your numbers are still climbing. Can you hang on for another thirty?" Nordic skiers, being the competitors they are, rarely gave him the thumbs-down; they just kept running until they couldn't keep up with the treadmill any longer, sometimes staggering off the back or being caught by an assistant before they landed in a heap on the floor in a tangle of hoses and wires.

As I gulped air through the restrictive tube, my legs felt like cement, and I knew the accumulated lactic acid was going to bring my test to an end soon. The thirty seconds seemed like thirty minutes, and when I heard the computer spit out its latest reading, I grabbed for the handrails as I was about to fall off the back of the machine.

It was a good test. I had given it about all I had. My VO_2 max score was 64.4. I had been hoping to be above 70 (which would have been respectable among my Dartmouth team members), but I was confident that shedding 10 pounds would enable me to break the 70 barrier. When I was tested at CU in 1975, I had one of the higher readings on the U.S. Ski Team, with a 76. I was encouraged that in fourteen years I hadn't lost more conditioning.

In evaluating my general fitness as of September 1989, I was guardedly optimistic. A personal best, 2:43 (2 hours and 43 minutes), in the marathon the previous May was encouraging. Foot running is not ski racing, but I had run almost twenty marathons since college, so establishing a personal record at age forty-three indicated a certain level of endurance. I was also encouraged by the results of the VO_2 max test in Whit Mitchell's lab. I would be no threat to the twenty-year-olds on the U.S. Biathlon or Cross-Country Ski Teams, but I hadn't totally lost my conditioning since 1976. Finally, I was philosophical about my weight and percent of body fat. I figured if I cut out desserts and my evening beer, I could drop the 10 pounds.

Goals for the 1990 Season

Once you establish where you are, the next step is to envision realistic goals. As the Dartmouth men's coach, I had helped my athletes establish and achieve all sorts of goals over the years, and I was familiar with many of the pitfalls. To be effective, the goal must be a stretch rather than easily attainable, but the athlete must believe that the goal is achievable. It is not wise to tie a goal to another person or team (no matter how convenient that may seen).

In fact, I was having trouble with this. Over the years there had been a couple of my former college and U.S. teammates who had stayed fit and competed actively. Both had done well at previous Masters National Championships and even won medals in World Masters competition. Occasionally during my tenure as Dartmouth coach, the opportunity to race would materialize, and I would still be competitive with my former teammates. It was difficult not to focus right in on these rivals and say, "My goal for the winter is to blast What'shisname's doors off." I resisted the temptation and settled on four mutually supportive goals. I'm a big fan of multiple goals, as long as they don't fragment your effort.

The U.S. Ski Association maintains a national ranking list based on percent back from the winner in every nationally sanctioned race. All registered racers receive points, relative to the winner, each time they compete. Theoretically, a racer in Vermont can evaluate himself against his counterpart in Alaska, even though they have never actually raced against each other. The Spring 1989 USSA Cross-Country Point List ranked me fifth in my age group (Master III, 40–44) with 19.81 points (at the time, the top-ranked cross-country skier in the nation, Audun Endestad, had 0 points). By looking at the national list carefully and noting the points of skiers whom I knew well, I determined that, with conscientious training and a more extensive race schedule than previous winters, I should be able to cut my national points by 25 percent. My first written goal was to finish the 1990 season with national points under 15.

Once, while the Biathlon Training Center was still functioning near Anchorage, Alaska, Coach Sven Johanson entered several of us in tryout races for the U.S. Cross-Country Ski Team. One of the tryout races was a 10K, twice around a difficult five-kilometer loop. This was back in the kick-and-glide days, probably still on wooden skis. I remember winning that tryout race in 30:00, exactly three minutes per kilometer. Sven was not big on flattery or overly generous with his praise; he simply expected us to work as hard as he did and to do our best. But that day he came up to me with a huge grin, sparkling eyes, and a bear hug saying, "Tree minnets a K! Now you really skiing, John!"

I've never forgotten his enthusiasm over that milestone. With today's skating technique, faster waxes, sophisticated training programs, and flawlessly groomed trails, three minutes per kilometer is an easy mark for a good high school skier. But I figured at forty-three years old, coming off a fifteen-year semiretirement, trying to master a new technique as well as polish up my rusty old diagonal style, striving to average three minutes per kilometer in the races would be a worthy goal.

Since cross-country ski races involve countless variables like terrain, snow conditions, wax, weather, and course length, it is difficult to evaluate race results. For example, one of my former Dartmouth skiers might ski the race of his life and still be on the second page of the results if the U.S. Ski Team and a representative number of Scandinavians are also competing. At another time and place that same Dartmouth skier might finish second among less-competitive racers when, in fact, the first result represented better actual skiing.

To help my skiers evaluate their races with some consistency, I began figuring their "percentage" of the winner. I soon discovered that one outstanding skier who often won would throw the system if he did not compete, so I averaged the top three times in each race and divided the Dartmouth skier's time into that average (or base). With this method, the winner of the race would be represented by slightly more than 100 percent (because of the averaging of the top three times), and every other racer would earn a figure that represented his or her percentage of the winner's performance. This system, to a large degree, eliminated the variables of weather, snow condition, size of the competitive field, length of course, and terrain.

Jumping ahead to my first three races of the season, I figured my own percent of the winners with the following results: 86.3, 87.6, and 85.6. With these figures in hand, I established my third goal: to finish consistently within 90 percent of the winners.

As I mentioned earlier, I try to be realistic in my expectations, and I felt each of these three goals was achievable. But they were also theoretical, heavy on the number crunching and not especially straightforward. After all, the obvious objective of a race is to win. Multiple goals are fine, but in the words of Howard Buxton, president of the U.S. Biathlon Association, it was time to "fish or cut bait." I was going to the Masters Championships to win! No more pussyfooting around. No more false humility. I believed I was capable of winning, so I came right up front with it and wrote it down as a goal. I didn't announce it in the local newspaper, but in my mind I acknowledged that I was going to Sun Valley, Idaho, in February to win the Masters National Championships.

The Training Plan

My next step was to establish a plan. I developed my schedule by backplanning from the ski season. I knew I wanted to compete at the Masters National Cross-Country Championships, hosted by the Sun Valley Nordic Center. If the races went well there, I was intrigued by the World Masters Championships in Östersund, Sweden (the same city that had hosted the World Biathlon Championships twenty years earlier). I had also envied Dartmouth graduates and other skiing friends who spoke on glowing terms of the American Birkebeiner, perhaps the largest and most famous ski race in the nation. There would be several early season races in the East to help me get back in the competitive groove and develop the capability of racing several events in succession.

Another necessity would be early-season, on-snow training. For an easterner, that meant traveling west or north. I decided to go to West Yellowstone, Montana, in November. This was where national team athletes and hopefuls congregate every fall to get a jump on winter. In December I would drive to Mount Ste. Anne, Quebec, for another five or six days on snow.

But before I slapped on the boards, I had a lot of dry-land work to do. If I had been training conscientiously all summer, it would have been time for intervals, pace training, and speed work, but since my "real" training was just beginning, I had to emphasize endurance. If I could pile on enough hours and kilometers before the snow flew, there was a good chance the early-season racing itself would quicken my tempo. If I didn't concentrate on endurance training, there was no easy way I could race well into March and avoid burning out. So my dry-land schedule for October and November emphasized hiking, long runs, mountain bike rides, hill striding with poles, and hours in the woods with my chainsaw.

I'm fortunate that my home is ideally located for cross-country ski training. Within an hour's drive are at least a dozen mountains that provide excellent hiking. Since so much of cross-country racing depends on the uphills, I'm a strong advocate of vertical training, and hiking in the mountains is one of the most enjoyable means to achieve this training.

A second personal reason for hiking in the fall was in preparation for the annual Dartmouth Ski Team Moosilauke Time Trial. Dartmouth College owns one of New Hampshire's White Mountains, 4,802-foot Mount Moosilauke. Over the years Dartmouth students have hiked, skied, explored, camped, built cabins, studied acid rain, and in just about every way possible, used the mountain. Sometime in the mid-1960s Al Merrill, the Dartmouth ski coach at the time, inaugurated the Moosilauke Time Trial, a timed run from the Ravine Lodge to the summit up the steep, rocky Gorge Brook Trail. It became a test of leg strength, stamina, and pure willpower. Al felt it evaluated overall conditioning, and he let the Nordic racers know that any of them who couldn't reach the top in less than fifty minutes could forget about skiing for Dartmouth. The event really took on some prestige when Al, then serving as coach for the U.S. Ski Team, hosted a National Team training camp in Hanover that culminated with the Moosilauke Time Trial. The nation's best cross-country skiers scrambled to the summit in a blinding November blizzard.

Jim Page had kept the tradition alive during his tenure as Dartmouth ski coach, and I wasn't about to stop it after almost twenty years of annual results. Logistically, however, the event had its drawbacks. At least two coaches serving as timers would hike to the summit, loaded down with what felt like the athletes' entire wardrobe of dry clothes. If we were feeling cocky, we would give ourselves only a ten-minute lead on the first racers, figuring that, even with heavy packs, we could outdistance the early competitors, reach the top, change to dry clothes, and prepare our clipboards to record the times and finish order of the arriving racers.

My confidence was severely shaken one year when women's Alpine coach Tim Fisher and I were breaking out of the trees at least a quarter mile below the summit. I heard labored breathing and turned in horror to see a racer charging up behind us. Fisher was carrying the watch we had synchronized with the starting clock at the base.

"Quick, Fish, drop your pack and beat him to the top to get his time!" Before Tim could protest, the racer was past us, and Tim reacted. I grabbed his backpack full of clothes and struggled up behind them. In the lull that followed we learned that the skier (one of our better athletes) had been a late arrival. Without thinking of the consequences, a coach at the base had seeded him thirty seconds *before* the first scheduled racer! From that year on we allowed ourselves thirty minutes' head start and made sure the latecomers were added to the *end* of the list.

At any rate, I was looking forward to the Moosilauke Time Trial. My replacement, Ruff Patterson, had invited me to participate in any ski team workouts. I was determined to give him plenty of breathing room with his new team, but to run Moosilauke for time, rather than carrying up all the clothing, was something I wouldn't miss. So I plugged in at least one, sometimes two, mountain runs a week, anticipating the time trial.

After fifteen years of pushing papers, I knew I also needed strength work. But this was a problem for me. The most efficient method of improving general strength is through some form of weight lifting: Nautilus, Universal, or free weights. Many top skiers substitute a homemade strength circuit with stations for chin-ups, sit-ups, push-ups, and so on. Although I've never been able to remain committed to any type of conventional strength program, I truly enjoy working in the woods. Perhaps one of the nicest presents my wife has ever given me is a Swedish chainsaw. After almost twenty years, several new chains, and a couple of replacement bars, it is still going strong. We have two wood-burning stoves in our house and one in the workshop, as well as a wood-fired sauna, and I boil maple sap in the spring, so cutting and splitting firewood takes up a considerable amount of my "leisure" time. Working in the woods may not be great strength training specifically for skiing, but I can assure you it generates a healthy sweat and you can stagger home exhausted.

In terms of specific strength training, roller boards or the newer Vasa Trainer are the current rage. I felt that if I were going to be serious about this adventure, I had better have a roller board. So I built one, a real beauty, out of scrap lumber. I even used up an extra piece of formica countertop to make the rolling surface extra smooth and durable. I invested about thirty dollars in wheels and nylon rope. I set it up, tested it out, and used it once all fall! I guess I'd rather be in the woods than on an incline board three times a week.

Another thing my fall program lacked was roller skiing. Every top cross-country skier and coach can enumerate the benefits of roller skiing as pre-season training. Unfortunately, I didn't own any roller skis, although I did have a pair of roller blades. I intended to blade at least once, perhaps twice, a week but ended up skiing the roads only twice all fall. Those two workouts were good ones, and I admit my lack of enthusiasm for this form of training probably hurt my results on snow.

Before I left Dartmouth, I used one of my contacts in the ski industry to get a bargain price on a mountain bike. Cycling has always been a great supplemental form of training — wonderful variety, forgiving on jarred knees or strained ankles. But mountain biking added a new dimension. Now it was possible to explore back roads and trails, terrain much more like ski courses. The mountain bike was perfect for Vermont's network of dirt roads. It provided an excellent method of training over distance. A three-hour run could really stress knees, while a three-hour mountain bike ride, in hilly terrain, provided almost identical cardiovascular effort while minimizing stress on the joints. I tried to use my mountain bike at least once a week.

As the fall dry-land training drew to a close and winter approached, I had mixed feelings about my preparation. I clearly hadn't started early enough— May was the time to begin, not late September. I also tended to do what I enjoyed—hiking, running, and working in the woods—rather than what I probably needed to do, such as roller skiing and ski-specific strength exercises. On the other hand, I was clearly training with more consistency and dedication than I had at any other time in the past fifteen years.

Sunday, October 29, the day of the Moosilauke Time Trial, was one of those unforgettable New England Indian-summer days. It was clear, dry, and by midafternoon the temperature would reach 70°F. It would be my first timed effort since the marathon five months earlier. It was significant because mountain running is more indicative of Nordic skiing fitness than road running. Furthermore, I had been training specifically for skiing for the past several weeks, without the conflict of a full-time job. No excuses!

We were started at thirty-second intervals, and I was late in the order. This meant there were lots of people ahead of me to overtake and a few hotshots behind to hang on to, when (and if) they went by. From previous hikes on the same trail, I knew I could run to the halfway point. From there I concentrated on striding out over the relatively flat sections and taking quick, efficient steps where the mountain became steep. The trail was beautiful, still soft with moss and runnable in many sections. The weather was perfect, and I broke concentration while passing viewpoints to admire the panorama of the White Mountain range stretching to the east. I offered encouragement to skiers I passed and tried to keep the "hotshots" who went by in sight as long as possible. I reached the top feeling spent but not hopelessly exhausted. It had been a good effort; the pace was about right, enough left for a decent kick to the finish.

Later in the day when the results were posted, I learned I had been seventh of the thirty undergraduates, alumni, and friends who participated. I knew that several of the top returning Nordic skiers were not competing because of leave terms or off-campus programs, but nevertheless I was glad to be among the varsity athletes, at least in terms of conditioning. I may not have done all my dry-land training by the book, and I certainly got a late start, but the Moosilauke Time Trial assured me that at forty-three years old I wasn't too far over the hill in terms of fitness. I couldn't wait to get on snow.

3: Conditioning

Probably more has been written about conditioning for cross-country skiing than any other aspect of the sport (with the possible exception of technique). Because world-class Nordic skiers achieve truly impressive levels of aerobic fitness, they are the subject of evaluations, study, and analysis the world over.

Until sometime in the mid-1970s it seemed that the sports medicine people relished the opportunity to interview and test elite skiers in an effort to correlate the athletes' physical conditioning and race results with what the athletes had done for training. The general assumption was the harder and more extensive the training, the better the results on the treadmill and on the ski trail. Every winter, as a new Scandinavian or Soviet superstar burst on the scene, rumors would fly as to how many hours he or she had trained the year before. When Thomas Magnusson of Sweden bulled his way to victory in the 1974 World Championship 30K, some of the credit went to his revolutionary fiberglass skis. But Magnusson had also developed a reputation as a training madman, amassing more than 1,200 hours during the previous year! It was said that when weather interfered with Magnusson's plans to ski, he shoveled, *by hand*, a one-kilometer track. Before Mother Nature came to his rescue, Magnusson had skied more than two thousand kilometers back and forth on his one-kilometer strip.

A 1,200-hour training year averages out to 23 hours each week, or nearly 3¼ hours of workouts per day. We'll discuss later how weekly hours vary dramatically with the time of year and the phase of the training cycle, but for the purposes of this illustration, consider that Magnusson trained more than half the weekly hours that most Americans work. And those are "true" training hours, not including time spent working on skis or conferring with coaches. If a world-class cross-country skier records "3 hours overdistance skiing" in the training log, it means just that: 3 hours of skiing, uphill and down, probably nonstop and at a pretty steady heart rate. Several years ago Arthur Lydiard, the famous New Zealand running coach, determined that most elite runners would not profit from running more than 120 miles per week. Many of the world's best footrunners still adhere to Lydiard's advice. For comparison purposes, an elite runner probably averages a pace of 6:30 per mile, which computes to 13 hours weekly, or 676 hours of training a year.

How could Magnusson, and others like him, train such incredible amounts without breaking down? First of all, skiing is forgiving, without the jarring and pounding associated with running. Skiers can train long hours on snow without suffering negative physical effects. Second, like ultramarathons, triathlons, cycling, and the conventional 26.2-mile marathon, cross-country skiing emphasizes endurance. The three traditional events for men in cross-country skiing are the 15K (9.3 miles), or the 30K (18.6 miles), and the 50K (31 miles)—events that put a premium on long, slow distance, which, of course, helps build up impressive training hours. (Women's races are 5K, 10K, and 30K.) And third, since even elite racers don't ski on snow every day year-round, there is a built-in variety to ski training that permits greater volume.

Don't Just Train Hard, Train Smart

Everyone jumped on the "more is better" bandwagon, piling on hour after hour of training, until a significant breakthrough (at least for those of us competing in biathlon) was celebrated in the South Tyrolean village of Anterselva, Italy, at the 1975 World Biathlon Championships. For the first time in World Championship or Olympic competition, the Finnish team had taken both individual and relay gold medals. It was no small accomplishment, since the Soviet Union had won the relay seven of the last nine times. The Finns were ecstatic over their double victory. By coincidence, our team leader that year was Peter Lahdenpera, the son of a Finnish World War II general. Peter, fluent in Finnish, was instantly adopted by his former countrymen and included in all the celebrations.

After the events were over and we were driving from Italy to Austria for the pre-Olympic competitions near Innsbruck, Peter let us in on the news. "You know why those Finns were so damn excited?" he asked. "They have been working for several years on a scientific approach to training. Last year's World Championships in Minsk were encouraging to them. [Juhani Suutorinen had won two individual golds.] But they weren't sure whether their plan was working or Suutorinen was just an exceptional athlete. This year, with Heikki Ikola's individual gold in the 20K and the relay team's victory, they are sure the plan is working! For the first time, the doctors and sports medicine people are not just observing and analyzing what the athletes are doing for training—they are actually *telling* the coaches and athletes how to train!"

In retrospect, that revelation in 1975 represented a significant turning point in biathlon, cross-country, and perhaps all endurance sports. The victory would no longer go to the athlete who trained hardest but to the one who trained *smartest*. Granted, many athletes had not yet achieved the volume of hours that top European physiologists considered necessary to compete at a world-class level, but at last the international leaders seemed in favor of a more sophisticated balance of several types of conditioning.

Before that, what most American Nordic skiers had been hearing from coaches was "If you want to do well in Europe, you've gotta train harder!" The success of the Finns in Anterselva, and the reasons for that success, threw all our basic theories into question.

"Whadaya mean I won't get better if I train harder?" we asked, bewildered. It was like Columbus telling us the world was round when we had been sure for so long it was flat.

The evidence had been right in front of us all the time, if we had only realized it. Sven Johanson, our biathlon coach in Alaska, was a tough old Swede who believed in hard work. We began training on snow the first of October every year, high in the Talkeetna Mountains north of Anchorage. It was not uncommon to have twelve hundred to fifteen hundred kilometers on snow before our European team tryouts in January. Few other skiers in the country enjoyed the luxury of this extensive early-season skiing. As a result, we often did well against the U.S. Ski Team cross-country racers early in the season, when they were first getting on snow. But usually by midseason they were kicking our butts all the way back to Alaska. We were certainly putting in as many hours as they were — usually more — and we had had the advantage of early snow. The reason, of course, was that we were training hard but they were training smart.

So before I go any farther, let's agree on this first principle: *It is more important to train smart than to train hard.* I know this contradicts hundreds of years of the Puritan ethic and the American way, but it is basic to everything that follows. Don't despair — there will still be plenty of room for hard work. But guiding rule number one must be "Train smart."

I will be using the words *conditioning* and *training* interchangeably to refer to physical improvement resulting from adherence to a plan or an organized program. For simplicity I am dividing physical training into three major categories: endurance (or distance), strength, and speed. Although there are limitless variations and combinations of these three categories, it is important to know in advance which one is the main goal of a given workout.

As a racer or coach begins to develop a training schedule, there are several time-tested principles that come into play. Concepts like consistency, volume, variety, specificity, capability, visualization, technique, and others must be understood and incorporated if a conditioning program is to be successful.

There are many types of physical activity that are training options, including activities as diverse as hiking, windsurfing, roller skiing, and weight lifting. An overview of these options is necessary before a successful training program can be developed.

The Training Program
Stress and Rest

At its most basic level, training simply consists of stress and rest. Long ago a perceptive person realized that if a muscle was stressed (given more work to do than it could comfortably accomplish), then rested, the muscle would respond by growing stronger. That's really all there is to it. Debate surrounds details like how much and what type. But never forget that improvement results from judicious applications of stress *and rest*. If you go overboard on the stress, you will burn out and break down physically. On the other hand, if you are stingy with the stress and generous with the rest, you won't make much progress either.

The key to success is a delicate balance of stress and rest — so delicate, in fact, that it has to be carefully monitored. This monitoring takes the form of a training program that consists of a plan, records, and evaluations of both training and competition. To achieve top results, it is necessary to develop a training plan, establish benchmarks along the way, and record your progress conscientiously.

Endurance Training

The backbone of the plan will be endurance, or distance, training. Elite athletes are aware of two components to every workout: duration and intensity. Distance workouts increase endurance by conditioning the cardiovascular system to operate more efficiently, enhancing the body's capacity to take in oxygen, transport it to the muscles (where it is used to generate energy), and dispose of the carbon dioxide. These long, slow endurance workouts can take several forms and should probably make up more than 60 percent of a cross-country skier's annual training. Depending upon the method selected, such as hiking, cycling, or skiing, an endurance workout can last several hours.

If the premium is on duration, then the pace of endurance workouts must be relatively slow. Elite athletes carefully monitor their pulses to maintain the prescribed level of exertion for particular workouts. For those of us lacking expensive electronic heart-rate monitors, a good guideline for pacing a distance workout is the ability to carry on a conversation. If you and your training buddy are continually solving the world's problems on your noontime runs, then your pace is probably about right.

Strength Training

The second component of a successful conditioning program is strength training. An old expression often heard in the weight room — "Whatever your sport, you'll do it better if you are stronger" — appears to be true. It's not just football players and boxers who lift weights to improve their performance; distance runners, figure skaters, and Alpine skiers do it as well.

There are a couple of principles to bear in mind before embarking on a strength program. First of all, you can tailor a strength program toward either power or endurance. Football players, hockey players, gymnasts, and boxers all want explosive power and increased muscle bulk. This is achieved by lifting relatively heavy weights, with relatively few repetitions. A football lineman might bench press a 250-pound barbell to increase the size and strength of his chest, shoulders, and arms, but he might lift that weight only three times before exhausting his muscles.

Endurance strength training, however, favors lighter weights and more repetitions. A runner who wants to add more zip to his or her stride might do leg presses on a weight machine, but rather than doing just three repetitions with heavy weights like the football player, the runner would complete up to twenty-five repetitions with lighter weights. Like other forms of conditioning, strength training is effective only if the body is allowed to recover for a day or so following the workout. Most strength programs prescribe workouts on alternate days, or three times per week.

The second consideration centers around the issue of general versus specific strength. Generalists maintain that an athlete who is stronger overall will perform better in *any* sport, while proponents of specific strength training believe that only increased power specific to the movements of the particular sport is of any significant value.

Both sides have merit. In my years at Dartmouth I observed scores of incoming freshmen (some of them accomplished skiers) who were physically weak. A straightforward, three times per week, general strength program was just what they needed before they could even think about developing proper skiing technique. By the time they were seniors, many of them were significantly stronger—their dedication had paid off. At that point additional hours in the Nautilus room would have done little good in terms of improved skiing results, but ski-specific strength training would continue to produce benefits. (By specific strength work I mean roller board or Vasa Trainer workouts, pulling on an Exergenie or rubber armbands, even ski striding with poles up a steep hill with a backpack full of sand.)

A quick review: Concentrate on endurance strength work, twelve to twenty-five repetitions, and stay away from power lifting. General strength work is beneficial up to a point, especially if you are just getting serious about racing, but as your ability improves and your goals become more ambitious, you'll probably need some ski-specific strength training.

We usually think of strength work in terms of exerting force against resistance where some movement results. Push-ups, sit-ups, dips, and chin-ups are all strength workouts in which body weight provides the resistance. The U.S. Alpine Ski Team developed an excellent routine that consists of several exercises to strengthen the stomach and lower back. This routine is valuable for Nordic and Alpine skiers alike.

Partner resistance exercises build strength and team spirit without expensive equipment.
Dartmouth College Archives

For many years it was said that elite Scandinavian racers avoided strength training, but in fact they love strength circuits in the woods. Many community ski trails in Norway and Sweden are equipped with stations where, in summer, athletes stop to do sit-ups, chin-ups, dips, bench hops, and so on.

Strength work on your own can be convenient and productive, but partner resistance exercises offer additional benefits. Here, two people take turns providing resistance tailored to the other athlete's strength. If done properly, partner resistance exercises can be more efficient than weight lifting and at the same time build team unity.

Perhaps the most common image that comes to mind when we think strength training is weight lifting. At present there are three widely recognized weight-lifting options: Nautilus, Universal Gym, or free weights. The free weights (heavy weights, few repetitions) are often preferred by the power lifters. They don't have much value for cross-country skiers. Proponents of Nautilus and Universal each have their preferences. I think either system is fine for general strength. Both systems are safe when the equipment is used properly. Best of all, they are fast. The Dartmouth Ski Team had a Nautilus circuit involving ten machines, with a maximum of twelve repetitions on each machine, which took less than a half hour to complete.

A couple of hints for weight lifting: First, make a score card listing the specific exercises you intend to do, how much weight you lift, and how many repetitions with each weight. Like other forms of conditioning, weight lifting should be progressive; thus you must remember what you did last time before beginning the current workout. Also, start out light. If you plan to lift three times a week, it won't take long to increase to where you should be; starting light gives you a chance to get the feel of the equipment.

A general rule about progression is to stay at a weight until you can lift it twelve repetitions (twenty-five if you are emphasizing endurance rather than general strength). Once you successfully lift a weight that number of times, go to a higher weight increment in your next workout. That's where the score card comes in handy. Maintain the proper body position while lifting, and if you can't get the last few reps without writhing or jerking, don't bother. Do only as many as you can do *properly*.

Methods of sport-specific strength training are limited only by your imagination. Some of the weight lifting, partner resistance, or individual circuit stations may approximate skiing movements enough to be considered specific. Hill running, striding, and bounding with ski poles (especially while wearing a weight vest or backpack) are all forms of strength training.

Several years ago American skiers returned from Europe describing a new training device the Germans were using—the roller board. First, a long plank is attached to a wall or other support, creating an incline. At the top of the incline are attached two ropes with ski-pole handle straps at the ends. The

The roller board is easy to build, inexpensive, and very effective for strength training.

roller board, a rectangular board with four casters on the bottom, is placed on the incline, then the athlete kneels or lies face down on it and draws his or her body up the incline by pulling on the ropes. (The ski-pole handle straps make it more authentic and comfortable.) The workout can be made more difficult by increasing the slope of the plank or adding more weight to the skier using a weight vest. This is a highly regarded strength workout for skiers because the motion is very similar to that used in double poling on skis.

Rob Sleamaker, a physiologist from Burlington, Vermont, took this concept one step farther and developed the Vasa Trainer. With Rob's invention the athlete sits on a bicycle-type seat, more closely duplicating the body position of skiing. The Vasa Trainer can also be used for other exercises specific to skiing.

Years ago, when John Caldwell was coaching the National Team, he began nailing bicycle inner tubes to trees and had his skiers pull on them. They became known as Putney armbands. The concept is as valid today as it was thirty years ago. You can even attach ski-pole handles to them. You will need to experiment a little to determine how high to attach the tubes. (Start at about head level.) You can also double up tubes to increase resistance. If you want to get fancy, you can use shock cord from the hardware store.

To use the armbands, start out facing the tree and pull on them for a while. Concentrate on good skiing technique. Avoid hunching over or thrashing your body from side to side as you get tired. Then turn around with your

Roller Board

10'-0"   ELEVATION   END VIEW   2'-0"

4"

6"
12"
6"

PLAN

Sled

2'-6"   10"

1/2"   ELEVATION   END VIEW

15"   PLAN

NOTES:
1. Roller Board Top: 1/2" Plywood
2. Roller Board Frame: 2 x 4" Blocking
3. Tracks for Sled: 1/2" x 1" Strapping,
   9" Long
4. Castors: Heavy Duty
   Non-Swivel 1/2" Dia.

Construction details for a roller board, a low-budget alternative to the Vasa Trainer.

back to the tree and pull some more. You can attach tubes near the base of the tree and use the same principles for leg work. Looping a tube over your foot and extending it to the side is a great workout for skating. You can use this low-budget resistance device to install several stations along a running loop and create a circuit.

Another resistance device is the commercially produced Exergenie, a metal cylinder with the ends of a rope protruding from it. By twisting the

Rob Sleamaker demonstrates the Vasa Trainer, which he invented to provide ski-specific upper-body strength work. Rob Sleamaker

cylinder it is possible to adjust the resistance on the rope. The Exergenie is convenient because you can take it with you on trips. You secure a strip of nylon webbing in a door jamb, and your strength workout can begin right in your motel room.

Another option is simply a large rubber band with handle loops at either end. The most popular commercially produced versions are the Life Line Gym and the Sport Cord. Either can be used in many innovative ways to provide resistance. Although not as specific to skiing as the Exergenie, this type of device is valuable because of its versatility. Proponents say you can do a complete weight workout without the weights, a tremendous convenience when traveling.

The skating revolution has brought about all kinds of innovations. One of them, the slide board, is an idea borrowed from speed skaters. The slide board develops strength, coordination, and balance. The idea is to concentrate on good technique while doing many repetitions.

Almost any ski-specific workout can be adapted to emphasize strength. If you are on roller skis or roller blades, you can double pole up a hill (no striding or skating) and create a first-class arm-strength workout. On your bicycle try muscling your way up a hill in a higher gear than you would normally use. At the beach, running through knee-deep water or over sand dunes provides good strength work as well as variety. Be creative. Soon after I discovered cross-

Slide Board

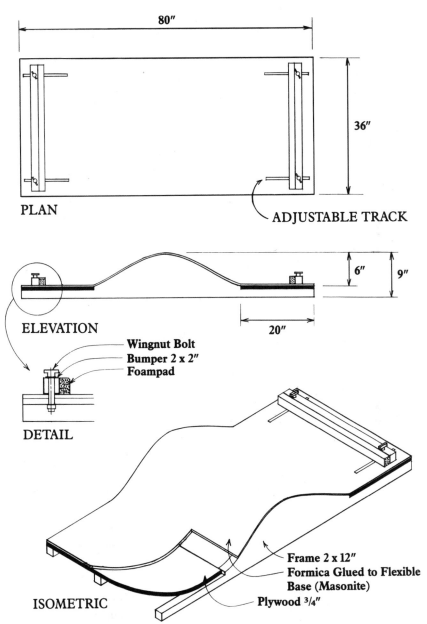

PLAN

80"

36"

ADJUSTABLE TRACK

ELEVATION

6" **9"**

20"

Wingnut Bolt
Bumper 2 x 2"
Foampad

DETAIL

Frame 2 x 12"
Formica Glued to Flexible
Base (Masonite)
Plywood ³/₄"

ISOMETRIC

The slide board, long used as a training device for speed skaters, gained popularity with skiers after the skating revolution. The bump in the middle forces the athlete to lift his leg when "skating" from side to side. Old, heavy socks are worn over sneakers when using the board.

country skiing, I figured I could increase my poling strength by training with old ski poles filled with sand. It wasn't a bad idea.

Finally, although not ski specific, one additional form of strength training should not be overlooked: old-fashioned, hard physical labor. Long before Nautilus machines and fitness centers, athletes looked for summer jobs involving physical labor. They sought employment with moving companies, hauling furniture up and down stairs all day; they threw sixty-pound hay bales high on wagons; they hauled lumber for carpenters. One of the best ski seasons I had in college followed a summer of road construction work. I had never worked that hard before (and not very often since). I worked from 7:00 A.M. to 5:30 P.M. six days a week building stone headwalls on drainage culverts running under an interstate highway. I hauled rocks, shoveled sand, mixed cement, and trudged up and down steep embankments all day. I came out of that summer strong as an ox, mentally tough, and loaded with money (for a college kid).

Although hard physical labor is not ski specific, it has two overriding advantages. First of all, strength developed through physical labor is broader based than most weight training. If you shovel dirt or split firewood for a couple of hours, you not only stress your muscles, you also improve your sense of balance and coordination. In addition, by working hard you often can make money. No one has ever paid me to lift weights!

Speed Training

So you have a good aerobic base, thanks to hours of long, slow distance training, and you are strong as an ox, thanks to a comprehensive strength routine. Are you ready to win ski races? Not quite. There is one more component of your training that needs attention: speed. Although cross-country skiing requires strength and endurance, the victory still goes to the fastest. To put it another way, we are in the business of building race horses, not work horses! One reason for those long hours of endurance training is to provide an aerobic base for speed work. In general, speed work is of shorter duration but higher intensity than distance training. There are several types of workouts that fall into this category: intervals; pace training; speed play, or *fartlek*; and races or time trials.

Intervals. Intervals are perhaps the most widely used form of speed training. The concept is to go as fast or faster than you could in a race, but to do so only for relatively short distances. The basic premise of training — stress followed by rest and regeneration — is important here. Each workout is a series of physically stressful segments of hard work followed by rest periods. The most common mistake made with interval training is shortchanging the athlete in the rest segments. If the idea is to go faster than is comfortable during the work segments, it is essential that the rest between intervals be long enough to provide adequate recovery. With well-trained endurance athletes, the break between intervals is usually adequate when their pulses have dropped back to 120 beats per minute. For a coach a more subtle yet equally reliable indicator is when your athletes resume chattering with each other.

How do you know when your athletes have done enough intervals? There is no fixed number; it varies with the athlete, the conditions, the difficulty of the interval, the time of year, and so forth. One good guideline, however, is that when consistent interval times begin to drop off, it's time to quit.

Let's say it's mid-January, the skiing is great, and I want to prepare for upcoming races. I have found a nice rolling loop exactly one kilometer long. After a warm-up of about thirty minutes, I'm going to do intervals on my one-kilometer loop. My objective is to do as many as I can, at a pace faster than I could race, but not so fast that my technique falls apart. I time my first interval: 2:50. I ski easily back and forth near the start of my loop until my pulse slows to 120, then start my second interval. I continue in this way, skiing, resting, checking my watch, and monitoring my pulse, until I finish a loop in 3:04. The previous loops have all been within a couple of seconds of 2:50. After a good rest my next interval is timed at 3:07. It's time to quit, regardless of how many I've done. Another twenty minutes or so of easy skiing provides the cool-down.

Like distance training, intervals can assume an endless variety in terms of method, intensity, and duration. One of the Dartmouth Nordic Team's favorites (using that word with a masochistic connotation) was hill running with poles. Not far from campus is a small Alpine ski area called Oak Hill. Once a week in the fall we would jog out to Oak Hill with our ski poles and stride, bound, and sprint up the Alpine slope. It was a great workout, stressing arms and legs together and even providing the opportunity for some technique work. Many Dartmouth skiers recorded their maximum pulse rates at the top of Oak Hill.

The Dartmouth Alpine Team used the same interval format for a famous workout on bicycles. They rode easily in a pack the ten miles from Hanover to Union Village, Vermont (an excellent warm-up). There they pedaled repeatedly up the paved access road of the large flood-control dam until their thighs were burning.

Another effective type of interval training developed out of necessity at Dimond High School in Anchorage. Before the city had a lighted ski trail, there were few options for training on snow in late December and early January. School got out at 2:40 P.M., ski practice began at 3:00, and it was dark soon thereafter. One choice was to ski under the lights on the football field. To combat boredom, we developed games, drills, and competitions.

One of the most popular was the three-person relay. The skiers were divided into teams of three. One skier from each team would be sent to the far goal line of the field; the others remained at the near goal line. When the coach said, "Go," the first skiers would sprint to the far end of the field, tagging their teammates as they crossed the line. Racer number two would ski back to the starting point, tagging number three, who then took off for the far end to tag number one. With three on a team, each skier got a rest roughly twice as long as the sprint. The three-person teams also seemed to increase the unpredictability of the results, generating excitement. We seldom announced a specific number of sprints in advance; we watched the athletes ski and stopped the intervals when it was clear they were getting tired. These short intense sprints taught the Dimond High skiers to move fast and, though done out of necessity, were especially valuable in preparing for mass-start races and relays.

Pace Training. Pace training is a variation of interval training. The concept is this: If you know how fast you need to ski a certain distance to achieve your goal but are unable to ski that fast for the full race, then shorten the distance to where you can perform at the desired rate. Let's say that by looking at results of the previous season, I discover I could do very well in my Masters age category if I could ski a 15K race in forty-five minutes. I haven't skied that fast in a long time, but it is not hopelessly out of reach. A forty-five-minute 15K race translates into three minutes per kilometer. After a little experimentation, I discover that I can ski a rolling one-kilometer loop in three minutes. A pace training workout would teach me what three minutes per kilometer feels like, so eventually I will be able to string fifteen of them together.

The procedure is much like conventional intervals: work alternating with rest. The major difference is that with pacing you have a specific target for each work interval. It is not a successful pace workout if your first kilometer is skied at 2:53 and your eighth kilometer at 3:15. If your target is 3:00 per kilometer, then you strive to hit 3:00 each time. When your time drops off noticeably, you've had enough.

One note of caution when skiing interval or pacing workouts: Snow conditions can play a significant role in your interval times. With my Dartmouth team, there were days when, after several difficult intervals, the skiers' times continued to improve even though I knew they were getting tired. In fact, the tracks were icing up as the sun went down, more than compensating for the fatigue of the skiers. In a situation like that you have to use your judgment and quit when you've had enough.

Fartlek. Fartlek is a Swedish concept that translates as speed play. Unlike running a marathon or 10K race on foot, where the level of exertion is relatively constant, skiing can be considered a series of sprints and recoveries. Like cyclists, skiers get more of a rest on the downhills than runners do. And because ski trails through the woods often have dramatic climbs and descents, there the sense of sprint and recovery is more pronounced. So the Swedes (who have a tradition of success in cross-country skiing, by the way) theorized that rather than training at a steady state all summer, a skier should be able to "turn on the jets" frequently, learning to be comfortable with varying paces. The resulting off-season workout might go like this: ten minutes of stretching followed by a forty-five-minute run on trails, cruising easily on the flats and downhills, but blasting hard on the uphills. Another variation would be running in a pack of athletes, each of whom attempts to outsprint the others for a minute or so during the course of a forty-five-minute run.

Before we had ever heard of *fartlek*, several college teammates and I were doing it at Middlebury. South of campus was a swampy forest. Early in the fall, before hunting season, we would head for the swamp to chase deer. Jogging through soggy grass, vaulting fallen logs, and splashing through streams, we would plod along until we glimpsed the magnificent white flash of a tail as deer spooked and bounded away. Then the chase was on! We would race off in the direction the deer had disappeared, hoping to catch another look. Often the animals were so curious they would stop for a glance back at us. I have heard that a well-conditioned person, with patience and determination, can eventually run down a deer since they are designed as sprinters rather than endurance animals. We never ran one down, but we certainly had hours worth of exciting sprints and recoveries in that swamp.

Racing. Racing can be a very beneficial part of your training program year-round. Even if your goal includes only one or two major competitions, preliminary races can play an important role in helping you achieve that goal. Racing gives you an opportunity to test yourself, to experiment with modifications in your technique, to gain confidence in new equipment. Racing can provide benchmarks to let you know how your training plan is working and point out areas that need additional attention. In some ways racing is the most specific form of training there is, since nothing else equals the rush of adrenaline, the concentration, and the intensity that "putting on a number" elicits.

But there are a couple of things to watch for as you plug races or time trials into your training program. First of all, prioritize your competitions, at least informally. I believe that every time you step into the starting gate with a number on, you should be committed to racing. I'm frustrated when I hear young skiers remark over their shoulder, "Oh, I'm just skiing through this race today. I'm peaking for the Nationals in two weeks." If you've got a number on, you'd better be "going for it," or you shouldn't be in the race. If you begin to race with the attitude that it's just training and it really doesn't matter, it's all too easy to fall into that way of thinking when the going gets tough in a race that *does* matter. Taking it a step farther, I'm against starting a race with this approach: "I'll see how I feel. If it's going well, I'll finish; if not, I'll drop out." No Russian or East German ever entered a cross-country race thinking he'd drop out after the first lap if things weren't going well! Part of the benefit of racing is to develop mental toughness, and you won't develop that attribute if dropping out is an option. If you are not fit, then don't race. If you do race, don't drop out!

Having said all this, however, there is nothing wrong with prioritizing your races. Early in the fall I had decided I wanted to win at the Masters National Ski Championships in February. In October, when offered the opportunity to compete in the Dartmouth Ski Team's annual Mount Moosilauke time trial, I was eager to participate. I knew my chances of winning were slim to nonexistent, but it would be a good evaluation of my conditioning and where I stood relative to other skiers. I ran hard and was happy with my seventh-place finish. But I didn't approach that event with the same intensity, concentration, or commitment I would reserve for the National Championships. Keep your races in perspective.

Finally, if off-season racing becomes part of your plan (which I support), be careful that it enhances, rather than detracts from, the overall program. Many skiers get into off-season competition, such as foot running, bike racing, canoeing, mountain runs, or triathlons. As a competition approaches, the athlete backs off on the training schedule to be rested for the event. If the competition was challenging (like a triathlon, hill climb, or marathon), the athlete may need several days of recovery before resuming normal training. If this scenario is repeated often throughout the summer, many effective training days will be lost.

This brings to mind a related observation. In my years of coaching at Dartmouth I noticed that most athletes fell into one of two categories: those who loved to race and trained only to improve their racing performance, and those who thrived on training and seemed to race only to justify the amount of time and energy they committed to conditioning. The former group might miss workouts because of academic conflicts but would beg to race even when coming down with pneumonia. The latter group would orchestrate elaborate, "iron man" type training events but often lacked confidence and self-assurance in the starting gate with a number on. The name of this game is *racing*. If you don't get a kick out of putting it all on the line, under the clock, then you have two choices. You can reassess your goals and motives—why you are interested in Nordic ski racing. By modifying your outlook and expectations, you may find racing increasingly enjoyable. On the other hand, if you simply don't enjoy the competitive side of it, don't fight it—focus on fitness, conditioning, and ski touring. Off-season racing can give you the opportunity to sort these things out and help you learn to enjoy the excitement and challenge of competition rather than dread it.

Training Principles

We now have the three basic building blocks of any training schedule for Nordic skiing: endurance, strength, and speed. But before we begin filling in the blanks on the training schedule, there are some training principles that deserve attention. Things get a little tricky here, as several of these concepts appear contradictory.

Consistency

This chapter began with a basic explanation of how conditioning produces improved results: stress followed by rest equals improvement. Now I'm going to tell you that the world's best skiers train almost every day year-round. In fact, for large parts of the year they train more than once a day! So much for the stress—what about the rest? These athletes (and their coaches) have discovered that nothing produces improvement like consistency. If you want to get good at something, do it a lot and do it every day. In terms of physical conditioning, this means it is better to do something every day, even in small doses, than to rest all week and beat yourself to a pulp on the weekend. But to avoid overtraining and to ensure the rest necessary for proper recovery, elite athletes will arrange their training plans so that successive workouts complement each other. Keep in mind the hard day/easy day rotation. Remember, in almost any workout you are dealing with duration and intensity, so it is possible to modify activities to fit a hard day/easy day schedule.

For example, my Dartmouth skiers usually regarded running, bounding, and striding with poles up Oak Hill as a hard workout. Although relatively short (forty-five minutes to an hour), the intensity was enough that the athletes were stressed aerobically and their arm and leg muscles felt the effort. The following day we might have scheduled a distance bike ride, two hours or more in length. I would pick a relatively flat loop and instruct the skiers to go slowly, ride in a group, and keep talking. The purpose of the workout was not speed, but endurance—just turning the pedals for more than two hours. Although it certainly qualified as a distance workout, it might almost seem like a recovery day after the tough Oak Hill workout.

Most adults are quite consistent about their eating habits: they eat at roughly the same times every day and develop preferences for certain types of food. Even busy individuals rarely miss a meal if they are accustomed to eating three times a day. When training becomes as much a part of your daily routine as eating—when you would no sooner skip a workout than skip a meal—then you have established consistency in your program and you will see positive results.

Volume

Closely tied to the concept of consistency is the idea of volume. Simply stated, those who succeed at cross-country skiing train a lot. This does not negate what was mentioned earlier about training smarter, it is just the acknowledg-

The toughest dry-land workout on the Dartmouth Ski Team's schedule is hill running (striding and bounding) at Oak Hill.

ment that among the world's foremost athletes, cross-country skiers (and biathletes) probably spend more hours training than almost anyone else. There is a very strong correlation between winning international performances and massive hours spent training in the preceding *years*.

An example is Gunde Svan of Sweden, who rose to the top of the Nordic world through year after year of massive volumes of training. Although I believe Svan was born with considerable talent, his inherited gifts might never have been evident had he not put in those countless hours of training. The point is, simply, if you want to succeed in Nordic skiing, you must be prepared to put in the volume; there are no shortcuts.

Capability

The concept of training volume leads to the related topic of capability. Success in cross-country skiing is a long-term investment. Developing the necessary technique and conditioning requires not weeks or months, but years. If this training is to be productive, it must be progressive and systematic. Just because the world's best skiers train 1,000 hours per year does not mean that everyone in America with aspirations to compete at the international level should train 1,000 hours next year. Massive volumes of training must be developed gradually, over several years. As a young racer responds successfully to a given work load, producing encouraging race results, the training volume can be increased gradually for the next year.

Most experts agree that a training volume increase of 15 percent per year is reasonable for promising young racers. For example, if a high school skier recorded 200 hours of ski training in a given year and was eager for improved results, a projected increase to 230 hours would be reasonable. With younger skiers it's important not to encourage dramatic increases in volume, especially if they are still growing or are up to their ears in academic obligations. It is all too easy for us as coaches to say that if the world's best are training 1,200 hours a year, our kids have to match that volume or we will never catch up. That may be true, but we forget that those mature, world-class competitors putting in 1,000 to 1,200 hours of training each year have built up to that volume over a long period and, very often, have few other demands on their time except to perform well internationally.

Several years ago U.S. Ski Team coaches Torbjorn Karlsen and Ruff Patterson distributed a paper titled "Training Planning for Cross-Country Skiers," in which they suggested training volume levels for various categories of athletes: national team members, 1,000 to 1,200 hours per year; national team hopefuls, 800 to 1,000 hours; college skiers, 600 to 800 hours; national caliber juniors, 400 to 600 hours. Since their goal was to make the U.S. Ski Team, and 600 to 800 hours of training was the volume the U.S. Team coaches suggested, my own national team hopefuls at Dartmouth were determined to match that standard. From the perspective of the U.S. Ski Team, it made perfect sense and was part of a logical progression, but for many full-time college students attending classes, studying for exams, and writing papers, the projected volume of training was simply too much. Any training schedule, to ensure success, must be within the capability of the athlete.

Variety and Specificity

The next two principles of training, variety and specificity, appear on the surface to be contradictory. The concept of specificity suggests that the best way to become a great ski racer is to do a lot of ski racing. All other forms of training are substitutes that to varying degrees fall short. This is actually a very significant concept for skiing because, for most of us, it is impossible to train in our sport year-round. Unlike world-class swimmers, who can be in the pool 365 days a year, or elite gymnasts, who can perform their routines in the gymnastics hall regardless of the weather, even the world's best skiers are forced to spend considerable parts of the year in alternate forms of training.

In the past decade there has been increased emphasis on summer skiing on glaciers in Austria and Alaska as well as on snowfields in Northern Scandinavia and Oregon. In addition, a Nordic racing schedule has emerged in the Southern Hemisphere, primarily in Australia and Argentina, so that skiers can actually race on snow year-round. For those without the means to get on snow in the off-season, roller skiing has become an increasingly important aspect of training because it is the closest thing to skiing you can do without snow.

To balance the principle of specificity, consider variety. This concept suggests that both mentally and physically there is great value to a training schedule that includes varied activities. The elite athletes who probably train more than anyone else are summer triathletes (swimming, cycling, and foot running). These competitors can put in such unbelievable volumes of training because their sport *demands* variety. It seems more likely that an athlete could enjoy training 1,500 hours a year if that training were divided between running, swimming, and cycling.

Skiers have the advantage of imposed variety because of the lack of snow in the summer. Although the inability to ski on snow may be considered a liability in terms of specificity, it forces skiers to include a wide variety of training methods in their programs. Variety in training ensures the development of broader athletic ability.

Several years ago a young Finnish student named Arno Laukenen dominated the Eastern intercollegiate cross-country ski circuit. I spoke with Arno several times about his childhood in Finland and how Finnish champions train. One comment I clearly remember referred to variety. Arno related that young Finnish athletes are encouraged to participate in a wide variety of sports. The idea, he said, was first to develop good athletes, then from those athletes develop great skiers. I'm afraid all too often in this country we spot a youngster with special ability in one area and immediately concentrate on that early promise, in the process narrowing the youngster's athletic experience. I know this is true because year after year at Dartmouth I saw incoming cross-country skiers who had been successful in junior programs but were virtually incompetent at other popular sports like swimming, tennis, soccer, volleyball, and even Alpine skiing.

The concept of variety suggests that, especially in the formative years, a wide range of athletic experiences will develop a competitor with broad abilities, ultimately resulting in stronger performance in a specific sport. A training schedule that permits a wide variety of activities will promote spontaneity, generate enthusiasm, and establish a strong base for more specific ski training later in the season.

The challenge, of course, is to successfully balance these two seemingly conflicting concepts. There are no hard and fast rules. As suggested earlier, it probably makes sense to emphasize variety for young skiers or those just getting into racing. At the same time, there is an increased need for specificity in training as the competitive season draws near. For example, roller skiing once or twice a week in July may be adequate, but four or five times a week may be appropriate in November. Finally, it's important to consider individual preference. I have known some athletes who were most content when involved in a strictly regimented routine with a minimum of distractions or diversions. Not long ago I spoke with a recreational skier from Quebec who has done the same forty-five-minute conditioning routine (push-ups, sit-ups, and calisthenics) in his basement every morning before breakfast — for the last twenty-six years! In contrast, I tried hard to add interest and excitement to the Dartmouth cross-country training schedule by changing locations, modifying workouts, inventing games, and disguising intervals as relay races.

Working on Weaknesses

It's simply human nature that we prefer what we do well. Success breeds success. To be successful in cross-country skiing, however, an athlete has to balance endurance, strength, and speed. Everyone tends to have a weak link somewhere. Rather than avoiding the weakness, the successful competitor acknowledges the area that needs work and focuses on improving in that area. A weakness can exist in any of the five areas necessary for success: conditioning, technique, equipment, nutrition, or psychology. A skier might be weak in the arms and upper body, be timid on the downhills, have a tendency to wax too warm, not drink enough water, or become mired in negative self-talk at the start of a race. You may have one vulnerable link in an otherwise strong chain, which could prevent any significant improvement. So acknowledge your weaknesses and work on improving in those areas.

Uphills

Not long ago the guidelines for laying out a cross-country racing trail suggested that the loop should be roughly one-third uphill, one-third downhill, and one-third flat. Since the advent of the skating technique, the tendency has been to increase the climb component. This brings up the next training concept, that *races are won on the uphills*. This is important to remember when planning your training. A competent racer can ski a typical fifteen-kilometer course in forty-five minutes. At first thought we might assume that the skier spent equal amounts of time on the flats, the climbs, and the downhills. But, obviously, more time ticks by when a skier is laboring up hills than when he or she is zooming down, and it may be that fifteen minutes were spent on the flats, five on the downhills, and twenty-five on the climbs. The greatest potential for improvement lies in the twenty-five minutes of climb. Taking it a step farther, I would suggest that more than 50 percent of your training should be oriented toward vertical power and endurance. It may be possible to lose a race on the downhills by falling or riding slow skis, but I firmly believe that to win, an athlete must be strong and confident on the uphills.

Arms and Legs Together

There appears to be significant benefit to activities that stress the arms and legs together. Cross-country ski racing puts demands on the entire body; the arms and legs work in concert to propel the competitor down the track. Under the heading of variety, we might assume that a long-distance bike ride would be great for the legs, while a Nautilus routine emphasizing the upper body would improve arm strength. That assumption is true; however, workouts in which arms and legs are stressed simultaneously seem to have a more significant aerobic impact than workouts in which arms or legs are stressed alone. This is not to say you should eliminate any workout that concentrates on either arms or legs. For planning purposes, however, put a star next to those workouts in which arms and legs are stressed together, such as roller skiing, hill striding with poles, rowing (in a shell with movable seat), or hard physical labor. You get more than your money's worth from these workouts.

Technique

The significance of ski technique will be discussed at length in chapter 5, but it should be mentioned here that one goal of dry-land training should be improvement of technique. Specificity is important in workouts because such exercises offer the opportunity not only to become physically stronger but also to improve one's form. Whether roller skiing down a country road or bounding with poles up a grassy pasture, skiers can imagine themselves on snow and actually improve their skiing technique.

Visualization

It has been proven beyond a doubt that visualization, or mental imagery, can enhance performance. Examples of visualization can be observed throughout the sports world: Ingemar Stenmark, eyes closed, leaning on his ski poles at the top of a slalom course, body swaying as he mentally runs through the gates again and again; Greg Louganis poised on the edge of a ten-meter platform, eyes closed, picturing his convoluted twists, turns, and flawless entry into the water; or Michael Jordan on the foul line, eyes riveted on the rim, imagining the swish of the net several times before he poises the ball for the shot.

If confidence on fast, icy downhills is a problem for you, summer is a great time to work on it through visualization. Every time you run, bike, or roller ski down a hill, imagine yourself on skis, confident, assertive, and with excellent technique, gaining time on your opponents. (More about visualization in chapter 11.)

Warm-up, Stretching, and Cool-down

I am part of a generation that, by and large, considered warm-up and stretching superfluous. I can remember many workouts with biathlon teammates or U.S. Cross-Country Team skiers in which we just blasted off on runs or hikes as if shot from cannons. Much has been learned since then about warming and stretching the muscles before strenuous exercise. You not only perform better if properly warmed up, but you also dramatically reduce the chance of strained or torn muscles. The ideal formula calls for five to ten minutes of light exercise (such as jogging, hiking, cycling, or skiing), followed by a stop to stretch. It's always better to stretch after the muscles have been warmed up slightly.

After a challenging workout or a competition, it is important to cool down for a few minutes. Strenuous effort, especially in endurance events lasting an hour or more, generates lactic acid, which accumulates in the muscles. Anaerobic effort, like sprinting to the finish line, also creates lactic acid, but light aerobic exercise (easy jogging or skiing a cool-down loop in dry clothes) stimulates the circulatory system to begin purging the muscles of lactate. Even after an exhausting competition, a gentle cool-down will significantly speed recovery. Watch any major endurance event and you will see the top athletes finish, put on their warm-ups, and walk, jog, or ski for ten to twenty minutes before they call it a day.

Rest

Earlier in this chapter I talked about physical conditioning in its most basic form—stress followed by rest and regeneration. Without rest you won't achieve any long-term improvement. We Nordic skiers have become experts at the stress part of the equation but have largely ignored the rest.

Leave it to the Russians! Not long ago John Caldwell (perhaps America's foremost authority on cross-country) was invited to tour several elite athlete training centers in the Soviet Union. He expected to see Soviet athletes training at the limits of human endurance, and he wasn't disappointed. But what *did* surprise him was their new emphasis on rest. Caldwell saw large sleep rooms papered in restful murals depicting birch forests. Soft sounds of leaves rustling, a brook gently babbling, and songbirds chirping filled the air. He even experienced a type of electronic stimulation that took him from being wide awake to a state of deep sleep in a matter of seconds. Although the Russian approach may sound like science fiction, the concept has merit. It seems logical to me that if we could improve the *quality* of our rest, recovery might be quicker, thereby allowing an increased level of stress. Never underestimate the training benefit of rest.

The Soviets have also led the way in the use of massage to speed recovery. My biathlon friend Alexander Tichonov once invited me to join him after a workout while the Russian team masseur gave him a rubdown. At the time I regarded the scene decadent, and it made me feel uneasy. But I have since learned that massage helps the muscles flush the lactic acid that results from a

Roller skiing in a train, as these Dartmouth athletes demonstrate, can teach poise and balance as those following try to outstride the leader. Notice the helmets and reflective vests.
Clayton Gates

strenuous workout or a race, thus speeding recovery. If recovery time is reduced, then training volume and intensity can be increased. I have come to have a high regard for the rejuvenative effects of massage, whirlpool baths, and saunas.

Methods of Training

What successful ski racers actually do for training varies considerably with the athlete. It is possible, however, to generalize to some degree. Several popular methods of training used by most top skiers are listed below, from most to least specific in terms of ski racing.

Skiing

It may seem obvious, but the best training for ski racing is skiing. Increasing numbers of elite racers and hopefuls congregate at places like Dachstein Glacier in Austria throughout the summer to ski on snow. Several European national teams schedule one-week-per-month training camps on snow during the summer. An early-morning skiing workout (before the sun has softened the snow to slush) will typically be followed by an afternoon dry-land workout in the valley below. Skiing in the off-season not only is terrific in terms of specificity, but it also is tremendous motivation, reminding the athletes what all the long hours of dry-land training are really for.

Roller Skiing

The next best thing to being on snow in the off-season is roller skiing. There are dangers, both in terms of auto traffic and the possibility of developing bad habits technically, since roller skiing, though similar, is not exactly like skiing on snow. Still, all the world's best racers roller ski extensively during the off-season. Pay attention to safety! Wear a helmet and a reflective vest, and stay to the side of the road when roller skiing or blading.

Ice Skating

Since the advent of freestyle as a bona fide skiing discipline, ice skating in winter and roller blading in the summer have taken on additional value as training options. In fact, there are few forms of human-powered locomotion more exhilarating than V2 skating (with poles) across a frozen lake early in the winter. It's great for balance, poise, and control, and you can cover distance quickly and smoothly. High Peaks Cyclery in Lake Placid, New York, recently began marketing a speed-skating blade designed to be used with cross-country ski boots and bindings. It looks like a great idea, especially if the unpredictable weather of the past decade persists.

Roller Blading

Roller blades — ice hockey boots with in-line plastic wheels — are a popular new training option for skiers. Roller blades are less expensive than roller skis (plus boots and bindings), and as most skiers would admit, are more fun. Roller blades, however, can encourage technical bad habits that cause problems later on snow.

Hill Work with Ski Poles

Perhaps the best bargain in the conditioning market is hill work with poles. First of all, it's cheap (you don't need to buy expensive gear or a plane ticket to Austria). Second, if done properly, incorporating visualization, it can be remarkably specific to cross-country skiing. Also, by working arms and legs together, you are getting an aerobic bonus in your training. And finally, hill work with ski poles is wonderfully versatile — you can spend all day hiking in the mountains for an endurance session, or you can put yourself under anaerobically in twenty minutes doing uphill interval sprints. There are four distinct forms of hill work with poles.

Walking with Poles. This is just what it sounds like — you walk with your poles, synchronizing the poling motion with your stride. It's appropriate for a distance hike in the mountains.

Ski Striding with Poles. This is similar to walking, except that you make a concerted effort to take *long* steps. Good diagonal skiing technique emphasizes a powerful stride forward, down the track. Striding, especially uphill, duplicates this reaching movement with the arm, the hip, and the leg. Be sure to emphasize the length of your stride rather than your stride rate, or speed.

Bounding. Perhaps the most valuable of all hill work with poles, bounding re-creates the explosive power needed to drive the skier down the track. Like striding, bounding emphasizes stride length rather than rate, or speed, but also puts a premium on balance and poise. I encourage skiers to hesitate slightly between bounds to emphasize balance and isolate each explosive step. Concentrate on bounding forward, visualizing "down" the track, rather than up, which seems to be the natural tendency with bounding. As fatigue sets in, athletes tend to compensate by shortening the stride length and speeding up. Guard against this by counting steps up a slope (the fewest being the best) rather than taking times. Hill bounding with poles up a moderate slope, if done properly, can bring an elite athlete to his or her knees after only ten one-minute repetitions of a climb.

Lungburners. Primarily a coordination and quickness drill, lungburners (or eggbeaters) consist of flat-out sprints with poles up a moderate hill. Twenty-five to fifty meters is plenty, depending upon the severity of the slope. The idea is that every time a foot strikes the ground, the opposite pole must be

One of the best forms of endurance training is hiking in the mountains. At the Biathlon Training Center in Alaska we enjoyed many spectacular workouts like the one pictured here in Seward.

planted. Athletes quickly learn that it takes coordination, concentration, and strength to make their ski poles move as quickly as their legs. To add spice and excitement, pair up skiers and have them race (leave plenty of room between them, so they aren't impaled by each other's flying ski poles).

Rowing

Although restricted to some degree by geography, rowing is surprisingly good training for skiing. An authentic rowing shell with a movable seat enables the training of arms and legs together. The delicacy of the shell also guarantees some balance development. Rowing also offers significant psychological relief, since the setting — calm rivers, lakes, or ponds — is much different from the rolling trails and roads where most other ski training takes place.

Hiking

Perhaps the best method of accumulating hours of quality, overdistance training is hiking in the mountains. These excursions can last from a couple of hours to all day, or even all weekend. I'm fortunate to live in a part of the country where a virtually endless network of hiking trails rambles through the mountains and hills. Not only do these trails provide excellent vertical training on relatively soft footing (rather than asphalt or concrete), but the beauty of the forests, streams, and panoramic vistas provides inspiration to the spirit as well.

Running

I'm not great at it, but running certainly constitutes the lion's share of my off-season training. It lacks specificity for skiing, but it can be infinitely variable and it is wonderfully uncomplicated: put on your shorts, a T-shirt, your running shoes and go. I've been concerned in recent years about promising young skiers who can't or won't run in training. Some claim that knee or ankle injuries prevent them from running, and others state that running lacks specificity and should be replaced by roller skiing. I may sound old-fashioned, but I firmly believe that running should be the cornerstone of a successful off-season conditioning program.

Cycling

Cycling can provide excellent aerobic work without the pounding associated with running on foot. The skating revolution has also made the pedaling motion more specific and thus more valuable. The mountain bike, a fairly recent technological breakthrough, has opened up exciting new opportunities. Now it is possible to ride back roads (virtually free of auto traffic), logging roads, and even ski trails and gain almost the same natural interval feeling that you receive from skiing. Although the motions used in riding a mountain bike differ from those used in skiing, the tactics of sprint and recovery on hilly, wooded terrain are remarkably similar and therefore valuable. I expect mountain biking to become a greater part of Nordic skiers' off-season training.

Other Sports

Several other sports or competitions have gained significance in off-season training for skiers (although not especially valuable in terms of specificity).

Orienteering is very popular in Scandinavia, and many top cross-country skiers or biathletes are also highly successful in orienteering competitions.

Mountaineering and rock climbing are both great for strength and confidence. Climbing requires strong hands, arms, and shoulders as well as self-assurance and forethought.

Windsurfing has taken the summer by storm during the last decade. It's fun and exciting, and it hones athletic skills such as balance and coordination.

Kayaking puts a premium on upper-body strength. It is also great for balance and anticipation.

Soccer is a great diversion from more specific ski training as long as the emphasis is on skill and teamwork. An afternoon of soccer can be a tremendous workout (especially on an oversized field), but less-experienced players often become frustrated and occasionally aggressive, causing injuries. For years soccer was an integral part of the Dartmouth Ski Teams' training, but more off-season injuries resulted from inadequately supervised soccer games than from all other forms of dry-land training combined.

Tennis is a favorite of many skiers in the off-season and provides a valuable diversion.

Swimming is wonderful aerobic exercise. It has been said that swimming develops long, supple muscles rather than the compact, explosive power required for running and skiing. But this might be used to a skier's advantage, especially if the athlete is stiff and mechanical. Swimming is also excellent for rehabilitation following an injury. Knees or ankles that are too sore to withstand the pounding of running or the uneven ground of hiking might be perfectly capable of sustaining considerable effort in a pool.

Triathlons (swimming, cycling, and running) ensure variety in training. A commitment to triathlons also requires careful planning to balance the demands of the three components.

Strength-training options, explained earlier in the chapter, should be included on this list of conditioning activities.

And finally, don't forget *hard physical labor* (also discussed earlier).

There you have it—all the pieces you need to construct the puzzle we call a training program! But although we have all the pieces and some suggestions on how they should fit together, the process is not an easy one. To be effective, a training schedule must be personalized—custom-made for the individual athlete. I couldn't even design a generic summer training plan for the "typical" Dartmouth skier. What do you do when one of your athletes goes home to Putney, Vermont, to paint school buildings (flexible schedule, ideal terrain for hiking and roller skiing, inspiring training partners), a second works as a legal assistant in New York City (long hours, limited time to train, no roller skiing or hiking), and a third spends the summer at ROTC Summer Camp at Fort Campbell, Kentucky (no free time at all)?

Designing Your Own Program

What it comes down to is that you, the athlete, must devise your own schedule using the above pieces and suggestions as they best fit your individual goals and situation. Regardless of your aspirations or geographic location, you can design a training plan that will help you achieve improved results in cross-country skiing. I recommend the book *Serious Training for Serious Athletes*, by Rob Sleamaker, which provides excellent, detailed, and comprehensive guidance for developing a training plan. I will just touch on the book's highlights here.

First, you need to establish your goals. You can't very well chart a course if you don't know the destination. (See chapter 11 for a detailed discussion of goal setting.)

Once your goals are defined, evaluate honestly where you are now. Are you a promising U.S. Team hopeful coming off a successful racing season? Or are you a forty-four-year-old drawn back to the sport because your clothes have become too tight and your cholesterol level has climbed too high? In general terms, if you've kept a log and last year went well for you, an increase of 15 percent in annual hours of training would probably be in line. If you haven't kept a log or haven't exercised on a regular basis for some time, consult your doctor before you design a training program.

Another consideration for those both earning a living and raising a family is how much time per day you can reasonably devote to training. It makes no sense to develop a beautiful 600-hour-per-year training schedule when, realistically (considering your other commitments), the most you can devote to training is about an hour a day. That works out to 365 hours a year, somewhat short of your plan. So, considering your current physical condition, what type of training you've done in the last year or so, *and* your available time, arrive at a target number of hours for the year's training.

Now comes a process that in the army was known as "back planning." In his book Sleamaker talks about the five training stages of the year: recovery, base, intensity, peak, and racing. He assigns time commitments to each stage as follows:

Recovery,	four to six weeks
Base,	sixteen weeks
Intensity,	sixteen weeks
Peak,	four to six weeks
Racing,	eight to twelve weeks

Using back-planning techniques, look at your next racing season. When do you anticipate your earliest race, and when will the racing be over for the year? Let's assume that the first race that really interests you is right after Christmas, and your last major event is scheduled for the second weekend in March. Those two events delineate a racing season of eleven weeks. You have established your racing stage. Now work backward through the peak, intensity, base, and recovery phases, blocking out segments of time that seem reasonable to you, using the above guidelines.

You now have the fifty-two weeks of the year (or that part of the year remaining before your next racing season) divided into different training stages. Using the terminology from Sleamaker's book, your next job is "periodization within weekly cycles." The body responds better to gradual stress increases, interspersed with planned low-stress weeks, better than it deals with random "killer" training weeks back to back. Sleamaker advocates a four-week cycle: three weeks of gradually increasing volume and intensity, followed by a week of low volume for R and R (rest and recuperation). At Dartmouth we used a three-week rotation; easy week, moderate week, hard week. I believe in the value of such cycles, whether they be three weeks or four.

Periodization Within the 4-week Cycle

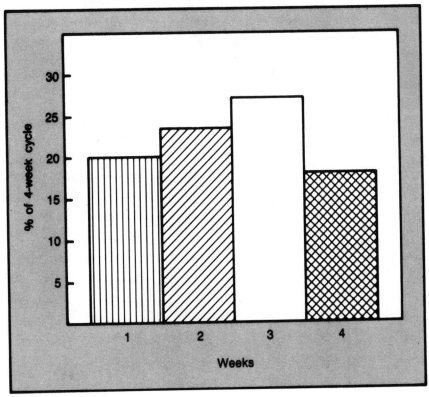

Finally, remember hard day/easy day rotation. This is more complicated than it sounds. During your training year a two-hour distance run might constitute a hard day at one point, whereas several months later a two-hour distance ski might be considered a recovery day following a race.

Now it's time to start crunching numbers. Using two graphs borrowed from Sleamaker's book — "Periodization Distribution between Training Cycles" and "Periodization within the Four-Week Cycle" — start breaking your target yearly training hours into appropriate percentages for each stage, and then each four-week cycle within the stage. Don't be afraid to modify the suggested percentages to your own situation. These graphs are most often based upon training information gathered from national-team athletes and coaches. What works for them doesn't always work for the rest of us.

If you know that the holidays will require a lot of family time and other obligations, write this into your program. Perhaps you can schedule a low-volume training week over Christmas and back-plan from there.

Periodization Distribution Between Training Cycles

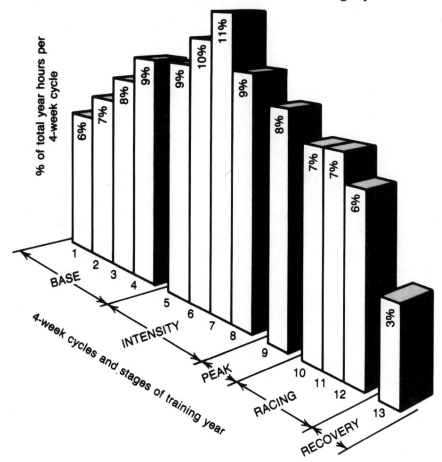

Once you've filled in your weekly targets, you can schedule individual days and specific workouts. This is where the juggling act becomes exciting, as you try to fit the various pieces of the puzzle together: strength training three times a week, at least one overdistance day, a couple of roller-ski workouts, a local foot race on Saturday—all taking into account hard day/easy day, specificity, variety, and so on. But take heart, there is no right or wrong way to develop your training plan; there is only what does or does not seem to work for *you*.

When your plan is finally hammered out, remember it is not much more than a road map to your goal. It is a *guide*, not the gospel. *You* made it, and you can change it if necessary. Olympic medals have been won using a staggering

(D) WEEKLY TRAINING LOG Date:_____ Week:_____

| Date | DISTANCE | | | | SPEED | STRENGTH | OTHER | sleep pulse weight | TOTAL DAILY TIME |
	SKI or BIKE	SKI roll / blade	RUN	Other: hike, swim, paddle, erg, etc.	high intensity : race / interval / speed		Biathlon: shooting		
Mon									
Tues									
Wed									
Thurs									
Fri									
Sat									
Sun									
Sub-Total distance/ hours					distance hrs:	speed hrs:	stength hrs:		Total Weekly hrs:
Total distance/ hours									

Sample page from a training log. It can be as simple or complex as you want, but it should include type of workout, duration (both in distance and time), and how you felt.

array of training programs. The one thing they all had in common was that the successful athlete believed in the plan. Don't be too quick to adjust, modify, or throw out your plan, especially if you put a lot of thought and energy into creating it. Cross-country skiing is a long-term investment. A sound, carefully designed training program may not show immediate results, but it might be responsible for a major breakthrough a year or two down the road.

Don't be a slave to your training program, however; life is full of unanticipated surprises and it's important to adjust to them. Let's say, in spite of all reasonable precautions, you come down with the flu. You know you should rest for several days, but you don't want to screw up your carefully designed program. Don't sweat it. Give yourself a chance to recover, then get back on the program. Don't try to make up for lost time or train twice as hard—just pick up the schedule where you are. Remember, the training schedule is just a means to an end: better racing results. Don't let the training schedule become an end in itself. If your races are mediocre, nobody is going to care that you never missed a workout. On the other hand, if you "smoke the field" at the races, the four training days you missed in November visiting your grandmother are not going to seem too significant.

Now that you've established your goals and developed a plan to help you achieve them, you're more than halfway there. All that remains administratively is keeping track of what you've done and, at the end of the season, evaluating your results. Keep a training log to provide a record of your training, racing, and state of mind. If you've had a tremendous racing season, your log documents the training that supported that success. If, on the other hand, your race results weren't what you had hoped for, the log contains clues that will help you discover the shortcomings in your plan, and you can revise it for the next season.

Training logs for elite athletes can become ridiculously detailed, recording everything from total vertical climb in every workout to daily urine color. If you keep your log simple, you will be more likely to keep it filled in. It can be helpful to know what your resting pulse was each morning, what you ate each day, or how many hours of sleep you got each night, but the really important things are what you did for training, how long it took, and how you felt. If you consistently record these three items, you're well on your way to achieving your competitive goals.

At the end of each season, review and analyze your conditioning plan and training log. If you were happy with the winter's race results, try to determine what were the key ingredients to your success. If not, think about what changes you should make in the plan for next year. The training plan and log are valuable tools only if you use them to improve your program each year.

Keep It Fun

I've saved the most important until last. Keep it fun! I mean it! As I've mentioned several times before, success in Nordic racing is a long-term investment, requiring *years* rather than weeks or months. Inevitably, promising American competitors retire from competition long before they have reached their physical peak. Audun Endestad, age thirty-eight, and Nancy Fiddler, age thirty-five, both multiple National Champions, are notable exceptions. The only way to ensure such longevity is to make certain that your training is fun. Obviously there will be individual workouts (a three-hour distance hike in the pouring rain or a 10K classic time trial in a blizzard at 32°F) that you won't recall as a "barrel of laughs." But in general you must look forward to your workouts and enjoy the people with whom you train. In short, you must celebrate the lifestyle of the conscientious athlete. When training becomes drudgery or obligation, your race results will certainly suffer and, before long, your competitive career will be over.

If your training becomes a vital and enjoyable part of your daily routine, if it instills in you a sense of accomplishment and feeling of self-worth, if it keeps you physically fit, and if it puts you in contact with motivated, energetic people who share your enthusiasm, then you probably can look forward to a racing career like those of Dr. John Bland, who skated to a sixth-place finish in the 70–74 age category at the 1990 World Masters Ski Championships in Östersund, Sweden, and Loren Adkins, National Champion and a 1990 U.S. Masters Team member in the 80+ category. Just keep it fun!

4: On Snow

L IKE THE SWALLOWS returning each year to Capistrano, the faithful elite cross-country skiers of America are drawn to West Yellowstone, Montana, every November for its early snow. The small town grew up around the western entrance to Yellowstone National Park. Summer is its big season, when more than a million tourists come to see the natural wonders of our oldest and largest national park. Perhaps twenty years ago a second tourist season began to develop in the winter to explore the park and its surroundings by snowmobile. Then in the mid-1970s the U.S. Ski Team was looking for an early-season training site, and Neil Swanson stepped into the picture. Neil, a West Yellowstone businessman and restaurateur whose sons loved to ski, drummed up some community support, cut and groomed a couple of cross-country trails, and invited the Ski Team to try them out. It proved to be a great arrangement. West Yellowstone usually had snow by early November, and if not, a twenty-minute drive to a plateau 1,000 feet higher could guarantee terrific skiing. Neil and his crew set and groomed trails for the skiers, who filled rooms that otherwise would be vacant between the summer crush of tourists and the winter influx of snowmobilers. Over the years the trails have been extended, more-sophisticated grooming equipment has been purchased, and the skiers flock to West Yellowstone in greater numbers.

Success hasn't spoiled Neil Swanson, who still operates his cozy log cabin restaurant on one of West Yellowstone's main streets. A wood stove heats the small dining room, while a generic sign over the building both directs and commands "CAFE EAT." Neil had planned to close up after a busy summer and fall, but the biathletes persuaded him to stay open through their training camp.

Biathlon Team coaches Bill Spencer and Max Cobb met me at the airport. We threaded our way to West Yellowstone through the starlit Gallatin Canyon, barely avoiding a disastrous collision with a thousand-pound bull elk. It was late when we arrived, so we agreed to meet for breakfast in the morning and turned in.

We headed up to the plateau by midmorning. I had established two general goals for my week in the West: to spend as much time on skis as reasonably possible and to concentrate on improving my technique and balance. I was not interested in going fast but in going long. This was always more difficult than it seemed since it was fun to train with others, many of whom had been on snow longer and were ready to pick up the pace. Additionally, every person skiing in West Yellowstone in November is a current or former competitor. It is almost impossible for these people to ski with each other hour after hour without occasionally "turning on the jets" just to see how their training partner will react.

The rolling Forest Service roads of the plateau were perfect for me: gradual, gentle terrain where I could cruise for hours without putting myself under in the thin air. That first morning I skied a total of twenty-eight kilometers in 1³/₄ hours. I felt clumsy, my balance was awkward, and my arms ached before I was finished, but it was great to be on snow again.

It was well past lunch when we arrived back in town. A blustery cold wind bringing snow squalls encouraged me to forego an afternoon ski in favor of an exploratory foot run around town. With the snow whipping at me, I ran through the deserted streets of West Yellowstone toward the park's massive entrance gate. The gate, toll booth, and ranger station were made of huge logs, some more than two feet in diameter, and were truly impressive. Like the adjacent town, the entrance appeared closed for the season as I ducked under the barrier and jogged into the park.

I was reminded of a training camp almost twenty years earlier, when several of us entered the park without permission and, in a few hours of youthful fun, committed violations totaling thousands of dollars. We hadn't realized that it was a punishable offense to enter the park when it was closed, skijor behind four-wheel-drive vehicles on the snow-packed roads, take close-up photos of the wildlife, or skinny-dip in the thermal springs. Somehow John Caldwell, then head coach of the U.S. Ski Team, smoothed things over with the park rangers. Even now it made me nervous to be in the park with the barricade down, so I retraced my steps and made a clean escape.

Just outside the gate I stopped to do calisthenics and some stretching. I was sore and tired from the morning's ski, but I had known from previous years what to expect. As long as I didn't overdo it, the aches and pains would diminish after a week or so on snow.

I would have been happy taking all my meals at Neil Swanson's, but the package rate I'd purchased at the Three Bears Lodge included food. Actually it was a great deal. The U.S. Ski Team had been staying there long enough that the chef was well versed in the nutritional requirements of endurance athletes. There was a wide variety of wholesome food: breads, pasta, veggies, fruit, yogurt, and juices. In fact, there was such a selection of healthy options, it wasn't until several days into my stay that I noticed the absence of junk food. There was no soda pop, no burgers and fries, no sugary desserts, no bacon or doughnuts for breakfast. Growing up in a generation much less conscious of what we ate, I was impressed with the nutritional knowledge and resolve of the younger athletes. And I discovered to my surprise that even after several days of hard training and meals at the Three Bears, I wasn't overcome by an insatiable urge for a Big Mac or a hot-fudge sundae.

Mealtimes at the Three Bears provided a chance to catch up with old friends and get to know some of the promising newcomers. One of my favorite U.S. Team members is Leslie Thompson. As a Dartmouth skier, Leslie quickly earned a reputation as a hard-working student and an organized, no-nonsense skier. Anything she may have lacked in natural athletic ability she more than made up for in dedication, self-reliance, and determination. At the 1988 Olympics in Calgary she demonstrated what she was really made of.

The cross-country trails at Canmore were like a giant roller coaster: punishing climbs followed by stomach-churning descents. The snow was "bullet proof" after weeks of freezing, thawing, and grooming. Just days before her first Olympic race, Leslie sat back slightly on the most treacherous downhill, was launched off the next roll, and slammed face first into the hard-packed surface. By the time she reached the start/finish stadium, the left side of her face was badly bruised and her eye was swollen shut.

In the dining hall that evening Leslie looked more like an Olympic boxer than a cross-country skier. Within the next few days, her eye still swollen shut and her confidence severely shaken, Leslie was back on skis. She raced all four women's cross-country events, including a strong leg in the relay, which helped the American team to a commendable eighth place. Courage is generally associated with bobsledders, ski jumpers, and downhillers; but day after day I watched this spunky cross-country skier from Vermont exhibit raw courage on the icy trails at Canmore.

Dining at the Three Bears also gave me a chance to speak with Nancy Fiddler, the astounding thirty-five-year-old who, several years out of Bates College, decided she'd try for the U.S. Ski Team. In 1986, the first year of her comeback, she won a National Championship event, and she did it again in 1987. In 1988 she earned a spot on the Olympic team, and at the Nationals in 1989 she won three of four races against women more than ten years younger. Nancy reminded me of America's best-ever female cross-country skier, Martha Rockwell, who also discovered the sport relatively late but had phenomenal success.

Audun Endestad was there, too, and we shared stories about Alaska. He makes his home in Fairbanks and enjoys the surrounding hills and nearby mountains for summertime overdistance hiking and hunting trips. Audun is a softspoken, transplanted Norwegian who is just reaching his stride at age thirty-eight, as evidenced by his four victories at the 1990 U.S. National Championships. "Lower Forty-eight" skiers regard Audun almost as a reincarnation of some mythical Norse god, running and skiing unimaginable distances in workouts and returning to his small cabin in the woods to carve a slab of meat off the frozen hindquarter of a caribou hanging on the back porch. The Alaskans just consider him one of their own.

The next day I was up early for my morning run to the park entrance. I had slept well and had awoken before six because of the change in time zone, but I was stiff and sore. I knew the easy jog and calisthenics before breakfast would loosen the aching muscles. It was a cold, clear day and the early-morning sky above the Rockies was bright pink. After breakfast it was back to the plateau for a classic-skiing workout. The sun was bright but the snow was cold, and the waxing was straightforward hard wax. I skied a short, two-kilometer technique loop that U.S. Team Head Coach Steve Gaskill had put in for his national-team members. There was limited traffic, and only Audun cruised past me occasionally. At one point Steve pulled me aside to give me a pointer. He was good-natured, even joking about the suggestion that I extend my gliding foot slightly to lengthen my stride. I felt slightly awkward at this first acknowledgment that I was no longer a coach, but once again a racer. I was grateful for Steve's advice, and I knew he was right. I concentrated the rest of the morning on extending that stride.

After lunch it was back to the plateau. I had mapped out a plan emphasizing distance workouts, variety, and classic skiing. Classic, or diagonal, skiing provided the foundation for technique. An excellent classic skier will almost always be a successful skater as well, but good skaters are not all good diagonal skiers. Therefore, it pays to spend the technique time on classic. Furthermore, if there was any snow at all in the East when I returned, it would probably be adequate only for skating. So it made sense to capitalize on the good classic tracks while I was in the West. One significant benefit of the skating revolution is the variety it adds to training, both on and off snow. In the old days it was just kicking and gliding every day, the only variation being length or intensity of the workout. But now we can alternate classic with skating, providing an important physical variation as well as mental relief.

I skated for about an hour in the strengthening wind and brilliant pink sunset. Back at the lodge I did sit-ups and push-ups before showering and going to supper.

Thursday was a repeat of Wednesday: a morning run with stretching, breakfast, and the drive to the plateau. Max led me to a magnificent Forest

Service road, seven rolling kilometers with double tracks out to a turnaround point. I made two trips before I headed up to the parking lot to catch a ride to lunch. The afternoon was another hour of skating, but I was beginning to feel the fatigue, my balance was still shaky, and I looked like a wounded rhino trying to V2 skate.

Jim Stray-Gundersen, one of the U.S. Team doctors, saved the workout for me. I was about to quit in frustration when he suggested we ski a loop together. Jim has a thriving sports medicine research lab in Dallas and (like a coach) doesn't have enough time to train. But he loves skiing and races when he can, even though he knows he is not in condition to do his best. We skied a second loop together, solving all the U.S. Ski Team's problems in our seven-kilometer conversation. It wasn't until after we had finished that I noticed how much better I felt the second loop than the first. When I had relaxed with Jim, taking my mind off technique with our conversation, my skiing had smoothed out and my balance had improved. It reminded me of an old lesson: You can't work hard at cross-country skiing; you have to relax and let it flow. When I was working at my skating technique on the first lap, I couldn't stay out of my own way; but when Jim got my mind off my skiing, my skating improved.

By Friday morning I was beginning to fall apart. Since I had done very little roller skiing in the summer and fall (and none of it was classic technique), my groin muscles were killing me. My lower back was stiff and sore from skiing, and I had slightly pinched a nerve while stretching on a morning run. Finally, I was developing a huge blister under the big toe on my right foot, an annual occurrence whenever I began classic skiing.

The Friday morning run was torture. The muscles on the inside of my thighs felt as tight as banjo strings, the blister on my toe hurt, and the pinched nerve in my back shot pain through my spine every time I twisted slightly. But I guess that's where experience is an advantage. I knew the aching groin muscles and the blistered toe would eventually subside. In fact, these minor inconveniences were all part of training at a high level. Many younger athletes train hard until the first hint of injury or illness, then stop. Of course, some maladies require complete rest, but it is also true that minor aches and pains are part of the territory if you are going to train 600 to 1,000 hours a year. The real champions in any sport can distinguish the potentially serious injuries and illnesses from the more routine inconveniences, and they don't let the minor problems derail their entire training programs. I once heard it said that "Olympic medals are won on strains, sprains, and blisters."

By this time the full Disabled Nordic contingent had arrived, including their enthusiastic and gregarious chiropractor, Paul Westby, from Minneapolis. I asked Paul if he could check out my back, and within two minutes he had adjusted my spine and relieved the pain. That morning, another beautiful western day on the plateau, I skied diagonal with Joe Walsh, a former Dartmouth Development Team member and winner of several medals in National and World Championships in the sight-disabled category. We skied together for an hour and a half. It was a great workout.

At some point after you feel comfortable on your skis, it is productive to ski with someone else (of about the same ability), or even in a "train." The leader tries to ski long and smooth (not fast), and those following try to match or exceed the leader's stride. Emphasis is on poise, balance, and gliding rather than stride rate. Joe and I exchanged the lead several times and forced each other to concentrate. It was a very satisfying morning, enough so that we repeated the workout that afternoon.

An endurance training program should have at least one overdistance workout a week. I knew I would be racing at least a couple of 50K events during the winter, so I needed to plug in some endurance workouts of three hours or more. Since the diagonal tracks were so good on the lower road, and no one knew for sure what the weather was going to do, I decided Saturday morning would be an overdistance workout. I concentrated on carefully stretching the sore muscles during my prebreakfast run, then really fueled up on oatmeal, toast, orange juice, and coffee. I smuggled a couple of bananas out of the restaurant and filled two water bottles with Exceed. I also added to my backpack a decent selection of kick waxes; conditions were variable and I would almost certainly have to rewax during the morning.

A thin film of sleet like miniature ball bearings covered the tracks. When I finally found a wax that kicked, the skiing was great. I skied three round-trips on the lower road, stopping for part of a banana and some Exceed after each loop. The workout took three hours, and I covered more than forty kilometers. What was especially satisfying was that I had bulled through some tricky waxing conditions. It was a great confidence builder!

By this point my roommate, Joe Ranari, had arrived. He was a sight-disabled skier from Delaware who skied in the B-2 class (his vision was more restricted than Joe Walsh's, but he was not totally blind). Ranari was not just a legally blind person who skied—he was a bona fide athlete. He had been a very successful runner, swimmer, cyclist, and triathlete before he discovered the Disabled Ski Team. Even with his limited experience on snow, he was America's best in the B-2 class and would have been a serious threat in the World Championships if his home were in New England or the Rocky Mountains. But Joe's job and family were in Delaware, so he roller skied a lot and relished the chance to ski on snow when training camps or competitive trips allowed the opportunity. His optimism and enthusiasm were contagious, in spite of the fact that he had recently discovered he was diabetic and was still experimenting with insulin dosages for workouts and races.

As I observed my roommate over the next few days—a guy for whom the world was a gray blur and who joked with me about being a junkie as he carefully injected his insulin—the minor discomfort of my strained groin muscles and blistered toe vanished. I was living with an athlete who, in spite of the challenges he faced, never complained about anything. It's been said a thousand times, but we sure do take things for granted!

With the weekend had come an influx of athletes and teams taking advantage of the Thanksgiving break. Several ski academies, prep schools, and even a couple of colleges were represented. In response to the population explosion, the locals opened up a freshly groomed Forest Service road high in the hills several miles west of town. Sunday morning was reminiscent of the California gold rush, with vans, cars, and ski-team Subarus all racing bumper to bumper to the new tracks. It was well worth the drive for a flawlessly groomed ten-kilometer section of rolling terrain.

The excitement was so infectious it was difficult not to race to the end of the road just to see where it went. The out-and-back route was great for socializing. During a couple of round-trips you could see everyone from U.S. Team elite to high school hopefuls. Coaches congregated along the trail. Steve Gaskill gave U.S. Team members technique suggestions. Dennis Donahue and West German ace Walter Pichler watched America's best biathletes and discussed their observations. Dr. Jim Stray-Gundersen had set up his mobile lab and was testing national-team athletes' blood lactate levels. As I skied past, he called cheerfully, "Morty, pull in here for a blood test."

"No thanks, Stray Cat. I gave to the Red Cross, and, besides, I need every drop at this altitude!"

Far out on the loop was a solid, heavy-set guy in a U.S. Team uniform whom I didn't recognize. A couple of kilometers later, the light bulb switched on in my head. He was Nikolai Anikin, one of the top Nordic coaches in the Soviet Union who, along with his wife, was serving as a consultant to the U.S. Team. He stood somberly studying the American skiers from his vantage point several yards off the track. As I skied past him for the second time, I looked up and made use of my very limited Russian: *"Strasvitcha Nikolai!"*

Like the sun coming out from behind the clouds, his face broke into a grin and gold teeth sparkled. *"Da, da, strasvitcha,"* he responded as I skied past.

It was another morning of great skiing (skating this time) and good fun. That afternoon, I reverted to a coaching role by helping a couple of Disabled Nordic Team members with their classic technique. The Disabled Nordic World Championships were coming up in January, for the first time hosted by the United States. Our athletes were already wired, and it was only November.

Monday was my last day in Montana. After breakfast I returned to the recently opened road and skied in perfect western conditions. I skied classic for 1½ hours nonstop, knowing it would be my last on-snow workout for some time. The pain in my groin muscles was gone, and it was pure pleasure to cruise out and back on the perfect tracks.

A few hours later, as I settled into my window seat for the flight to Salt Lake, the first leg of the trip back, I reviewed my training log. In seven days at West Yellowstone I had completed just over 18 hours of training, a total of 234 kilometers on skis. Of those 234 kilometers, 146 (or 62 percent) were classic, about what I was shooting for. In terms of training time, I had devoted about 2½ hours to foot running, 11¼ hours to classic skiing, and the remaining 4½ hours to skating. In general, I was very happy with the week. Even though the trails in town had been unskiable, I had not missed a workout in a full week. I'd worked through the normal aches and pains of the annual transition to snow, I'd caught up with scores of friends, and best of all, I'd be home with my wife and daughter for Thanksgiving.

By November 27 there was skiing available in Vermont at the higher elevations, but it meant a minimum forty-five minute commute each way. I mapped out a training schedule that alternated skiing days with dry-land workouts. After all, it was only November! About that time a neighbor in Thetford who is an enthusiastic citizen racer let me in on a wonderful secret: The Vermont snowmobile association has been gradually developing a beautiful trail network throughout the state. Until recently that was of no interest to Nordic skiers except that it kept the snow machines off our ski trails. With the advent of skating, however, the snowmobile trails have taken on new significance. Many of the trails are old logging roads that are groomed by large Sno-Cats pulling long, heavy drags to level and smooth the snow. The result is some of the best skating available anywhere. Many of us who were outspokenly critical of snowmobilers when they obliterated our diagonal-skiing tracks are now going hat in hand to ask permission to skate on *their* trails. And you know what? We haven't been turned down yet.

A neighbor, Tom Ozahowski, told me about a section of snowmobile trail not far from Killington Ski Area that gets great early-season snow and is often groomed, even when the ground is bare in the valleys. Tom gave me careful directions and I easily found the trail. The skating was as good as any I had experienced out West, and it was only November 27. Two days later Tom and I returned together for another skating workout. It was cold and windy, so by the end of two hours we were ready to head home. It was the first time in more than a decade that I had skied in the East on well-groomed trails before the first of December.

One of the nearby touring centers, known for early snow, is Mountain Top in Chittenden, Vermont. Perched right on the spine of the Green Mountains just north of Killington and Pico Alpine areas, Mountain Top clearly benefits from its elevation. A few years ago, when Mike Gallagher decided to give up his position as head coach of the U.S. Cross-Country Team to spend more time with his family, Mountain Top gave him a job. It was a match made in heaven. Mike is probably the most extroverted, enthusiastic Nordic racer America has ever produced. From the early 1960s through the mid-1970s, Gallagher was clearly the leader. During his career he won more than a dozen National Championships, an accomplishment only now challenged by Audun Endestad.

Mike has probably seen and skied with more of the world's best racers than any other American. So when I heard that Mountain Top was open on December 1, I threw my skis in my pickup and headed over. Gallagher was in typical form, scrambling to get his ski shop and rental equipment in order before the weekend rush. He gave me a trail pass and directed me to the loops that had been groomed. It was a cold, windy day (not much above 0°F, if at all), but the views both east and west were terrific. After an hour or so I returned to the lodge to warm up. Gallagher was raring to go. I thawed out my fingers and toes and followed him back into the cold.

During the next forty-five-minute tour (in spite of the bitter temperature and howling wind), we seldom stopped talking. Mike was extremely excited, perhaps envious, about my project for the winter. He had joined Bob Gray and Mike Elliott the previous winter at the World Masters Championships, hosted in Mount Ste. Anne, Quebec, and the old threesome had "kicked butt" in the relay. Before long our tour had become a lesson, and Mike was filling me in on the latest nuances of the skating technique. I was reassured that not much was new or different from what I had been advocating to my Dartmouth skiers the previous year.

I left Mountain Top exhausted but energized by Gallagher's enthusiasm. There are a handful of Americans who have truly dedicated their lives to cross-country skiing, and Mike Gallagher is a charter member of that group.

It had been a productive week. The biggest plus had been the availability of decent skiing — a real luxury in late November. I alternated skiing days with the hard physical days in the woods — clearing a trail and gathering firewood.

During the first two weeks of December my training followed pretty much the same formula: skiing every other day, alternated with strength work in the woods. The weather was both an ally and an enemy. We had been blessed with early snow — by December there was even enough to skate on the Hanover Golf Course — but then the mercury dropped, eventually establishing a new record for the second-coldest December in history. The meager snow cover remained, but training in temperatures that seldom rose above 0°F was exhausting. Part of my plan had been to spend a few days at Mount Ste. Anne, Quebec, about six hours' drive north of Thetford, but I began to have misgivings and felt uneasy about the whole idea.

Ste. Anne, within site of the mighty St. Lawrence River, had the tendency to be very cold. As December continued to set new temperature records, I could imagine what it was like at Ste. Anne, and I wondered whether it would be worth the trip. My ten years in Alaska had taught me that, properly dressed, it is possible to train in almost any weather. But if you have an alternative, the value of training while waddling around bundled up in all the warm-ups you own, socks over your boots, bulky mittens, and face masks comes into question. I *could* stay at home and continue to scratch around on the golf course or snowmobile trails.

The Dartmouth Team had gone to Quebec on schedule and had been there for a week. I phoned my successor, Ruff Patterson, for a weather report. He admitted it had been cold, but the skiing was great (including classic tracks) and they were having a productive training camp despite the temperatures. I decided to go. On December 14 I threw my gear into the back of my truck and headed north.

After almost two hours I reached the Canadian border. I had learned long ago to be polite and friendly to the customs officers, to answer their questions and not be a wiseass about it. Once, in the early seventies, a Biathlon Team member joked about the ten thousand rounds of ammunition we were carrying, and we were subjected to a two-hour inspection. The official who stopped me this time, however, merely asked my destination and length of stay, then wished me a pleasant trip. Next stop: Drummondville.

On our first pilgrimage to Ste. Anne, after three hours in the van, we were looking for a place to eat, stretch our legs, and use the bathroom. We pulled into the McDonald's at Drummondville. Given free rein in ordering, my eleven athletes amassed an awesome array of Big Macs, fries, fish fillets, shakes, and sundaes.

When they finished, a couple of the guys discovered that they weren't quite full, so they returned for one more fish fillet or cherry pie. But finally, happily stuffed, we waddled back to the van for the remaining two-hour drive to Mount Ste. Anne.

As I pulled out into the traffic, our team captain, Kirk Siegel, burst out excitedly, "Hey Morty, there's a Dunkin' Donuts! Let's get some for the road!"

I slammed on the brakes in disbelief.

"You've got to be kidding! How could you eat doughnuts after what you just put away at McDonald's?"

Kirk responded with assurance, "I could eat a dozen doughnuts right now, no problem!"

There was silence in the van as I swerved into the Dunkin' Donuts parking lot. The van came to a stop in front of the huge plate glass window displaying scores of sugar-coated, glazed, jelly-filled, and chocolate-covered confections. I turned to Kirk with a smile and said, "You're on! I'll buy you a dozen doughnuts just to see you eat them right now! But if you don't finish all of them, you pay. Whadyasay?"

A lively discussion followed. Kirk maintained confidently he could do it, and Colin McNay (who weighed all of 140 pounds) chimed in, "Yeah, me too, no problem." Reason prevailed, however, when the other guys envisaged the remaining two hours in the van if Siegel and McNay got sick trying to fulfill the challenge. We settled for two dozen assorted "road doughnuts," which we shared over the remaining two hours of the trip.

More than a year later I was headed home (with another group of skiers) after a great ten-day training camp. Of course, tradition demanded that we stop in Drummondville. The first hint that something was up came when we placed our orders at McDonald's. Several of the guys were noticeably restrained: "Uh, I'll have a Big Mac, small fries, and a medium Coke please." Then, before everyone had finished, several of the group headed for the door, cheerfully shouting as they left, "Morty, we're going across the street to Dunkin' Donuts. Will you pick us up there?" When I pulled the van into the Dunkin' Donuts parking lot, they piled in loaded with boxes of doughnuts, announcing with a flourish, "The Drummondville Dunkin' Donut Challenge is about to commence!"

For the next twenty miles the skiers debated rules, finally agreeing on a forty-minute time limit in which to consume a dozen of the most disgusting, sugar-coated, cream-stuffed, jelly-filled doughnuts I had ever seen.

When it came right down to it, I was having some severe misgivings. Is this something a prudent and responsible parent would endorse? Could someone have serious repercussions from an overdose of sugar? I gave them my "everything in moderation" speech, to no avail. They listened politely, and as soon as I had finished, their self-appointed announcer reviewed the rules and introduced the contestants. The attention focused on two freshmen as the contest unfolded. Complete with official timekeeper, a competition jury to settle disputes, and their announcer giving the play-by-play, the competition commenced. For several minutes I watched in the rearview mirror as the freshmen, Tim Derrick and Tom Longstreth, happily consumed doughnuts. Longstreth showed signs of strain first. Even though it was bitterly cold outside, he opened a window and leaned his face into the freezing air. He was working on doughnut number eleven when he plaintively mumbled, "Morty, could you pull over for a minute?"

He assured us he wasn't sick, he just needed air and the chance to stretch his legs. Meanwhile, Derrick just kept eating. As Longstreth paced beside the van in the freezing Quebec wind, a weak whistle sounded from the middle seat. Derrick had done it! One dozen doughnuts, after a full meal, in less than forty minutes! Even the upperclassmen were impressed. Amid slaps on the back and congratulations, Tim calmly reached for Tom's remaining doughnut.

"Just so none of you will think I had trouble with the first dozen," he said, as he finished off number thirteen.

This is a somewhat lengthy explanation as to why, almost against my will, completely alone in my pickup truck, I was drawn to the Drummondville McDonald's. And I confess that after a prudent meal there, I crossed the street for a coffee and two plain doughnuts to go. The power of tradition is a frightening thing.

From Drummondville, Quebec, north the countryside is flat, with huge metal towers marching across the farmland carrying high-tension electric lines. There is an impressive bridge across the St. Lawrence, spanning two high cliffs where General Wolfe defeated Montcalm more than two hundred years ago. From the bridge it's easy to see what a gutsy decision it must have been for Wolfe to cross the powerful St. Lawrence, which flows swiftly through the narrow gorge, and climb the sheer rock face to attack the well-fortified French garrison in the dead of night.

About ten miles south of Ste. Anne de Beaupré you can spot the blinking red lights atop the twin spires of the cathedral. It is one of the most impressive buildings of its kind in North America, and it looks even more impressive dominating a small town on the banks of the mighty St. Lawrence.

A couple of miles past the cathedral you leave the river valley and turn north into the hills for a couple of miles as you approach the base of the alpine mountain, the highest point so close to the St. Lawrence for many miles. At sunset the view from the top of the mountain is unforgettable, with the skyline and twinkling lights of Quebec City visible to the south and the broad expanse of the river to the east reflecting the alpenglow.

I felt both relief and regret when I saw the Dartmouth vans lined up at the Chalets Montmorency. It was hard to believe, after eleven years, that I hadn't driven one of them. This year, however, my only reason for the trip was to ski, and if I got cracking, I could squeeze in a workout before dark! I checked in, changed clothes, and was on the trail within thirty minutes. I skated on perfectly groomed snow from the chalet up the bike path that linked it to the touring center. It was cold! By the time I returned, in the dark, my fingers and toes were numb.

The next morning was clear and frigid. I decided to forego the morning run in an effort to maximize the time on snow. After years of supervising a dozen athletes, it was refreshing to get my own breakfast, wax my skis, and head out. In the morning I skied classic for 2½ hours, putting in about forty kilometers. I had to stop several times to swing life back into my fingers and toes. After plenty of hot soup and a rest at lunch time, I was back out at three o'clock for 1¾ hours of skating. This time I pulled socks over my ski boots to keep my feet warm (an old Alaskan trick) and wore bulky Alpine ski gloves rather than the skimpy cross-country variety. Having licked the cold, I could now concentrate on technique. The bike path was perfect for working on stride length, long glide, riding a flat ski, and balance. I skied several minutes worth of no-pole drills. The Dartmouth Team had just about finished its camp and asked me to race in the final time trial Saturday morning. It would be a good test, just over eight kilometers, classic.

Ruff invited me to join the team that evening for a technique and video session. It was an interesting (and reassuring) session on skating. Since Ruff had worked with the U.S. Ski Team for several years and collaborated with Torbjorn Karlsen on several articles, I considered him an authority on the skating technique. It was reassuring to hear his presentation and view his video analysis. I had been advocating the same principles that he now presented to the team. Some of the upperclassmen even grinned at me as Ruff used phrases they had heard before. The meeting broke up with some good-natured ribbing about whether or not I would perform well enough in the next day's time trial to make the carnival team. The upperclassmen whom I had coached were eager to tease me, and I enjoyed giving it right back to them.

The next morning was cold and overcast. I ate breakfast, waxed my skis, and headed for the trail. Although the time trial would start and finish up at the touring center, I felt that the seven kilometers along the bike path would be a good warm-up and loosen muscles stiff from Friday's double workouts. I stopped once to rewax; my guess at the chalet had turned out to be too slippery. I arrived at the touring center to find Ruff and Cami Thompson, the Development Team coach, standing alone in the windswept start area. With the combined impetus of the temperature and the wind, the athletes had been eager to get the workout under way. I quickly stripped off my warm-ups and Ruff started me several minutes after the last team member.

We skied a nice, rolling 8.1-kilometer loop. Racing alone against the clock gave me the opportunity to concentrate on using smooth, powerful strides, rather than the quick scrambling that tends to develop when one races head to head. I could feel that my balance was off and I wasn't comfortable on my skis, but I was able to work hard without letting up. As I coasted past Ruff, who was standing frozen in the field hunched over his clipboard, I felt it had been a good test, and I was conscious of how much more I enjoyed skiing than freezing while recording times.

As the Dartmouth skiers loaded the van for the chalet and a quick lunch before heading back to Hanover, the time trial being the culmination of their ten-day camp, I put on my warm-ups and headed around the loop again. It was great skiing. I wanted to maximize my time on snow, and a good long cool-down after the time trial would help dissipate the lactic acid. I cruised the loop easily, then headed back down the seven-kilometer bike path to the chalet. About midway I ran out of gas, and I struggled in feeling light-headed and weak in the knees. I had skied about thirty kilometers, eight of them at full bore, for a total of 2½ hours.

I felt much better after a hot shower and lunch, but since it was snowing hard, I decided to bag the afternoon workout. While I was finishing lunch, the Dartmouth vans were being loaded for the trip home. Ruff showed me the time-trial results. I was happy to see I had been sixth out of twelve, but more important, I had met my goal of skiing under three minutes per kilometer. I didn't have any misconceptions about the time trial. Several of Dartmouth's top skiers were not in Quebec but home for Christmas in Alaska or Colorado. Also, it had come at the end of ten days of hard training for them, and they were all but exhausted. Nevertheless, I was reassured to be reasonably competitive with college skiers roughly twenty-four years younger. As I shook hands and wished the guys a good trip back, Pete Althausen, a gregarious freshman, shook his head, saying, "Two seconds, Morty, you got me by just two seconds."

I put my hand on his shoulder and said with mock seriousness, "That's right, Pete, only two seconds, and you'd better enjoy it because that's as close as you're going to get to me all season!" It broke them up, and they were still laughing and waving as the van disappeared into the snowstorm. I didn't envy Ruff standing, freezing, taking times on his clipboard, and I certainly didn't envy him the more than six-hour drive he faced in a blizzard with a very full van, but I had to admit I would miss the jokes, discussions, debates, and pranks with the Dartmouth skiers.

Sunday morning arrived with continued cold temperatures and six inches of new powder snow. I felt the urge to drive down to the cathedral, as I had with the team for the past nine years, but since my stay in Quebec was limited, I opted for a long ski tour. Endurance is a prerequisite for Nordic skiers. Although some of the great moments in cross-country involve duels between legendary athletes and dead-heat finishes with national honor at stake, the truly awe-inspiring feats almost always have to do with endurance.

As a college racer I remember hearing of an exploit attributed to Norwegian Olympian Harald Groenningen. Groenningen was entered in a 50K race in the valley next to his own. The weather looked good, so he decided to bush-whack the thirty kilometers over a pass to the start of the race. Leaving before dawn, he arrived in time for the start—well warmed up, no doubt. Legend has it that he won the race, attended the awards ceremony, and with his trophy in his backpack, started home over the pass. He was high in the mountains with darkness approaching when a snow squall blew in. Rather than lose his way in the whiteout, Groenningen dug a snow cave and spent the night with no sleeping bag, food, or stove. I can't guarantee the authenticity of this story, but, knowing several Scandinavians and Soviets, I find it completely credible.

Another story recounts the misadventures of Juha Mieto, the most famous Finnish cross-country skier of modern times. A veteran of several Olympic competitions and scores of World Championships, the six-foot-five giant was a charismatic favorite of Nordic fans everywhere. When the events of the 1979 pre-Olympics at Lake Placid were threatened by severe cold, Mieto influenced the competition jury by training in the subzero weather with his racing suit unzipped to the waist. He lost a layer of skin on his chest to frostbite, but the races went off on schedule in spite of the bone-numbing cold.

This stubborn Finn was competing in front of a very partisan crowd of more than a hundred thousand Norwegians at the Holmenkollen Ski Festival in Oslo. The final, showcase event was the men's 50K — among Scandinavians the true test of Nordic ability and endurance. Unfortunately, heavy, wet snow at 32°F made for very tricky waxing. This is a racer's (and a coach's) nightmare, especially for fifty kilometers! Wax too warm and your skis will ice up hopelessly, eliminating any chance of gliding; wax too cold and your skis will have no kick, demanding the slow arduous herringbone step on even the slightest uphill. Furthermore, in such a long event, conditions can change dramatically, making what was great waxing at the start hopeless an hour into the race.

With grim racers soaked from the heavy, wet snow even before the start and frantic coaches scrambling to make last-second wax changes, the race got under way. The course looped back through the start/finish stadium several times, and a computerized scoreboard reported to the crowd the standings at various points in the race. It was clear at ten kilometers that Mieto, like many other prominent racers, had missed the wax and was hopelessly out of the running.

As Mieto struggled into sight, sweating profusely, his huge body bent almost double in an effort to muscle his way to the stadium with his arms, the Finnish-team coach approached the track. But rather than pull over and save his strength for another race as so many others had done, Mieto just hunched lower and kept going! His coach ran alongside, becoming increasingly agitated, obviously imploring his athlete to call it a day. With his gaze fiercely set on the track ahead, Mieto ignored the frustrated coach and plowed on. As the scoreboard flashed Mieto's interim time, a hush fell over the Norwegian crowd; the giant Finn was not just seconds or minutes out of it, he was scores of minutes off the pace! But he would not give up.

Almost three hours after the start the medal winners crossed the finish line to the loud cheering of the Norwegian crowd. The scoreboard clock kept on ticking, yet few of the thousands of spectators, soaked by the wet snow, left the stadium. They were waiting for Mieto. This colossal Olympian and World Champion would finish dead last in this Holmenkollen 50K, a result that many elite athletes would consider a terrible disgrace. But Mieto plowed into the stadium to a Norwegian crowd on their feet and roaring their approval. These knowledgeable fans cherished determination, courage, and mental toughness in their skiers, and when they found it, even in a rival Finn, they were generous with their praise. Years later many who were there would be hard pressed to remember who won the medals, but no one would forget Mieto's exhibition of *sisu* (Finnish for courage).

So my last full day at Mount Ste. Anne I had reserved for a tour. I packed a lunch, my water bottle, and a dry shirt, and set out to explore everything that had been tracked for classic skiing. Although there had not been enough snow to track all the racing loops, several long touring trails had been set overnight in the new snow and were perfect. I worked my way out to Refuge de la Seigneurie, a beautiful log cabin on the high point of a nineteen-kilometer touring loop. I shared the warm cabin with several French tourers while I had my lunch. After half an hour it was back on the tracks until the brilliant pink alpenglow in the sky and on the trees warned me it was time to head back to the chalet. That evening, checking the trail map, I determined I had skied more than sixty-three kilometers in 5½ hours. Tired and sore, I enjoyed the comforting feeling that I had just made a significant deposit in the "training bank."

Monday morning was another clear, cold beauty. After a short "recovery" ski, I made a quick lunch, packed my gear, and was headed back to Vermont by early afternoon. It had been a good camp. In just under a week I had skied 192 kilometers in about 14½ hours. I had also skied in my first time trial, with encouraging results. Counting West Yellowstone, Quebec, and the Hanover golf course, I had covered about 500 kilometers. Not much to brag about, until I remembered that this probably represented more skiing than I had done in the previous ten years! I celebrated my preseason success with another stop at the Drummondville Dunkin' Donuts, just for the sake of tradition. As the French girl gave me my coffee and two plain doughnuts, I couldn't help asking if a green van full of college boys had stopped Saturday afternoon?

"*Oui, oui,*" she said with a smile.

"And they bought a lot of doughnuts?" I responded.

"*Oui, oui, beaucoup doughnuts!*"

5: Technique

I WAS FIRST EXPOSED to cross-country skiing as a high school sophomore in 1962. I was hooked immediately. It soon became apparent, however, that simply "running on skis" from start to finish, regardless of your level of physical conditioning, would not win races. The name of the game was technique. As I worked my way up through college racing, to the Eastern Team, and finally, to the National B Team in 1967, technique continued to be the deciding factor. Everyone trained hard (though in retrospect, not always wisely), but the races were usually won by the competitor with the best technique. For many years that was Mike Gallagher.

Yet, though Mike was clearly the top American at the time, he was still well behind the best Europeans. Mike reasoned that if he trained with the Norwegians, he would learn the subtleties of the sport from them and thus improve his results. He spent a summer training in Scandinavia, during which he participated in several foot races, competing very successfully against the Norwegian skiers who routinely beat him on snow. More than once his Norwegian friends suggested Mike should quit skiing and compete in track. The message was clear. In terms of conditioning and competitive drive, Mike Gallagher was the equal of his European rivals, but in his ski technique he was significantly behind them, even though he was clearly America's best.

So the coaches of that era—John Caldwell, Dolf Kuss, Al Merrill, Sven Wiik, and others—harped endlessly on technique. U.S. Team coaches Caldwell and Merrill brought Norwegians, Swedes, Italians, and Swiss to America for races, primarily so we could watch them and emulate their technique. If you got two or three American skiers together, inevitably the conversation would turn to some exotic aspect of technique.

And it worked! By the mid-1970s a new crop of younger Americans was gaining the attention of the Europeans. Martha Rockwell, Tim Caldwell, and Bill Koch had benefited from training with Bob Gray, Mike Gallagher, and Mike Elliott, as well as racing against the imported Europeans for several winters. Martha recorded an impressive tenth-place finish at the 1974 World Championships in Falun, Sweden, and two years later Bill set the Nordic world on its ear with his dramatic, silver-medal 30K performance at the Innsbruck Olympics. In terms of technique, the Americans had arrived!

But the saga doesn't end there. Bill Koch, his American teammates, and the Canadian cross-country team would lead the way in a technical revolution: skating. After disappointing results at the 1980 Winter Olympics in Lake Placid (the American public and media expected gold medals after his silver four years earlier), Bill cut way back on his competitive schedule for the 1981 season. He did, however, compete in two of the World Loppet events, finishing first at the Engadin in Switzerland and second at the Rivière Rouge in Quebec. It was during those events that he observed Pauli Siitonen, a tough, older Finn who had specialized in skiing marathons. Bill noticed that Siitonen conserved energy yet generated more speed on the long, flat sections by using an innovative skating step combined with double poling. Siitonen took one ski out of the track, placed it diagonally on edge, and pushed off, generating more power with less effort than he could pushing off his wax in the tracks. This technique became known as the marathon skate.

Between the 1981 and 1982 seasons Koch perfected the marathon skate and began experimenting with skating to both sides, ignoring the tracks altogether. This gradually led to his discovery that skating could not only supplement diagonal technique in specific terrain (long, flat stretches), but could actually replace diagonal technique altogether! Once athletes perfected skating and developed the confidence and the conditioning to skate for the entire race, they could dispense with kick wax completely, making their skis much faster than those of their competitors, still waxed for diagonal.

With his newly perfected skating technique, Koch returned to the World Cup circuit for the 1982 season, and emerged as the overall champion! The FIS was in an uproar. They couldn't decide whether skating was a blasphemous aberration of the previously graceful sport, or a natural outgrowth of the new, faster fiberglass skis and more sophisticated trail-grooming equipment. The conservative Scandinavians and Soviets ignored it as a silly fad, while the Americans and Canadians, inspired by Koch, embraced skating with a passion. Although Bill dropped to third overall in the 1983 World Cup standings, other Americans and Canadians moved up on the international points list before the Europeans and Soviets recognized that skating was here to stay. By the second half of the decade the FIS had settled on a set of compromises that would establish two separate cross-country disciplines: **classic** (the traditional diagonal technique) and **freestyle** (skating). Major international competitions like the Olympics and the World Championships would include both classic and freestyle events, encouraging athletes to master both disciplines rather than specializing in one or the other.

By the start of the 1990s the skating controversy seemed to be behind us. The balanced approach between the two disciplines is working well, embracing the dynamic speed and excitement of skating, but not ignoring the graceful diagonal tradition. But a couple of very interesting developments have emerged from the chaos of the skating revolution. First of all, we seem to have come full circle on the issue of technique. Because skating was new, different, and relatively easy to learn (without the hassles of exotic kick waxes), we are now confronted with a generation of young racers who can skate like rockets but have seriously flawed classic technique. They may be strong and motivated, but they will never succeed against their European counterparts until they perfect the diagonal technique. (Sounds like what I was told by John Caldwell and Marty Hall back in 1966!)

Second, as it became apparent during the mid-1980s that skating was here for good, the conservative Scandinavians and stolid Soviets went to work perfecting the technique. It was soon evident that the best classic skiers were also among the best skaters. Gunde Svan of Sweden won both classic and freestyle World Cup events with amazing regularity. The Soviets, always in contention in diagonal races, were the dominant team at the 1988 Calgary Olympics in both classic and freestyle events.

In the spring of 1987 Anchorage, Alaska, hosted both the NCAA Ski Championships and the USSA Junior National Cross-Country Championships. Those events overlapped, so many college coaches were able to watch the nation's best juniors show their stuff on the same courses on which the collegiate racers had competed. There was general enthusiasm among the NCAA coaches over the speed and strength of the younger athletes in freestyle competition. Their optimism turned to disbelief, however, as racer after racer struggled awkwardly in the next race, a classic event. The colleges were about to welcome a new generation of American competitors that was woefully inadequate in terms of classic technique. Several major universities had for at least a decade drifted into the relatively lazy approach of recruiting their athletes ready-made (usually from Norway) rather than locating promising American athletes and developing great skiers. We also suffered from a shortage of qualified coaches who could demonstrate and critique proper classic technique.

The result has been several years of mediocre-to-poor international racing for the Americans. Thanks to *glasnost*, the U.S. Ski Team has responded innovatively. Not long ago Nikolai Anikin of the Soviet Union was hired as a consultant and assistant coach to the U.S. Cross-Country Team. This is exciting for two reasons. First, after more than a generation of the Cold War, it's intriguing to think that the movers and shakers of American skiing would be willing to admit publicly that the Russians know more than we do about anything (except maybe vodka and borscht). Second, having been brought up to fear and distrust Americans, I'm amazed that Anikin would be willing to share the secrets of Soviet success in Nordic skiing with his country's longtime political adversary. But Anikin and his wife, Antonina Anikina (also a former skiing champion), have spent two winters in the United States and will be back for more. They have even put together a short book on Soviet principles of technique and methods of training for cross-country skiing. Anikin says in his book that *"classical style of cross-country skiing is the foundation of the overall training of skiers."* There you have it from one of the most successful, highly respected coaches on earth: Classical technique is the basis for everything else.

There are several excellent books dedicated to technique that I would recommend for the motivated newcomer to racing or the experienced veteran who wants an update on the latest nuances. John Caldwell, who has probably watched and coached more world-class skiers than any other American, has written *Caldwell on Cross-Country*. Lee Borowski, though lacking Caldwell's background and experience, studied skating like a scientist and produced *Ski Faster, Easier*, which contains excellent information especially on freestyle techniques. The skating revolution was also responsible for collaboration between international speed skater John Teaford and cross-country multiple National Champion Audun Endestad. The resulting book, *Skating for Cross-Country Skiers*, is an innovative look at the skating technique.

I will not attempt to accomplish in one chapter what these books and others have already successfully achieved. My goal is to give the basic principles of sound skiing technique to illustrate how it fits smoothly with the other four components for success discussed in the preface: conditioning, nutrition, equipment, and psychology.

To keep this discussion straightforward and to minimize confusion, I've broken it into three major parts: classic, freestyle (or skating), and downhills (which are skied pretty much the same in both classic and freestyle races). First, however, I want to mention several general concepts that apply to both disciplines.

General Concepts of Cross-Country Technique
Explosive Power and Relaxation
Cross-country skiing is a beautifully delicate balance of explosive power and relaxation. In a race, cyclists or foot runners don't think about relaxing between power strokes; to win they simply keep "turning it over" and pouring on the power. In skiing, however, the power stroke creates glide and the champion is that athlete who can relax and take advantage of the glide before applying the next stroke. In young, inexperienced skiers it is relatively common to see a generous application of power but an inability to capitalize on the glide. The single most basic principle of cross-country skiing is to generate a concentrated, explosive drive, then relax and capitalize on the resulting glide. This is true for skating as well as diagonal. The extremes on either side of this ideal

are "Dr. Tempo," who basically runs on skis, lacking the balance or patience to glide at all, and "the tourist," who walks on skis, never generating enough power. Truly masterful cross-country skiers instinctively discover the delicate, almost balletlike, balance between explosive power and relaxation during the glide.

Stride Length and Stride Rate

If you're striving to improve your performance over a given distance, you can increase the frequency of the steps you take, called your stride rate; increase the amount of ground covered with each step, your stride length; or increase both.

The first American to study this concept scientifically was Dr. Chuck Dillman, a biomechanical specialist. Taking advantage of the pre-Olympics in Lake Placid, New York, where the world's best cross-country skiers raced on the courses scheduled for use at the 1980 Winter Olympics, Dillman and his crew set up sophisticated movie cameras in three strategic locations: a steep uphill, a gradual uphill, and a relatively flat section. Each was carefully measured and marked with brightly colored poles. During the pre-Olympic race series, the scientists filmed every racer each time they passed through the designated zones.

Back in the laboratory, upon careful study of miles of film, several interesting discoveries were made. Since the cameras ran at a constant rate and the zones were consistent for all skiers, it was possible to count steps and measure the stride length of each racer. For years coaches had been telling their athletes, "You're too slow, pick up the tempo" (meaning stride rate). Interestingly, Dillman and his crew discovered that most of the racers at the pre-Olympics had similar stride rates. Among the world's best, it seems, there is relatively little variation in tempo. There was a significant difference, however, in stride length. The winners and racers close behind them had considerably longer stride lengths than the less-successful skiers.

Dillman's innovative study produced important results. For the first time in my experience we were given specific scientific information relating to technique, which could lead directly to improved performance. Years earlier, after a dismal biathlon race in Europe, I had asked Sven Johanson in desperation, "Sven, what do I have to do to win races over here?"

"Yon," he responded sympathetically, "You yest gots to ski faster!"

Dillman's study confirmed how to ski faster: maintain a reasonable stride rate and concentrate on increasing stride length. But that is not as easy as it sounds. Picking up the tempo is relatively straightforward; swimmers, runners, and skiers do it all the time as they peak for big competitions by concentrating on interval training. Increasing stride length in skiing is much more difficult to accomplish. It involves generating more explosive power from the arms and legs as well as improving poise and balance on the gliding ski. These traits are not developed in a couple of weeks before a big race but, rather, over several years.

About now someone is saying, "This stride length stuff might have been true in the wooden-ski and wool-knicker-socks days, but with the skating revolution it no longer applies." Obviously, it's counterproductive to overstride when your skis are pointed forty-five degrees away from the direction of travel, which is often the case with skating. But I will contend that Gunde Svan and other international champions succeed not because they have a faster tempo, but because, even in skating, they cover more ground with every step. In fifteen years of coaching I encountered not more than half a dozen athletes whose strides were too long. All the rest, literally hundreds of skiers, could have bettered their race results by improving their explosive power, their poise, and their balance on the gliding ski.

Weight Transfer

Closely related to stride length is weight transfer. The great cross-country skiers subtly and gracefully commit their entire body weight to the gliding ski. This requires balance, timing, and a certain confidence that beginners often have difficulty achieving. A common fault of inexperienced skiers, or even seasoned veterans faced with exhaustion in the late stages of a difficult race, is "straddling the track," or inadequate weight transfer. The best method of diagnosing and correcting this technical shortcoming is skiing without poles. Although ski poles are essential to every race, they also conceal a myriad of technical difficulties. Arm and shoulder power definitely contribute to a racer's success, but inadequate leg power, poor balance, and insufficient weight transfer can all be masked by the upper body. Skiing without poles is a great way to develop poise and balance, explosive drive, and confidence on the gliding ski.

One of America's top biathletes, Raimond Dombrovskis, emigrated from Latvia in the late 1970s. Rai had been one of Latvia's most promising junior biathletes and had competed in several Soviet National Championships. Rai tells the story of skiing without poles on a snow-covered lake with members of his club early in the season. The young Soviets skied round and round the lake without poles day after day until the coach was satisfied that each athlete had developed the balance and power to ride a flat ski. One by one he excused his charges, giving them their poles and sending them off to ski the hills and valleys of the conventional ski course. Raimond recounts with chagrin that he was the last young skier to be released from the lake, *after more than a month of skiing without poles!* For the better part of the last decade Raimond was one of America's top biathletes: a National Champion, a North American Champion, and a member of the Calgary Olympic Team. If you want to improve your technique, spend some time skiing without poles.

No-pole skiing is great for balance and timing, especially early in the season.
Jeff Robbins

Drive Forward

The concept of driving forward could be mentioned just as appropriately in the chapter on psychology as here. In the early 1970s U.S. Ski Team head coach John Caldwell visited Alaska and conducted a clinic. This preceded the skating revolution by almost a decade, so most of the technical discussion centered on kick. Athletes and coaches debated late kick, early kick, kicking down through the track versus kicking back, and so on, ad nauseum. Finally Caldwell, in his no-nonsense, straightforward, Vermonter style, made the following observation: The finish line is down the track, ahead of you. Why worry about kick, which is going on behind you? Think only about driving forward, hips, knees, feet, and arms, toward the finish line. If for no other reason, it makes a lot of sense psychologically.

Caldwell's contention was that concentrating on the forward-drive aspect of the motion was a psychological advantage, since mentally it drew the racer closer to the finish line. His suggestion resulted in an overnight improvement in my skiing. Simply by concentrating on driving forward rather than worrying about kick, my ski times dropped dramatically. The effect on my own skiing was such that in subsequent years as a coach I seldom, if ever, mentioned kick. Caldwell's advice is just as valid today (with slight modifications for skating). If the racer's concentration is focused on driving forward down the track toward the finish line, most technical difficulties will resolve themselves.

Technique versus Style

Although good technique is essential to winning races, we are all built differently and therefore have slightly varying styles of skiing. One of the marks of an experienced coach is the ability to differentiate between individual style and technical flaws. Bill Koch had the habit of bending his knee at the end of a pendulum swing. It was a stylistic nuance having no significant effect on his technique, which was excellent. But it was visually distinctive, and for a while we had a whole generation of young skiers bending the knees at the end of every stride because, "That's the way Kochie skis." Although Bill didn't allow this stylistic quirk to hamper his stride, many of the kids imitating him lifted the trailing foot off the snow, thus shortening their strides and wasting energy.

A common mistake of inexperienced racers is bending too far forward at the waist, or "jackknifing." In 1980 I stood beside the trail during the Olympic men's 15K event at Lake Placid as the world's best competitors blasted past, and I admired their power, strength, and flawless technique. I cheered loudly for the four Americans entered in the race. Then I watched in disbelief as a huge, bearded bear of a man lumbered up the hill toward me, arms driving forward more like a swimmer than a skier, and bent nearly horizontally at the waist. As he drew closer, I recognized the Finnish giant Juha Mieto and wondered to myself how a famous champion could have achieved so much success with such poor technique. Mieto lost the gold medal in that event to Thomas Wassberg of Sweden by *one one-hundredth of a second!* Obviously his technique was not too shabby. In fact, his size made him appear to hunch over more than smaller men, but all the basics of technique were flawlessly executed. Mieto's body position was a stylistic variation rather than a technical flaw.

Learn to separate good technique from individual style, a distinction that is not always easy to make. Concentrate on the basic principles of good technique and don't worry about stylistic differences.

Classic Technique

Flat Terrain

The classic technique used on the flat is the basis for *all other* types of skiing. To assume the correct body position for cross-country, imagine yourself as a classic "nerd," with poor posture and nonathletic. Your knees should be slightly bent, back somewhat rounded forward, shoulders hunched, head and arms relaxed. Next, pinch your buttock muscles together, forcing your hips forward under your torso. Finally, with the help of ski poles or your hand against a wall, lean your entire body forward from the ankles until the point at which you would fall on your face were it not for your poles or the wall. This body position can be described as relaxed, up, and forward. It has some advantages: the forward lean generates momentum down the track; the relaxed torso ensures that maximum energy is devoted to arms and legs generating speed down the track rather than holding the body in an awkward, unnatural position; and the high and forward position of the pelvis requires good balance and complete weight transfer from one gliding ski to the next. The most common problem in body position is jackknifing. Occasionally beginners ski without enough forward lean, but this is rare among racers.

With the proper body position, the arms and legs appear to pivot naturally forward and back from the shoulder and hip joints. One can imagine the arms, in diagonal skiing, as the pendulum of a large clock swinging naturally forward and back, reaching comfortably down the track in front and allowing the arm to trail directly behind at the conclusion of the poling motion. Observing a skier approaching head-on, you should see a minimum of crossover by the arms. It is normal to see the hands come slightly in toward the center of the body, but the leading hand should not cross far over, which would encourage the upper body to bob from side to side.

If the ski pole straps are properly adjusted, the arm can be completely extended and the grip on the pole relaxed at the end of every poling motion. As the hand and arm then pendulum forward for the next pole plant, the handle comes back to rest comfortably in the hand. This release of the pole at the end of the motion is important for two reasons. First of all, it corresponds with an

The proper body position for classic resembles poor posture: knees slightly bent, shoulders forward. Jeff Robbins

Alexander Tichonov of the USSR, winner of dozens of Olympic and World Champion-ship medals in biathlon, had the habit of crossing his arm in front of his body instead of reaching down the track. This was a stylistic trait, not a technical flaw.

important reach forward of the other hand, the absence of which would signifi-cantly shorten the racer's stride. Second, it provides an instant of rest for the muscles of the hand, arm, and shoulder, which, when multiplied by the num-ber of strides in a race, becomes significant.

Corresponding to this relaxed follow-through of one arm is the relaxed but assertive pendulum swing forward of the other arm. An assertive reach forward every stride with the arm almost straight until the very end of the motion guarantees a dynamic, athletic, forward body position that generates momentum. There are some great skiers who bring their hands up short, but in those cases it seems to be stylistic variation that doesn't affect body position.

I believe for most skiers that the correct image to have is of a racer charging down the track, swinging his or her arms naturally forward in such a way that if a glove slipped off at the farthest point of the motion, it would shoot straight down the track ahead of the skier rather than looping up into the air or flying across the track into the woods.

The largest muscle mass in the human body is found in the buttocks and upper legs. Regardless of all the attention skating has drawn to the upper body, with the use of longer poles and the need for stronger arms, shoulders, and back, it is still your legs and butt that are going to do most of the work. As I explained earlier, I don't talk about kick. John Caldwell also deserves the credit for a graphic description of the forward motion of the skier's leg, which he compared to a softball pitcher's windup. At the start of the windup the ball moves slowly, deliberately up and back, away from the plate. Then in one smooth, fluid motion, quickly gathering speed and power, the ball describes a natural arc until, low, fast, and with the pitcher's weight behind it, it is released directly toward the plate at maximum velocity. The leg motion of the skier is much the same. At the end of a stride the leg and foot are relaxed, hanging gracefully above the snow behind the skier. As the foot begins to swing forward under the body, its motion is slow and relaxed at first, but as it traces its arc back toward the snow, it picks up speed and power. At the instant the accelerating foot passes its mate, the skier's weight shifts, generating additional speed and forward power. As the ski speeds down the track supporting (and powered by) the entire weight of the skier, the racer subconsciously tries to milk every inch out of the stride before friction decreases the forward momentum. Then the other leg drives forward, repeating the process. At the final instant the best skiers imperceptibly rotate the driving hip forward and slightly flex the knee, thereby gaining another couple of inches.

It used to be popular to describe knee drive when discussing classic technique, and it certainly is present in the best skiers. But too much attention to knee drive had the unfortunate backlash of causing skiers to drop their butts. It is important to glide in a dynamically forward position, body weight up and over the camber of the ski. Most top racers these days finish the gliding phase of a stride on an almost-straight leg.

Now we have come full circle to my first general concept of technique, the delicate balance of explosive power and relaxation. The drive forward of arm and leg down the track must be dynamic, assertive, and explosive, and yet the glide phase of the stride must be poised, graceful, and quiet. The upper torso of an experienced racer, even at full speed, is remarkably stable. There is very little up and down or side to side movement. The distinction between being relaxed and being lazy can also be difficult for the less-experienced skier. The experts exert explosive power, then relax, capitalizing on the glide they have generated. Often the very good skiers appear to have slower tempos because of

Classic technique is a beautiful balance of the explosive power of the stride down the track followed by the quiet relaxation of the glide. Jeff Robbins

their poise, balance, and ability to glide. The novice sometimes emulates these slow, graceful movements without reproducing the explosive power stroke, and thus doesn't go anywhere. The relaxation is necessary but so is the power, if the goal is to win races.

Thus far the discussion has focused on the basics of diagonal or classic technique on the flat (in slow snow) or on slight climbs. Before modifying this technique for steeper uphills, I need to mention a couple more options for the flats.

Change-ups. Back in the wooden-ski days, when it was the custom to apply kick wax from tip to tail (even red klister in wet snow), skis didn't glide nearly as freely as they do today. If the snow was slow, it was often the "ox" who would win, usually on pure determination rather than technique. The endless repetition of stride after stride up a gradual hill would wear down even the strongest skier. One method of breaking up the monotony and providing a little relief for the muscles was the change-up. This consisted of bringing both arms forward during a normal stride in a syncopated type of rhythm. This motion would provide enough variation that, when the skier resumed the normal diagonal stride, he or she would have a little extra zip. It was not uncommon to see a good skier throw in a change-up every ten strides or so on a long, gradual climb. Change-ups are far less common today because skis and wax are so much faster and racers are better trained and less willing to rest even for a few strides during a race.

Double Poling. What has become more common is double poling, in which both poles are used simultaneously. Thanks to plastic bases and mechanical trail grooming, double poling is now used on sections of flat trail that once were skied diagonal stride. There are three common variations of double poling. The first is simply poling. The feet and legs remain stationary on the skis while the racer is propelled down the track by pole power alone. This technique is appropriate in a couple of specialized situations. When the tracks are fast enough that taking a step is awkward or slows you down but not quite fast enough to tuck and coast, you can generate a faster tempo double poling alone than with either the one- or two-step double-poling technique. If your wax is worn off or not working and you have no kick, you can always make it to the finish by double poling.

The other two modifications are the one-step and two-step double pole. They are just what they sound like and are used if the tracks are slightly too fast for diagonal striding. In the one-step version you take a powerful step, reach up and forward with both hands, plant your poles, and commit your upper body weight onto the poles, thus propelling yourself down the track. The two-step double pole is the same, except that the snow speed dictates two steps between poling compressions. A common error among beginners is to use just the arms to generate power. The champions initiate the double pole by committing their hips, backs, and shoulders, as well as their arms, up and forward—so much so that if their poles were to slip out or break, the skiers would land face first in the snow. It is this concentration of upper-body muscular strength and weight that generates the power in a good double pole. The

When initiating a double pole, the arms should be fully extended forward and the body weight committed over the front of the skis. Jeff Robbins

Completion of the double pole motion. Willie Carow, two-time Olympic biathlete, demonstrates excellent compression and follow-through with his arms. Eric Evans

top skiers also complete the motion, compressing the upper body to a horizontal position parallel to the snow, trailing both hands fully extended behind the body.

Double poling is one aspect of technique that can definitely be improved by roller skiing, and many elite competitors think nothing of heading out on the breakdown lane of a highway for a sixty- to ninety-minute double-poling workout!

Uphills

By this point you should have a pretty clear picture of classic cross-country technique on flats or slight climbs. But as I said earlier, races are won on the uphills. More actual time is spent on the uphills than either the flats or the descents (maybe even both). So it makes sense to master uphill technique if you want to win races. In fact, diagonal hill-climbing technique is very similar to that for skiing the flats, with a couple of modifications. First and most important, as the slope increases, stride length decreases and tempo picks up. Imagine a cyclist roaring down the highway in high gear, hunched over the handlebars to reduce wind resistance, applying smooth, powerful force to the pedals. As the cyclist approaches a hill, he shifts down so that he is exerting roughly the same force but now at a higher tempo. Keep this image in mind as you approach a hill on skis. You don't want to let up—in fact, if possible, you want to pour on the coal—but you do it by "shifting gears" to a shorter stride and quicker tempo. Be selective and sensitive as to how and when you shift, though. Don't shorten your stride any more than you have to. Remember, even on the uphills it is still stride length that makes the significant difference.

If the hill is steep or if the kick wax is marginal, there is a natural tendency to jackknife forward and muscle your way up the hill with arm power. Resist that temptation by settling your hips a little lower to the snow, directly over your boots. In the old days coaches would talk about "kicking a soccer ball up the hill" or "sneaking up the hill like an Indian warrior." These may be exaggerations, but it is true that the appropriate body position for the flats—up and forward—moves your center of gravity forward of the wax pocket on an uphill, resulting in slippery skis. If you settle a little lower on the skis and look toward the top of the hill, keeping head and shoulders up rather than jack-knifed forward, the wax will provide adequate kick and you will bound smoothly up the hill.

Even with excellent body position and appropriate wax, there are times when the kick is borderline. On those occasions the experienced racer will "cushion his skis," or carefully apply weight to each stride, sensing just how much the wax can hold before breaking loose. This is more an intuition that develops from years of experience than a technique to be learned in an afternoon.

As a hill gets steeper, it is common to see less-experienced skiers gradually shorten their strides until they are literally jogging on skis. Their arms come through scarcely beyond their noses, and there is no glide whatsoever. Occasionally this state of affairs is inevitable, even with experienced racers, if the hill is very long and steep, the course is especially difficult, or the racer has missed the wax. The champions, however, almost always reach forward with their arms and push for at least a couple of inches of glide, even on steep hills.

There are occasions when the hill is so steep or the snow so sugary that no wax will hold, and even the best racers resort to the herringbone. This is an awkward, almost comical technique named after the design left in the snow when the skier has passed. With arms and legs pretty much spread-eagled, the skier tries to scamper quickly to the point where he can resume diagonal skiing. The comedy comes in (if you are a spectator rather than a participant) when racers are herringboning up a hill in deep new snow or powdery snow well churned up by previous skiers, or when they are part of a crowd, as is often the case early in a mass-start race. It's hard to imagine all the things that can go wrong as ski tips, pointed almost sixty degrees from the desired direction of travel, catch continually in soft, deep snow; a skier plants his poles just

You don't get anywhere by rushing when you have to herringbone. David Brownell

ahead of his own skis; or a racer slaps a ski down on another's pole basket just as the pole is about to be drawn forward.

The best advice concerning the herringbone technique is to avoid it if possible. If there is no alternative, do it calmly and deliberately. Any advantage you gain by rushing or scrambling will more than likely be lost when you stumble, get hopelessly tangled up, and fall on your face. Straddle the track rather than shifting weight from one ski to another as you do with diagonal technique, maintain your composure, and conserve energy. If you end up following someone slightly slower than you would like to go, herringbone patiently behind him; a herringbone hill is almost certainly a hopeless place to pass another racer—you're sure to get tangled up and fall. And remember, since the advent of skating, once a ski is placed in a herringbone step, it must not glide; that constitutes skating and is grounds for disqualification in a classic race.

This brings up another interesting point. For as long as people have been skiing cross-country, there have been step turns. When performed on a down-hill or on fast snow, a step turn becomes a skating turn. This created a problem for the FIS when they tried to divide the sport into classic and freestyle. It wouldn't really be fair to eliminate an efficient and appropriate form of turning from a classic skier's repertoire simply because it was *so* efficient that it gave birth to a whole new form of skiing. In major international classic races, sections of the course are marked with signs and colored lines across the track where step turns are permitted. If a racer puts a ski diagonally to the prepared tracks anywhere outside of these predesignated zones in an effort to gain speed, it will result in a disqualification.

For local or regional classic races a good rule of thumb is this: Step turns are permitted for changing direction or overtaking a slower skier. In spite of race organizers' concerns, the transition to the two disciplines has been smooth, with a minimum of illegal skating in classic races. Perhaps Nordic skiers are an honest group, or perhaps by now the two disciplines are distinct enough in everyone's mind to minimize confusion. I suppose it is not often that a swimmer throws a couple of crawl strokes into a butterfly race.

One final observation on skiing hills, and this applies to skating as well as classic. As a coach I spent hundreds of hours on cross-country courses standing alone in the woods at the crest of hills. That is where the races are won, it's where the skiers most need encouragement, and, I believe, it's where you see the difference between the champions and everyone else. If the uphills are the most significant part of a ski race, then the transitions—from the flat into the hill and over the top to the descent or flat beyond the climb—are the most critical parts of each hill.

Psychologically, most of us recoil in dread as we approach a hill. We take a deep breath or sigh, and throttle back a little to compose ourselves for the strenuous effort to come. At the crest of a hill we tend to straighten up, take deep breaths in relief that another climb is behind us, throw in a half-hearted double pole for the spectators, and wait for gravity to take over. The champions, on the other hand, don't throttle back approaching a hill; they downshift and "put the pedal to the metal." And at the crest of a hill the champions don't let up—they keep charging, looking for all the world disappointed that the climb didn't continue for another kilometer! And they keep pushing over the top and down the other side, building momentum until gravity really does take over. Even among elite competitors the visible differences in these transitions are more apparent than anywhere else on a racecourse. Without knowing the start interval or split times, an experienced coach could predict with some accuracy the leaders in any race simply by watching the top of one tough hill. In more than fifteen years of coaching athletes of all abilities, beginners to Olympians, I'll bet I didn't see more than one out of ten competitors ski the transitions well in a race.

Freestyle

The skating revolution of the mid-1980s was probably the most exciting (and confusing) time in the history of Nordic skiing. Not even the emergence of fiberglass skis in 1974 and 1975 sparked the widespread interest and bewilderment that skating did. Most of us, coaches and athletes, were caught totally off guard. Predictably, the coaches, who were older and more conservative and had a wealth of experience in diagonal technique, were slower to embrace skating than the younger athletes. I clearly remember telling my Dartmouth skiers, "Skating is just one more technical option you should have in your bag of tricks, like the two-step double pole or a good, tight tuck on the downhills, but it will never replace the diagonal stride on a challenging cross-country course! There is no way a racer could skate [with bare skis] a 15K race on a trail like Van Hoevenberg at Lake Placid."

In the first race of the very next collegiate season, a skier did exactly that: he skated fifteen kilometers with skis glide waxed from tip to tail for speed. On the trails designed for the 1980 Olympics at Mount Van Hoevenberg, he not only skated the entire race, he also soundly beat the best college racers in the East. That did wonders for my credibility as a coach! The only consolation was that most coaches were in the same boat. It was uncharted territory. None of us knew what good skating technique should look like. Many of us shook our heads in disbelief as our skiers hacked the tips off their skis so they wouldn't catch in the powder at the edge of the trail and scrambled for longer and longer ski poles. I remember watching one of my racers standing in the starting gate, his hands gripping ski poles just even with the top of his head! It was a dramatic, even comical, evolution from conventional pole length, which had been armpit height for more than half a century.

The media must have relished the skating revolution. It seemed that every week *Ski Racing* would publish some new tidbit. Once it reported that World Cup leader Gunde Svan was seen after a major event in Europe experimenting with a single ten-foot pole, propelling himself down the track like a gondolier in Venice. Gunde no doubt did it as a joke, but the sport was in such turmoil and the public was so gullible that the day after the story appeared half my team was practicing with bamboo slalom poles equipped with homemade handles resembling the ends of canoe paddles. As comical as this all seemed at the time, it wasn't total insanity. Not long thereafter, Swix introduced the T-handle grip, specifically for skating, which permitted a biomechanical advantage over conventional ski-pole grips. The Swix T-handle was almost exactly what my skiers had fashioned on the ends of their bamboo slalom poles.

It was a turbulent, confusing, but invigorating time for cross-country skiing. Skating drew new participants who had been intimidated by the complexities of waxing or the nuances of diagonal technique. As it matured, the skating technique was regarded as easier to learn than diagonal; after all, most people in northern climates had some familiarity with ice skating even though they may not have tried skiing. And even old, hard-core "kickers and gliders" like me found the speed and freedom of skating exhilarating once we had mastered the technique.

Although skating and diagonal technique are significantly different visually, they share some fundamental principles. The basic body position is the same: up and forward. Stride length is more important than stride rate. Here there is a point of diminishing return in skating, since the racer is not striding directly toward the finish line as in diagonal technique; but even so, the champions glide farther than everyone else.

Also, it is critically important to ride a flat ski. The Alpine skiers probably discovered this first on icy slalom courses: a sharp edge carving a turn is slower than the flat bottom of the ski skimming over the snow. As a result, Alpine skiers are on and off their edges as quickly as possible when a turn is necessary. For traditional cross-country skiing, the deep-set, machine-packed tracks made gliding on a flat ski almost obligatory. With skating, since kick and glide were part of the same motion, it wasn't so clear; however, it was quickly learned that the more-successful racers were spending most of each stride gliding on a flat ski and only at the last instant turning it on edge for the kick.

Complete weight transfer is also important in both disciplines. Coaches look for a vertical nose-knee-toe alignment in skaters, indicating that the athlete's weight is fully committed to the gliding ski.

Of course, there are major differences. Perhaps the most visible distinction is that in skating the skis are parallel only while coasting downhill. Also, the longer ski poles—mustache rather than armpit height—are immediately apparent. If you viewed a skater from directly overhead, it would be clear that, unlike classic technique, skating is often asymmetrical. In the most widely used skating steps one ski pole is planted close to the foot, with the shaft almost vertical and the hand not far from the face. This is usually described as the "hang pole," and as the stride evolves, it absorbs a considerable amount of force generated by the weight of the upper body. The other pole, called the "push pole," is planted farther back and takes a longer, smoother power stroke from the unweighted arm and shoulder. The best skiers are ambidextrous and can smoothly switch from "power left" to "power right" as the terrain dictates.

Another difference that would be readily apparent from overhead is the direction of travel of the racer's torso. In classic technique the upper body is very stable and moves steadily down the track toward the finish line. In skating, however, the torso describes a gentle zigzag down the track, much like a snake, as weight is committed to first one ski then the other. From a side view yet another difference is apparent: the classic skier's body is quiet, with a minimum of bobbing, but the skater is constantly compressing, using his upper body to generate power to the poles.

Anne Jahren of Norway demonstrates good weight transfer (nose, knee, and toe alignment) while skating in the 1985 World Championships at Seefeld, Austria. Eric Evans

Norwegian Annette Boe initiates a marathon skating step: her left ski remains on the track, her right ski is being positioned for the push-off, and her upper body weight leans toward the skating ski. Eric Evans

Here she completes the marathon skate step with full upper body compression, weight back over the gliding ski, and arms fully extended behind. Eric Evans

The skating revolution spawned countless lively discussions, thousands of hours of videotape analysis, and a landslide of articles, academic papers, and books. As could be expected with anything so new and different, skating has been analyzed, broken down, reconstructed, measured, and tested. At one point I heard that the Norwegians had isolated fourteen distinct skating techniques! Five years after its widespread acceptance, skating technique is still maturing. Six distinct skating steps, almost like dance steps, have emerged. These are important moves that an experienced racer should be able to perform.

Marathon Skating

As mentioned earlier, the marathon skate, or scooter step as it is known in Scandinavia, was a product of the long, flat sections, often frozen lakes, found

This photo of Johan Danielsson of Sweden is a great illustration of complete weight transfer and planting of the hang pole. David Brownell

in several of the ski marathon events of the World Loppet series. It was discovered that by keeping one ski in the track, placing the other on edge diagonally to the track, and pushing off (much like an old-fashioned child's scooter), skiers could cover long flat sections faster and with less effort.

The marathon skate is initiated by allowing the weight of the upper body to "fall" over the diagonal push ski. As the push-off is completed and the poling motion is almost spent, the body weight is transferred back to the gliding ski in preparation for another push step. Although the top competitors can marathon skate with equal ability to either side, they usually let the terrain dictate and will switch from one side to the other only to break up very long flat sections. Although marathon skating has been overshadowed by faster skating steps, it is still very useful, especially in longer events and around corners.

V1 Skating

V1 skating has become the standard, most commonly used skating step. Watch any skating race and for the most part you will be seeing V1 technique. Unlike marathon skating, in which one ski remains in the track, in V1 the skis form a V, with the opening pointing toward the finish line. But like marathon skating, V1 is noticeably asymmetrical, with a hang pole, a push pole, and a power side, and the skier's movements appear syncopated. Dick Taylor, a longtime U.S. Team coach, described V1 skating as "galloping." If you were setting cross-country skiers to music, classic technique would have a steady beat — *da . . . da . . . da . . . da* — while V1 would require a beat more like *ta da . . . ta da . . . ta da . . . ta da.*

Almost everyone, beginner or expert, tends to favor one side as the power side, but it is important to be versatile. Inevitably the terrain or traffic on the course will necessitate shifting the power stroke to the other side, and the accomplished skater can make the switch without missing a step. I'm not embarrassed to admit that learning to power stride to either side has been the most difficult aspect of skating for me. Probably 99 percent of my V1 skiing is power left, my left hand high, upper body compressing on the left ski pole, right pole serving as the push pole. I'm not especially coordinated (otherwise I probably would have stuck with slalom and downhill in college), and switching to power right is still awkward and confusing for me. It is somewhat reassuring to learn from other, more-successful skaters that they had difficulty with this move as well.

V2 Skating

V2 skating is the most graceful and visually pleasing form of skating to watch. It is also the most difficult to master, requiring tremendous balance, poise on the gliding ski, and considerable strength. V2 is similar to speed skating on ice — long fluid power strokes to each side, rhythmically interspersed with long, smooth glides on each foot. But the skier has the additional benefit of poles, which generate even more power with every stroke. At first, V2 was used by only the most-experienced skiers (those with perfect balance) over flats, very gradual climbs, or slight downhills in slow snow. By the 1988 Olympics in Calgary the world's best biathletes were V2 skating much of Canmore's hilly course. This may have been because biathlon competitions are all free technique, thus giving biathletes more opportunity to perfect V2 than their counterparts in cross-country, who split their training time between skating and classic. It is also possible that biathletes subconsciously favor V2 skating because the smoother, more-fluid movements result in less back and forth bouncing of the rifle.

Unlike V1 skating, V2 is symmetrical. The athlete, balanced on the gliding ski, reaches forward with both arms and poles powerfully in the direction of glide. As momentum dissipates, the gliding ski is turned on edge, the athlete shifts weight to the new gliding ski, and once again reaches forward in the direction of the glide. If V1 "sounds" like *ta da . . . ta da . . . ta da*, then V2 skating "sounds" like *varoom . . . varoom . . . varoom*.

Skating with Diagonal Poling

Skating with diagonal poling is another step that is easy to identify. It is a V skate with alternate poling, as in diagonal skiing, rather than the double poling of V1 and V2. This technique was originally used on steep climbs but has all but disappeared as athletes becomes stronger with V1. In fact, this step is sometimes called "coaches' skating" because old, out-of-shape coaches are the only ones who use it anymore. One exception might be on a steep hill, early in a mass-start race, when competitors are backed up and struggling in line up the slope. In such a situation the prudent approach is to conserve as much energy as possible until the opportunity appears to pass the slower skiers ahead. The most energy-efficient method of climbing hills is the skate with alternate poling.

Skating without Poling

Fast fiberglass skis, glide waxed from tip to tail, and firm, smooth, mechanically groomed trails have led to another form of skating: in a tuck without poling. In classic cross-country, when a downhill becomes fast or steep enough that double poling is no longer adding to the racer's speed, the athlete simply compresses into an aerodynamic egg position and coasts. With modern grooming equipment, the course for skating often resembles a corduroy carpet, and almost regardless of the speed the racer can go even faster by skating. On relatively gentle slopes at slow speeds the skier may swing his arms like a speed skater (although the poles never make contact with the snow). At higher speeds where the reduced wind resistance of a tuck is advantageous, the skier may keep the poles locked under the arms, hands in front of the face, and take long, smooth skating steps to generate speed. Riding a tight tuck down a long hill requires strong thigh muscles, and skating in that low crouched position, even more strength. But if you can handle it, skating without poles is definitely fast.

The Gunde Skate

For the second half of the past decade Gunde Svan, a tall, young Swede, dominated the sport like few before him. In two Olympics (Sarajevo 1984 and Calgary 1988) Gunde earned six medals: four gold, one silver, and one bronze. It was Svan who perfected the sixth and newest form of skating, aptly named the Gunde Skate. As mentioned earlier, the V1 skate is used the majority of the time by most racers. Its syncopated rhythm is appropriate for hills, twisty courses, rutted trails, or weaving in and out of traffic. But for the seasoned competitor the fluid grace of the V2 is more efficient, with the skis in a narrower V, covering more ground with each stride. Gunde Svan extended the typical V1 stride, with its pole plant every other step, to the length of a V2. The resulting Gunde Skate is longer and more efficient than the conventional V1 (and minimizes the distinction between the hang and the push pole) but doesn't require the perfectly groomed trail or flawless balance of V2 skiing. I would not be surprised in future years to see the Gunde Skate replace V1 everywhere but on the steepest hills.

Downhills

I've saved downhills for last for three good reasons. First, downhills are clearly the most fun, and it's good psychology to get the work out of the way before enjoying the fun. Second, with one minor exception the technique for skiing downhills is identical for both skating and classic, so it makes sense to discuss the two together. Finally, in a technical sense I regard downhills as relatively unimportant in comparison with the flats and uphills.

While races are usually won on the uphills, however, they can certainly be lost on the downhills. If the time spent on downhills in a typical 15K race is only five minutes, then the spread between the great skiers and everyone else is going to be relatively minor — only a few seconds. The superstar might aggressively accelerate into the downhill, ride a perfect aerodynamic tuck, and carve smooth, crisp turns on a predesignated line, while a less-able skier might air check slightly going into the descent, drag his poles to increase stability, and slide his skis around all the turns. Still, the difference in their elapsed times won't be overwhelming. What does create an overwhelming margin is a fall. It doesn't matter what causes the fall — lack of concentration, overconfidence, slower skiers in the track, or a poorly groomed course — if you fall on a descent, you can lose a race that otherwise was "in the bag."

I am by no means suggesting that downhills should be approached with a dread of falling. In fact, champions attack the descents with confidence. But the great racers ski the downhills prudently, realizing that what they stand to lose going flat out far outweighs what they stand to gain. For every success story like Bill Koch's (who probably won his Olympic silver on the final three-kilometer downhill at Seefeld), there are dozens of disappointments as a racer catches an edge, slips out on a patch of ice, loses concentration for an instant, or gets tangled up overtaking another skier. My advice for the downhills is this: Be assertive and confident, but be prudent.

The ideal body position for descent is the tuck, or egg, borrowed from Alpine downhill racing. With the legs slightly apart, the upper body compressed tightly down on the thighs, and the hands held out in front of the face,

The "downhill tuck" position: chest on knees, elbows in front of legs, back and poles parallel to the ground. Jeff Robbins

the racer assumes the most aerodynamically efficient profile possible. A good tuck can make a difference on a long downhill. If you don't believe it, tuck a hill next to a friend who skis it standing up. There are some disadvantages, however, to the classic downhill tuck. It is an awkward and stressful position to maintain for more than a minute or so. It's difficult to keep your balance and react to obstacles when in a tight tuck. It is also impossible to breathe deeply with your chest compressed against your knees. In spite of these drawbacks, the traditional tuck is great for long, smooth downhills where there is potential for considerable speed but little risk of a fall. In these circumstances your speed can be increased even more by riding on your heels and pulling up on the toes of your boots. This takes some resistance off the tips of your skis, thereby increasing your velocity.

It is also especially important at higher speeds to keep your hands up, out in front of your face rather than down between your knees. There are two reasons for this. Ninety-nine percent of the falls on fast downhills result from sitting back. As the speed increases, the skier subconsciously recoils, loses balance, and falls on the tails of his skis. To avoid this, keep the hands out in front. Many racers visualize themselves driving, steering a race car around a turn. If your hands stay forward, your body weight will stay forward over your skis. If your hands are down near the snow, your pole shafts and baskets will be high above your back, generating the very wind resistance you're trying to minimize with the tuck. Keep your hands up and out, in front of your face, and your ski poles will go straight back along your body.

As always, it's important to keep everything in perspective. When I was an eager, young biathlete on my first trip to Europe, I was astounded to observe what I regarded as very sloppy downhill tucks by some of the top Soviet and Scandinavian competitors. They were hunched forward, but their chests were nowhere close to their thighs; their forearms were resting on their knees, hands often crossed, poles pointing carelessly to the sky.

It was years later that I learned the wisdom of these champions. Remember for a moment that the downhill racers whose aerodynamic tuck we have copied only race flat out down a mountain for two minutes. That's their entire event! The downhill sections of a cross-country race, however, are a relatively minor segment of the contest, timewise. The top European biathletes had learned that the sacrifice of a couple of seconds of speed on the downhill in exchange for more power and stamina on the uphill was well worthwhile. Therefore, many top racers use a modified resting tuck, especially if the downhill is at all challenging or if they have really been putting out on the uphills. With a slightly higher body position they can breathe deeply, recovering from the last climb or in anticipation of the next one. The forearms on the knees provide support for the upper body, generating a minimum of muscular strain. The thighs are closer to vertical than in the downhill tuck, but this position generates virtually no muscle fatigue. A racer has a given amount of energy to expend in the course of a competition; the trick is to use that energy most efficiently. If that means losing a couple of seconds by riding a resting tuck down a hill in order to gain ten seconds on the next uphill, I call that a good allocation of energy.

Turns and bumps used to be a major concern in cross-country racing; the skillful athlete could accelerate out of corners and time his stride to kick off the back sides of the countless bumps in every trail. Now racecourses are usually groomed to resemble interstate highways. There are virtually no subtle bumps to work for additional speed, and the turns are usually wide, sweeping, and easily negotiable (until perhaps a few dozen racers scrape through to the ice or create some ruts). On those rare occasions on which you encounter a bump, or roll, on a fast downhill, the prescribed technique is exactly what Alpine skiers do: prejump, or unweight your skis as you approach the bump. As the bump slides under you, absorb it with a relaxed flexing of your knees. It helps to concentrate on keeping your hands well forward. On the back side of the bump, your body weight comes back to rest on your skis. You will have absorbed the bump much like the shock absorber of a car, without ever leaving the surface of the snow.

Theoretically, the fastest line around a turn is the smallest radius, so you should cut the corners tight. That's why we see Alpine skiers banging the gates so hard that they need to wear armor! There are a couple of other considerations in cross-country, however. First of all, cutting downhill turns tight might require more energy and involve more risk than it is worth. After only a few competitors, challenging turns are often rutted or scraped through to boilerplate or ice. Struggling with these conditions is seldom worth the effort. I have found it usually safer and faster to "ride the rut." If you stay slightly wider on a turn, you have the advantage of better snow. By putting a ski in the rut or on the berm created by the other skiers, you can confidently carve a turn much as a bobsled does: smooth, fast, and crisp. Why struggle with ice, ruts, and sometimes even rocks, when with one step to the outside you can have smooth sailing, and conserve energy for the next uphill in the process?

There is one more aspect of downhill technique that deserves mention: slowing down. Whatever your experience, talent, and ability, you will undoubtedly encounter occasions when you must reduce speed on downhills. It might be during a race on an especially icy trail or when a pileup of other racers is blocking the course. Whatever the reason, there is progression of methods to use for decreasing speed.

If you really need to slow down, apply pressure along the shafts of your poles with your forearms. Jeff Robbins

Assuming you are in a tuck when you decide to throttle back, your first move should be to stretch out your arms. This allows you to maintain balance and control, but offers enough wind resistance to slow you down somewhat. If that doesn't do the trick, stand up. Both of these methods are called "air checking" because, by exposing more body surface to the wind, you increase drag and slow down.

If more drastic deceleration is necessary, it may call for a snowplow. Anyone who has ever skied is familiar with this method of slowing down. But be careful: snowplowing is tricky on cross-country skis, especially if you have a full head of steam, if you are skiing in diagonal tracks, or if the snow is rutted and bumpy. Lots of good racers will "feather one ski," sort of a half snowplow, if they are going too fast to risk a full snowplow or if there are good, deep tracks. It's best to snowplow only if you really have to.

Finally, if you get into real trouble, try this trick Sven Johanson taught us in Alaska: Drag your ski poles in the snow, applying pressure to them with your forearms along the shafts. It's surprising how much drag you can create by exerting force on the baskets in this way.

Technique is definitely an important component of any champion's success. But remember that it's only one of five ingredients that must be kept in balance.

I remember watching a major international relay in which the Norwegians were fighting it out with the Russians for the gold. The Norwegian anchor man was widely regarded as the finest technical skier ever. Cross-country skiers all over the world watched films of his flawless technique and emulated his style. The Norwegian was pitted against a Russian who looked and sounded more like a freight train than a skier. As they entered the stadium for the sprint to the finish for the Olympic gold medal, the flawless Norwegian had a couple of strides on the pesky Soviet. Watching the leader's long, powerful strides, I turned to my Norwegian biathlon friend and said, "He's got it; the Russian will never catch him."

No sooner had I opened my mouth than the Norwegian put his ski pole between his skis, or missed a pole plant, or did something to send him spread-eagled in the snow. He did it entirely on his own. The Russian was well behind when the fall occurred, but he saw his heaven-sent chance and scampered awkwardly past his fallen rival to the finish line and victory.

I was stunned. My Norwegian friend put a hand on my shoulder and said, "It's all right, John, it was bound to happen. He is probably the prettiest technical skier ever, but he has no heart. This has happened before."

Polished technique is wonderful, but races are won by athletes with heart!

6: Off to the Races

I F YOU WANT to succeed at Nordic skiing, you must have a plan. Not only do you need a training program for the off-season, you also need a competitive schedule for the winter. It is important to know in advance which will be your major events. Will you have to perform well in December at tryouts for an Olympic or World Championship team, or will you train and race a progressive schedule throughout the winter, peaking for the NCAAs in early March?

My plan was to race as often as possible early in the season, focusing on the Eastern Super Series, in anticipation that those events would help prepare me for the Masters Nationals in Sun Valley. But where Mother Nature is involved, plans seldom work out as expected.

I returned from six days in Mount Ste. Anne tired but confident. I may not have had the hundreds of kilometers on snow I used to accumulate in Alaska, but I was certainly far better prepared than I had been in almost fifteen years. After a couple of days of rest and easy skiing, I felt I would be ready for the first of two Super Series events, December 22 and 23 at Lake Placid.

Lake Placid has always been an enigma to me. It was the site of some of my best and worst results in skiing. And my most recent commitment in Lake Placid had proven to be an emotional roller coaster. I had been asked to serve as the Biathlon Team leader for the 1988 Winter Olympics in Calgary and, in preparation, for the 1987 World Biathlon Championships (hosted, as in 1973, in Lake Placid). Since as many as half of the athletes on America's World Championship and Olympic Biathlon teams would be former Dartmouth skiers, and the projects could significantly enhance recruiting success for my college team, I was definitely interested. The Dean's office approved, so I accepted the volunteer position and lined up substitute coaches for the college team during my absence.

I had instructed my replacements on the possible challenges they would face with the Dartmouth Team while I was gone—a team whose intense and driven captain had quit during our training camp at Mount Ste. Anne. I asked the coaches to call me in Lake Placid if they had any problems.

The day of the 20K event — the first race of the series — broke sparklingly clear and bitterly cold. It was − 20°F as we left the village for Mount Van Hoevenberg and the biathlon course. The good news was the absence of wind, and thankfully it stayed calm. The competition jury postponed the start an hour to give the sun a little longer to work. Finally the race began, a few degrees below international guidelines, I'm certain. Raimond Dombrovskis was our first racer out, and in spite of grumbling about being in the slower first seed, he was doing well and would collapse in exhaustion across the finish line in twenty-sixth place, his best international result. Glen Eberle and Willie Carow were struggling and would finish further back in the field. But as Josh Thompson cleaned his targets, it was clear he was going to be a contender.

Although I was busy helping the guys as they finished, the radio chatter and what I could see on the range confirmed that Josh was "putting one together." As expected, Frank-Peter Roetsch of East Germany was in the lead, with a couple of Soviets close behind. But the interim splits on the course, combined with the shooting scores, indicated that Josh could be in a battle for second. As he coasted across the finish line, Josh turned to look at the huge electronic scoreboard. All the foreign names below Roetsch rotated down a notch, and THOMPSON–USA appeared proudly beside the number two! There were a few minutes of tense waiting while the remaining competitors finished the course, but Thompson remained second.

At the finish line the sense of euphoria was genuine. Athletes and coaches from other countries sought out Josh and the rest of the American team for a handshake or a slap on the back. Raimond, Willie, and Glen quickly put their personal disappointments behind them and joined in the celebration. After thirty years of international competition, much of it frought with frustration and disappointment, America finally had a medal winner! Sigvart Bjontegaard and Tracy Lamb, the Biathlon team coaches, hugged Josh as cameras recorded their joy. I stood away from the crowd and took in the whole scene: the small but loyal clutch of well-wishers surrounding Josh and the other team members in the finish area, the colorful international flags ringing the stadium, the scoreboard still displaying THOMPSON–USA on the second line just below ROETSCH–DDR. My eyes grew blurry with tears. For three decades we had struggled in a sport clearly dominated by Soviets, Scandinavians, and Germans. With his World Championship silver medal, Josh had given us some respectability. He had made those countless hours of training, coaching, and dedication seem worthwhile. He had made us proud to be Americans.

By ten o'clock that evening we had cleared the well-wishers out of the celebration in the rooming house and sent the athletes to bed for the night. The phone continued to ring for a while with congratulations from around the country. When I finally hit the sack, it was almost midnight. I was exhausted by the emotion and activity of the day. I smiled at the image of the illuminated scoreboard and the Stars and Stripes waving crisply against a cold blue sky.

Someone was shaking me.

"Morty, you've got a phone call!"

"Huh?" I didn't even know where I was.

Led to the darkened living room, I was handed the telephone. By then I remembered I was in Lake Placid, but I had the feeling it must have been two or three o'clock in the morning and that the call represented an emergency for me or one of the athletes. My mind raced.

"Hello?" I mumbled into the phone.

"Uh, Coach Morton, this is John Lynch. I'm sports editor of the *Dartmouth* and wanted to get your comments on an article we are running in tomorrow's issue."

"What?" I was still groggy and confused.

"Uh, well, Coach, we're running an article in tomorrow's paper that is, well, pretty critical of you and your coaching techniques, and, well, we wanted to give you a chance to comment on it."

Talk about experiencing the "thrill of victory and the agony of defeat": I'd had a full dose of both within twelve hours!

I didn't sleep much after the phone call, and before dawn I woke Sigvart and told him I had to return to Dartmouth for the day. It was Friday, February 13, a training day for the competitors at the World Biathlon Championships in Lake Placid, but the first day of competition at the annual Dartmouth Winter Carnival back in Hanover. I knew the newspaper article would tear the team apart when they read it. And I wanted to be on hand to make sure none of the guys overreacted. It was not a happy scene when I arrived, just before the start of the 15K individual event. My skiers were shocked by the article and were angry and frustrated over the quotes it contained. I was happy that I had made the effort to be there. I encouraged, reassured, cheered, and counseled. The Dartmouth Team didn't ski especially well that day, but since no one was beaten senseless, I figured it was a success.

As I drove back to the Adirondacks of New York, I wondered if I was jinxed, if biathlon was cursed, or if there was really something to "Friday the 13th." After waiting and working for nineteen years for international success in biathlon, I enjoyed it for a couple of hours before being hit between the eyes with the greatest challenge of my coaching career.

So on January 3, 1990, I was headed back to Lake Placid with mixed feelings. My carefully developed competitive schedule was not yet three races old and already it was falling apart. I had gambled that the Super Series races would be canceled because of the extreme cold the Northeast had been experiencing. Not wanting to drive almost four hours and waste money for food and lodging for nothing, I remained home in Thetford. As it turned out, Friday's race was postponed for an hour and then run on an abbreviated loop, out of the wind and avoiding fast downhills. (Several skiers who participated told me later that the temperature was about $-8°$F.) It warmed up a little on Saturday, so the relay went off on schedule. So much for my planning. There were no other races scheduled in the East until January 6, and that was the Lawrence Loppet, a 50K, mass-start citizens' race at, you guessed it, Lake Placid.

About then Jed Williamson, director of the U.S. Biathlon Association, asked if I would serve as chief of course for the Biathlon Team trials January 4 through 7 on the Olympic courses at Lake Placid. I told Jed I was planning to race the Loppet on the sixth.

"Great, Morty, that's a training day for us! If you serve as chief of course, I'll give you some transportation money, put you up in the Olympic Training Center, and pay your entry fee in the Loppet. Whada ya say?"

It was hard to turn down, since the schedules did seem to mesh so well.

"Remember, the Mount Van Hoevenberg crew will do all the work," he added, just in case I was still wavering. "All you'll have to do is give a brief report, answer questions at the coaches' meeting, and serve on the jury."

I agreed, and promised to be in Lake Placid in time to check out course preparations on the third. As soon as I arrived at Mount Van Hoevenberg, I found Greg Strafford, the manager of the cross-country and biathlon trail system, who briefed me on the loops they had prepared for the first tryout race. I put on my skis and headed out to inspect the course. This was the best part of these jobs. Everything looked great. They hadn't had a lot of snow, in fact it was marginal, but the trails had been groomed to perfection, thanks to a significant amount of man-made snow.

I hit the sack early, knowing I would be up before dawn to inspect the course prior to the race. Provided it is not actually snowing, grooming for major cross-country or biathlon races usually takes place during the night. This ensures that no tourists or misguided racers chew up the freshly tilled surface before it has the opportunity to set up. But as chief of course, it was my duty to ensure that the course was ready for the competition, which meant cruising the perfectly prepared "corduroy" trail as soon as it was light enough to ski. Greg and his people had done a magnificent job; the course was flawless.

The first tryout race went off without a hitch. I took a rake with me and skied around looking for trouble spots: ruts developing on downhills, bare spots appearing in thin-snow areas. After the race I skied the loops again, noting potential problem areas. I raked and shoveled for about an hour with some of Greg's helpers until I was confident we were ready to go for Friday's 10K event. Greg warned me that the forecast didn't sound promising—warm temperatures and rain overnight—but it could just as easily end up snowing. We agreed to meet at 6:00 A.M. to evaluate the course.

It began raining after supper and poured all night. When I left the Olympic Training Center (OTC) before dawn for Van Hoevenberg, I was prepared for the worst. It had never dropped below freezing; there were signs of flooding and standing puddles everywhere. The biathlon range and the large field behind the stadium was a mess. Greg and I stood in the predawn twilight tired, frustrated, and discouraged. He was ready to pack it in and chalk up one more for Mother Nature. He reluctantly agreed to stick around a few minutes more while I skied a loop. In spite of the nonstop downpour, the man-made snow that covered most of the trail in the woods had held up remarkably well. I returned more optimistic.

"Greg, the worst of it is right here in front of us. The trails are skiable! Could we make a bridge across this lake with man-made snow?"

"Yeah, we could, but not by the ten o'clock start time," he responded.

"We'll delay the start. How much time do you need?"

"Another hour or so."

"You've got it."

I drove back to the OTC to pass the word that the race would go on but the start would be delayed by an hour. Then I began recruiting workers. Parents, girlfriends, husbands, college roommates, everyone was put to work, and by eleven o'clock the second biathlon tryout race was under way. I shoveled and raked at one rough spot after another throughout the race, only vaguely aware of who was doing well. A postrace conference with Greg revealed the news that a cold front was expected within a few hours. It would be a lot harder to rake and shovel what little snow was left once it was frozen solid, so we agreed to keep at it while it was soft. I had been at the range before breakfast and returned to the OTC just before supper, most of my day spent raking and shoveling. This was *not* the approach an experienced racer, let alone coach, should take to the first race of the season, which against all good judgment was a freestyle 50K!

I arrived at the cross-country stadium the next morning in plenty of time for the 9:00 A.M. start. The waxing had been easy. Since the temperature had dropped well below freezing overnight and would rise only to the midtwenties during the race, the course was crushed ice and rocket fast. I got off by myself and did some stretching. It had been more than fifteen years since I had raced a 50K event, and I had never skated that far. My retirement following the 1976 Olympics had also preceded the growth in popularity of huge, mass-start races, so this would be a new experience for me. Not long before the start I learned that the rain that had all but wiped out the biathlon range had forced Greg to revise the loop for the Loppet. Normally the 50K event consists of two times around a twenty-five-kilometer loop, about half of that loop on gentle terrain and the remainder in the more-challenging foothills of Mount Van Hoevenberg. The revised course consisted of one twelve-kilometer loop, from the start stadium out onto the Porter Mountain Trails, back over Russian Hill, down Main Street, and back to the stadium. Normally the Loppet course contains a challenging 3,700 feet of total vertical climb, but this loop would have significantly more than that!

Because of the revised course, they also changed the start procedure. Rather than a mass start of the several hundred 50K and 25K competitors, they announced that the 25K racers would start thirty minutes after the others. As nine o'clock approached, I put on my number, gathered my gear, and headed for the starting line. My anxiety increased as the seconds ticked by. It was stupid to race fifty kilometers the first race of the year. I hadn't trained or even prepared properly the last few days, I wasn't confident about my skating, and the course would be harder than normal.

The gun went off and the stampede began. The course left the stadium and headed up — dramatically — into the hills. I knew I didn't want to go under in the first kilometer of a 50K race, so I didn't scramble to stay with the leaders. Even so, it was disturbing as hundreds of insectlike skaters, skis and poles splayed to the sides of the track, plodded deliberately up the long hill as the lead pack disappeared gracefully into the woods. There was no sense fighting the tide. I tried to stay calm, conserve energy, and reassure myself that I could make up for lost time later in the race.

The first twelve-kilometer loop went well. Although the lead pack was out of sight, I felt I was skiing smoothly — confident on the icy downhills and strong on the uphills. As we came through the start stadium, the race took on a new dimension. They had just started the several hundred 25K Kort-Loppet participants. Although there were many fine racers who had elected to ski the shorter event, most of the participants were less-experienced skiers who wanted to race but knew fifty kilometers would be too much for them. Many skied with heavy clothes and backpacks (as if they were prepared to spend the weekend on the trail, if necessary). As the leaders of the 50K race overtook the throng of 25K participants and threaded their way through the crowd, I envisaged Indianapolis race cars darting in and out on a clogged Los Angeles freeway.

At first it was fun. There were so many skiers walking the uphills, cheerfully chatting with each other, that it made no sense to yell "Track." The best approach was to ski for the daylight, calmly announcing, "Coming by on your right," as you approached. It was inspiring to pass so many other racers, and I felt even better than I had on the first loop (though I'm sure all the weaving and dodging slowed down my lap time). The real excitement took place on the downhills, as inexperienced skiers snowplowed in panic on the icy descents. The bottom of each hill was littered with competitors, spread-eagled across the trail or rolling out of the way. It was like a demolition derby. The main objective was to "thread the needle" through the wreckage and remain standing. There was an unbelievable sense of relief upon shooting out of a downhill turn unscathed.

Former biathlon coach Art Stegen let me know I was eleventh overall in the 50K. So now was the time. I had to concentrate, ski hard, and make up more than a minute and a half needed to overtake the leader in my age group. The apprehensions I had felt at the start had disappeared. The skis were fast, my skating felt okay, and I actually enjoyed the challenging course. I cut back on the cheerful banter with everyone I passed and concentrated on going fast. As I came through the start stadium to begin my fourth and final lap, I knew I had gained time on the leaders. But I had paid the price: my quadriceps were showing signs of cramping with every stride. I grabbed two cups of Exceed and a section of banana at the next feed station. My face began to feel cold and my eyes refused to focus. I knew I was in trouble.

In any endurance event lasting more than an hour, a constant threat facing the athletes is running out of blood sugar, commonly known as "hitting the wall." Even a highly trained competitor can sustain top effort for only about an hour before the body's reserves of blood sugar, or glycogen, become used up. Dehydration speeds the onset of glycogen depletion, so experienced competitors anticipating an effort of two hours or more usually start the event literally sloshing. It is also critical to drink during the event, because once you feel thirsty, it is too late. As Gene Morgan, one of America's toughest distance skiers during the 1970s, once said: "When you hit the wall, you probably don't have five minutes left at race pace. You'll be lucky if you have energy enough to *walk* back to the finish!"

A few kilometers into the fourth loop of the Lawrence Loppet, I had hit the wall. By this point in the race I knew precisely where the food stations were located, and I shuffled along like a zombie, desperate to reach the next one before I fell down.

Two things kept me going. I knew I had skied well for the first three laps, and even if I really throttled back I could probably finish respectably. Even more compelling was the realization that I was almost to the far end of the loop. It wouldn't be much harder to continue on the course to the finish than to ski back to the stadium against the traffic.

At the final food station on the far point of the loop I stopped to chow down. No grabbing a cup of water on the fly this time; I parked and washed down several banana and orange sections with cup after cup of Exceed. I knew the fuel wouldn't kick in until too late, but it would at least get me back to the stadium. I was light-headed, shaky, and desperately weak. My eyes wouldn't focus properly. I arduously walked every uphill and approached the downhills with a sense of dread. Other skiers passed me and I couldn't respond. I struggled one step at a time up Russian Hill knowing I was within a couple of kilometers of the finish. Then I remembered with horror the fast, icy S turn that led to Main Street and the stadium. The S turn had become increasingly challenging through each of the first three laps, as more skiers plowed snow off the underlying ice. I approached the turn in a wide, stiff-legged snowplow worthy of a first-time skier from Florida. Halfway through the descent I caught a tip and slammed into the ice in a heap. It felt so good to be off my feet and motionless that I seriously considered just staying there for a while. But more exhausted racers were plummeting down the chute, and I was right in the way. I struggled to my feet and coasted listlessly toward the stadium. A few minutes later it was over. I had no idea of my time or placing; I just knew I was very cold, hungry, and shaky, and needed to get inside. The ever-present ski patrolman at the finish line asked the endlessly repeated question, "Are you all right?"

Out of habit I answered, "Yup."

"No, you're not," he responded, and throwing a blanket around my shoulders, he walked me across the stadium to the warming house. He sat me down on a bench and went to fetch hot tea, orange slices, and a handful of cookies.

"I'll get your skis and poles. You stay here till you warm up and feel better!"

"Thanks," was all I could respond.

I did feel better after I had stuffed down about a thousand calories of cookies, oranges, and doughnuts. I was surprised to discover that in spite of my fourth-lap "death march," I'd ended up eighteenth overall, second in my age group.

My competitive comeback was officially under way. I spent most of the drive home evaluating the pluses and minuses of my fall training, early-season skiing, and first race. There certainly were things I would do differently another time around, but on balance, I figured things were OK. The last twelve kilometers of the Loppet were no fun, but the first thirty-six were great! That was encouraging, especially with the White Mountain Marathon coming up in three weeks.

During the days that followed the Loppet, I fought a case of the flu. It never had me completely sidelined, but the aches, cough, and scratchy throat made me cut back on my workout schedule. Marginal snow conditions didn't help either. I spent an hour or so each day cutting firewood or skating with my daughter on our pond. Saturday's Super Series race was relocated from Glens Falls to Prospect Mountain near Bennington. I wanted to go, especially since it was a classic race, but I was nervous about racing both Saturday and Sunday with the cold hanging on. I decided to play it smart for a change and race only at Putney on Sunday. Because of the snow conditions, the scheduled classic race was switched to skating, and we were to ski a 4.2-kilometer loop twice for 8.4 kilometers, rather than the advertised 10 kilometers.

One of my former Dartmouth Team captains, Chris Bean, had just completed medical school and was serving an internship at Mary Hitchcock Hospital in Hanover. His love for skiing was stronger than ever, although he seldom got a complete night's sleep and rarely had time to train. Since he had Sunday off, and the weather was clear, cold, and beautiful, he eagerly agreed to join me for the Putney race.

The nice weather brought out hordes of skiers: kids, parents, highschoolers, and college students, as well as the U.S. Ski Team and a couple of world-class Italians. We started at intervals over a hilly, twisty loop that showed the effects of lots of shoveling and raking. It was a real "lung burner": short, fast, and intense. In an interval-start race it is sometimes difficult to get a clear picture of how you are doing overall. Generally, if you pass athletes who started ahead of you and no late starters pass you, things are going well. The situation becomes more confusing when it involves multiple laps. Not long after I completed my first loop, Brad Bates, a promising Dartmouth skier I had once coached, passed me. He was just starting his first loop; I was beginning my second. I tried to hang tough, right behind him, but he pulled away. I spent the remainder of the race debating whether I was a wimp for letting him get away or just being unreasonable in trying to stay with a good college skier more than twenty years my junior.

Before the results were posted, I tried to evaluate the race. Coming off a week of coughing and headaches, I was happy to have finished strong in a high-tempo "lung burner." On the other hand, my skating felt sloppy, my balance, awkward. When the unofficial results were posted, Chris pushed his way through the crowd to get a look. He returned with a dour face.

"Let's head home. . . . You beat me by almost two minutes."

He had been working twenty-hour days for months at the hospital and knew I had been training consistently for the first time in years, but he still didn't enjoy finishing behind "Old Coach." I smiled to myself as we headed home; it was just this type of competitive spirit (admittedly unreasonable at times) that has made so many skiers so successful in their chosen pursuits. Dr. Chris Bean may never win a major cross-country ski race again, but he will become a brilliant orthopedic surgeon.

The weekend of January 20 and 21 the Super Series moved to Farmington, Maine, for two races: a 7.5K classic race on Saturday and a 15K skating race on Sunday. I was interested in these events because they offered the opportunity to race classic and freestyle back to back against roughly the same competitors. In planning my racing season, I was faced with an intriguing decision. I had grown up skiing classic and felt that my technique and experience would be an advantage. I had resisted the switch to skating and didn't feel as comfortable with the new technique. So at first I figured I should concentrate on classic races. Then I realized that all the masters my age probably felt the same way. In fact, coaching at Dartmouth I had had better exposure to skating than most of my opponents, so perhaps I should concentrate on freestyle. The Farmington races would let me know how I was doing in each technique.

The drive to Maine took longer than I had anticipated, and I arrived Saturday morning without my customary two-hour cushion for wax testing, warming up, and checking out the course. I rewaxed in the parking lot and ran to the start. It was another twisty, old-fashioned course on crushed ice. Before long the tilled crust had worn off most of my klister, and I was working hard to stay optimistic. I hung with it, convincing myself that others would be having wax difficulties as well. Besides, it had become a hell of a good arm workout. In a field of forty-one men I finished twentieth (compared with thirty-six of sixty-five at Putney). That evening I figured my percent of the top three Americans in the race and was pleased to see an improvement: 87.6 percent at Putney and 89.4 percent in the Farmington classic race.

The 15K skating race on Sunday was also challenging. I had glide waxed both classic and skating skis before I left home on Friday. The National Weather Service forecast had called for moderate temperatures throughout the weekend, around 20°F. For some inexplicable reason I had decided to experiment with a wax I'd never used before, but which seemed appropriate for the forecasted conditions. Just before the start of the freestyle race the temperature began to drop and a fine, crystaled snow started to accumulate. I pushed hard in the race, feeling the effects of the previous day. For most of the second loop I was nursing cramps in both quadriceps. I finished hard, feeling that it had been a pretty good physical effort but that I'd blown the wax. By the end of the race the thermometer showed 9°F, more than ten degrees below what I'd anticipated. When the results came out, I was listed twenty-eighth of the fifty-two men competing. Here I was 85.6 percent of the top Americans.

After fifteen years of coaching I had reconfirmed some very basic rules. First of all, at a classic race, arrive early. You need time to test your wax, and if it's a course you haven't seen, you should tour the loop as part of your warm-up. Arriving two hours before the start of a classic race is not a waste of time.

Second, waxing is important, even in a skating event. If you are serious about your results, pay attention to the snow conditions and be prepared to adjust if necessary. Resist the temptation to experiment with waxes in important races. It is easy to fantasize that some new concoction will provide that extra edge for a stunning victory, but more often an unfamiliar or unproven wax will prove disappointing. By all means experiment with new waxes and innovative applications, but do it in practice.

My results in these two races confirmed what I had suspected concerning my preference for classic over skating. Of course, under the circumstances it wasn't a conclusive test; but it did suggest that I'd better exercise some positive thinking and imagery if I had hopes of doing well in skating races throughout the winter.

In short, my "comeback season" was four races old and had a notable absence of impressive results. I had hit the wall violently at Lake Placid, had skated to mediocre results in two Super Series freestyle events, and had blown the wax in my first classic race. This was not much of an endorsement of my coaching expertise.

On Saturday, January 27, the Great American Ski Chase opened with the White Mountain Marathon, a hilly 30K freestyle event at Waterville Valley, New Hampshire. The Ski Chase is a series of nine mass-start citizens' events, spanning the continent from New Hampshire to Alaska. Some of the races boast more than seven thousand participants annually and become the cornerstone of week-long ski festivals in the host cities. A small number of elite athletes ski most of the nine nationwide events in an effort to earn recognition as Great American Ski Chase Champions. But since consideration for overall honors requires participation in at least four events (one in each of the three national regions) it means considerable travel and expense.

I had toyed with the idea of skiing the events necessary for overall consideration, but eventually decided against it. My schedule had room for two Ski Chase events: the White Mountain Marathon in New Hampshire and the American Birkebeiner in Hayward, Wisconsin. I was optimistic about Waterville. It was a 30K event, and I had skated well for the first thirty-six kilometers of the Lawrence Loppet in Lake Placid. On the other hand, my Super Series results had been nothing to write home about, and Waterville had been the scene of the worst waxing disaster in my coaching career.

Early in my first season at Dartmouth, while I was still trying to prove myself, the U.S. Nationals, or U.S. Ski Team trials, were held at Waterville Valley. New-fallen wet snow made waxing a nightmare. To complicate things further, the course included quite a bit of flat skiing before heading into the woods for a gut-busting climb followed by a long, thigh-burning downhill. I was putting every conceivable concoction on the Dartmouth boys' practice skis, telling them, "Go try it, make sure you test it in the woods, and let me know how it works."

"The U.S. Ski Team is using silver and red," my returning skiers announced breathlessly.

"What about these test skis?" I asked.

"Slipped, no kick at all!"

"Did you try them in the woods?" I asked.

"Didn't have time."

We were running out of time. Nothing I had tested worked well on the glazed tracks of the golf course, although I was afraid the snow in the woods would be drier and have a tendency to ice up. As the minutes ticked by, the guys became more insistent on the combination they had heard the U.S. Team was using, so we set up an assembly line and began applying the sticky, red and silver klister combination. I was still torching skis as the race started. I got to a strategic turn at the bottom of the long descent as the leaders came through. Many of the U.S. Team, college, and club coaches were also there. Minutes crept by without a trace of a green uniform. Finally, my first Dartmouth skier appeared, red-faced and sweating profusely, double poling laboriously where others had coasted around the corner. I ran along the side of the track offering encouragement. Eyes straight ahead, struggling on, the skier showed no reaction to my coaching. Something made me ask as he rounded the corner, "How's the wax?"

That got his attention! He almost stopped, turned his beet-red face over his shoulder, glared at me and the other coaches, and announced, "It SUCKS!"

There were some nervous chuckles behind me, and one of my colleagues asked in a deadpan voice, "So how do you like college coaching, Morty?" I stood on that corner for another half hour while the rest of my skiers hobbled down the hill. It was a very quiet ride back to Hanover.

I learned several important lessons from that race. Since then I always try to arrive at a race site with plenty of time to test waxes, and I follow my own instincts on the day of the race. I check the air and snow temperatures and I reread the instructions on the wax containers. I don't ask anyone else what they are using or what they have tested, and I don't want to know. While a coach, I would wax every conceivable combination on test skis and send my top skiers out to decide which combination was best. After all, they were the ones who were going to race on it. (It also cut down on postrace criticism if they were the ones who had made the decision.)

I had learned from my recent mistakes at the Super Series and planned to arrive in Waterville the day before the race, tour the course, test wax, and find a place to fuel up on spaghetti! Although I was not a member of the Fischer/

Salomon Marathon Team, I had been provided equipment by those two companies, and when I checked in with Jeff Clark, the team's manager, he invited me to stay with them Friday night in a rented house. I accepted and found it to be a very interesting, educational, but disorienting experience. There were Fischer/Salomon Team members from across the country, some of whom I had known for years and others I had never met. After a giant spaghetti dinner Dan Simoneau, Nordic racing coordinator for Fischer of America, and Jeff Clark called everyone together for a team meeting. It was the first time in many years that *I* hadn't called the meeting, that *I* wasn't responsible for arranging logistics, and that *I* didn't have to stick my neck out by recommending a wax for the race. It was disconcerting to sit quietly among the other racers listening to Dan's instructions. I was immediately impressed by his knowledge, his sense of organization, and the respect he commanded from his peers.

The wax combination Dan suggested was Solda orange under Cera F. I had never seen or heard of Solda, and Cera F was significantly beyond my budget. I took my skis and wax box out to the garage where the benches had been set up and athletes were preparing their skis. I figured I could always learn more about waxing, and even though I didn't own either of the suggested varieties, I could carefully watch the others apply it before using the best substitute on my own boards.

As the crowd began to dissipate, I took over a vacant bench. Dan came in to check on everyone's progress. As I was ironing on my choice, Dan asked, "Hey, Morty, what are you doing?"

"Well, I don't have Solda or Cera so I figured this would be the next best thing."

He went over to his team wax box, an aluminum footlocker filled to overflowing.

"Here, put back what you don't use," he said, handing me the Solda and Cera.

Even though I had never used either before, having watched the others carefully I had no problem applying the combination. As I consolidated my gear and went to bed, I thought, "Well, if exotic wax really makes a difference, I should have an advantage tomorrow!"

Saturday morning was beautiful, clear, and cold. A downpour two days earlier had necessitated minor course revisions, and a new wave start replaced the traditional mass start. Even though the bright sun was beginning to warm things up, the course was basically crushed ice that had been tilled and groomed most of the night. Wax shouldn't have been an issue. The waves were scheduled to depart at one-minute intervals, and each wave consisted of twenty-five or thirty racers. I was assigned to wave eleven and didn't know anyone else in the wave. As we moved up to the starting line, a familiar voice said, "Hey, Morty, have a good one." I turned to see John Broadhead preparing to start one minute behind me. John had beaten me at Lake Placid by twelve minutes and had given me a good ribbing afterward. Returning his greeting, I thought to myself, "Great, Sodhead will kill himself to make up that minute, then blow me off the track as he goes by! Well, I'll just have to hold him off as long as possible."

The starter released wave eleven and we were off. There was a long, grinding climb not far into the loop, so I had planned to be conservative early in the race. But only two hundred yards out of the start, as the trail narrowed, I found myself leading the wave. I was timid at first, thinking how risky it is to lead early in a race, but then I let positive psychology take over and just enjoyed it. Furthermore, my skis felt great! The sun was warming the snow slightly and my boards seemed to have a life of their own. As I worked into the first long uphill, I risked a glance back—no one in sight! Before long I was picking off the stragglers of wave ten. I knew then that it was going to be a good day. After almost twenty kilometers I had seen no sign of Broadhead, so I began to focus on finishing more than a minute ahead of him. About that time I noticed a small, quick skier in the distance. I slowly reeled him in over the next several kilometers until I recognized Murry Banks, a former Masters Champion of the Ironman Triathlon in Hawaii. Although Murry was a recent convert to skiing, he was a real competitor and would not easily let me slip by and pull ahead. After skating behind him for a while I called on all the experience and psychology I could muster. Rather than grunting "Track" as is often done, I casually remarked, "Murry Banks, how's it going? I gotta sneak by ya on this corner."

I did catch him off guard, at least for an instant. When I went by, I horsed it for all I was worth, knowing full well I could never keep that pace up for more than a couple hundred meters. Murry hung on gamely throughout my sprint and probably would have tailed me right to the finish line had it not been for a long, fast downhill and my super wax job. I held a tight tuck and let the skis run, barely avoiding disaster as I roared by less-experienced skiers, who checked dramatically to reduce their speed. I was so "pumped," I'm sure the last couple of kilometers of rolling terrain were my fastest of the race. I skated alone through the finish line, coasted to a stop, and turned to look at the display clock. A minute would have to elapse before Broadhead finished if I were going to beat him. The seconds ticked by. Even if he did beat me, it would be by much less than the twelve-minute margin he established at Lake Placid. Sixty seconds and still no Broadhead! Another two minutes elapsed before John charged through the timing light. I watched from a distance as he caught his breath and surveyed the exhausted finishers. When he spotted me, he waved and shuffled closer.

"Morty, nice going; I never saw you!"

"Yeah, I imagined you breathing down my neck at least half a dozen times," I said.

"Not today. Some better than Lake Placid, huh?"

"You can say that again!"

It was such a beautiful day and I was so excited (even though I had not yet seen times or placings), I corralled my old army friend Peter Hale, who had been demonstrating waxing techniques for Ski*Go since dawn, and we headed back around the fourteen-kilometer loop. We talked, joked, reminisced, and told lies the whole way around, teasing each other about how the twenty years since Fort Richardson had treated us. It would be one of my most enjoyable memories of the entire winter — the exhilaration of the race, perfect weather, a scenic trail, and good friends. That is the essence of our sport, and you can't do much better anywhere!

We returned in time for a quick change of clothes and a short walk to the awards presentation. The large convention room was crowded with gregarious, sunburned skiers, exchanging adventures. The results were posted on the wall. I had finished twenty-fifth of the 232 men competing and ended up top finisher over forty years old. I was thrilled! After an inauspicious start to the season, I had put a good one together, and a skating race at that! In less than a week I would be headed to Sun Valley, Idaho, and the Masters National Cross-Country Championships. Before the White Mountain Marathon I didn't have cause for much optimism over Sun Valley. But after my results in Waterville I began to think positively. I could have good results skating. I could hold my own in a mass or a wave start. And I could finish strong in a long event. For the first time since I had concocted the whole idea, I really was looking forward to the Masters Championships!

7: Nutrition

I'M NO EXPERT on nutrition. In fact, I'm a card-carrying member of the generation that was told a thousand times, "The normal American diet contains all the nutritional requirements for good health." When I was competing on an international level from 1969 through 1976, the only dietary concern most of us had was that we got enough to eat. We didn't much care what fuel we put into the "engine"; we figured we were training so hard we would burn up anything.

Nutrition didn't really attract my attention until October 1986. Kjell Kratz, a famous Swedish Nordic coach who had worked with Gunde Svan and with the very successful Swedish World Loppet Team, came to America to do a series of high-level coaches' clinics. I eagerly agreed to host one at Dartmouth. Coaches and athletes from throughout New England packed a conference room and listened attentively as the famous Swede explained the keys to the success of his nation's Nordic program.

When he called for questions, I asked him what he considered to be the most significant reasons for the success of the Swedish Team, noting that nothing he had described was dramatically different from what we were doing in the States.

Kjell paused thoughtfully. "Well," he began, "I see two important factors. The first is cultural. In Sweden all youngsters dream of being Olympic skiers. We are a small country, but the majority of our population skis and our National Team racers are regarded as Sweden's finest athletes. In America many people never experience snow and don't understand ski racing. And even in the North, where skiing is popular, many youngsters want instead to play football or baseball. You are a large country, but only a small percentage of your athletes ski."

"The other area where I think we have an edge on you," Kjell continued, "is nutrition. Our athletes train so hard year-round that we have focused quite a bit of attention and research on what foods are best for training and competition. We believe the proper diet allows our athletes to train harder, resist injury and illness, and ultimately race faster. Gunde is a great champion to a significant degree because he is very conscientious about what he eats."

His remarks were followed by a stunned silence. Most coaches had at least a casual awareness of nutritional requirements, but we were surprised to hear nutrition given as one of the two most significant keys to success in Nordic skiing!

Kjell offered some specifics. At training camps the athletes have four meals a day — the three customary ones and a late-evening snack. All of their meals are predominantly carbohydrates: bread, potatoes, rice, pasta, and a lot of oatmeal, which they believe aids in muscle recovery during stressful training sessions. They drink a tremendous amount of water to stay hydrated but don't go overboard on milk or on fruit juices, some of which are too acidic.

I heard a lot of interesting information that day, including suggestions about dry-land training and observations on the skating revolution. But nothing had as great an impact as Kjell's comments concerning nutrition.

They caused me to question what I had taken for granted, especially the often-repeated reassurance that the average American diet fulfills all nutritional requirements. What is the "average American diet" anyway? In 1986 many ski team members typically overslept and skipped breakfast, bolted down a lunch of burgers and fries, and ate everything in sight at supper, topping it off with a pint of ice cream! At the same time, others lived off-campus, surviving on low-cost pasta, and a couple were vegetarians. I began to believe there was no such thing as an average American diet.

To add to my confusion, the skiers who cooked for themselves or were vegetarians performed just as well in workouts and perhaps even better in physiology tests. After a couple of testing sessions, I realized the athletes with the highest body-fat percentage were those who lived on campus. I also noticed they were usually freshmen or sophomores who hadn't quite come to grips with the vast array of food available at the college dining hall.

Kjell Kratz's comments also supported two of my own nutritional observations, which I had never taken the time to carefully evaluate. The first involved my ten months in Vietnam. As a Mobile Advisory Team Leader in a remote village of the Mekong Delta, I lived, worked, and ate with my South Vietnamese counterparts for several weeks at a time. At first glance it seemed our Vietnamese hosts were starving because of food shortages due to the war. This was reinforced by their appearance (small of stature and very thin), as well as what they ate — mostly rice, garnished with what little meat or fish they could add to it: chicken, fish, dog, snake, eel, bats, turtle, or rat.

What was interesting, however, was that these small, lean Vietnamese could walk all day under the scorching Delta sun, knee deep in rice paddy muck, toting an M-60 machine gun almost half their body weight! In terms of actual physical endurance, the average Vietnamese soldier could perform circles around his typical American counterpart. At the time I thought it was the heat, the humidity, or some strange cultural adaptation, but time after time I saw the diminutive Vietnamese walk farther and carry heavier loads than their bigger, "stronger" American allies. Now I realize that their endurance was due to a significant degree to their high carbohydrate diet.

A final revelation came when my wife and I went on the Pritikin Diet. It was quite a change at first (since so much of what we routinely eat contains fat, and the Pritikin Program avoids most fat), but we persevered. The pounds didn't just magically disappear and I never got down to my Vietnam weight (the famous rice, sweat, and combat diet program), but I did feel fit and ran my best marathon to that point, a 2:43:05. When friends would ask, "Do you feel better, do you have more energy, are you more alert?" I would have to answer, "No, I feel fine, but I haven't noticed a dramatic difference since going on the program."

There was one memorable exception, however, when we went out to eat with my wife's folks. Rather than creating an awkward scene trying to decide what, if anything, on the menu we could eat, Mimi and I agreed to ignore the Pritikin diet for that one meal. I ordered a "normal American meal": steak, baked potato (with sour cream and butter), vegetable, salad (with blue cheese dressing), a beer, and dessert.

I may not have felt a dramatic change being on the Pritikin Diet, but I certainly felt terrible the day after that steak dinner! I felt heavy, bloated, slow, and lethargic when I tried to work out the following day. For me it was a vivid example of how what you eat affects your performance.

It has taken me a long time to recognize the significance of nutrition in achieving top results in Nordic skiing. Habits that have become established over the years are difficult to break. What adds to the problem is the millions of dollars spent on advertising food products, not all of them nutritionally beneficial. Thanks to repeated messages in the media, when we get thirsty, we tend to reach for a soft drink rather than water (which is not only less expensive but probably better for us as well).

As I became more concerned about the nutrition of my Dartmouth skiers, I sought the advice of several specialists on campus. Marcia Herrin, the college nutritionist, gave the team some guidelines for healthful eating. She recommended that the diet of male endurance athletes consist of up to 70 percent carbohydrates and 20 percent protein, and not more than 15 percent fat. My athletes did their best to comply, going heavy on the bread, rice, noodles, and potatoes. But a midwinter diet check was revealing.

An intern in the physiology lab conducted a computer analysis of my skiers' diets. They had to record everything they ate for three days, and during that time try to eat normal, representative meals. The results were interesting. Three skiers who ate primarily in the dining hall discovered their carbo consumption over the three days reflected 57.4, 54.0, and 39.7 percent of their total caloric intake. This was while they were striving for about 70 percent carbohydrates! If the relatively low levels of carbohydrates were surprising, then the amounts of fat ingested were alarming: 24.7, 31.8, and 42 percent.

This test confirmed a couple of things in my mind. First, that many people's diets were in fact unhealthy. They lacked sufficient carbohydrates to fuel an active lifestyle and contained far too much fat, a leading contributor to heart disease, which is our nation's number-one killer.

Second, simply knowing the appropriate target percentages for carbohydrates, proteins, and fat in the diet does not automatically make it possible to reach those target percentages. It is difficult to eat enough carbohydrates while avoiding the fat. It is also hard to translate 70 percent carbohydrates into servings of rice or spaghetti per week. To help make this transition, Marcia Herrin gave us the following chart. It is not meant to be a literal daily diet but a translation of percentages into actual servings. When we begin to visualize twenty servings of toast, three cups of vegetables, and four cups of fruit, we can more easily grasp the volume of carbohydrates we need daily.

Recommended Daily Food Plan for the Male Athlete 3,000 Calories

70% carbohydrates; 20% protein; 10% fat

20 servings of breads/cereals (20 slices of bread or 12 cups of spaghetti or 10 cups of cereal)

3 cups of vegetables

4 cups of fruit (or 4 large apples)

6 cups of milk or yogurt

5 ounces of meat or cheese

7 teaspoons of fat

I'm not an expert on nutrition. In fact, of the five components for skiing success, nutrition was the last one I recognized and acknowledged. There are many excellent books on diet and nutrition, providing sample menus, creative techniques for adding variety to meals, and strategies for maintaining diets while eating in restaurants. *Serious Training for Serious Athletes*, by Rob Sleamaker, has an excellent chapter on nutrition. *Training for Cross-Country Ski Racing*, by Brian Sharkey, also contains valuable nutritional information (although since it was published in 1984 estimates of carbo requirements have been revised upward from the 60 percent he mentions to 70 percent). *Jane Brody's Good Food Book, Nancy Clark's Sports Nutrition Guidebook,* and *The Athlete's Kitchen,* also by Nancy Clark, all contain valuable information for the competitor who is interested in learning more about nutrition.

Several years ago the Shaklee Corporation, which produces nutritional supplements, became a U.S. Ski Team sponsor and assumed responsibility for underwriting the sports medicine program. Of course, Shaklee was interested in promoting the nutritional supplements they produce, but company experts also spent time and energy evaluating the nutritional demands of elite U.S. skiers. The following is taken from Shaklee's "Nutritional Dos and Don'ts for Skiers," which I feel represents sound advice.

Nutritional Dos and Don'ts for Skiers
Breakfast

DO: Eat hot cereals like oatmeal or Cream of Wheat
Select whole-grain or high-fiber cold cereals
Eat breads, including muffins, biscuits, and bagels
Try milk, skim or lowfat is best
Choose fruit, including fresh, canned, and fruit juices
Drink hot beverages such as hot chocolate, hot apple cider
Eat pancakes, waffles, and French toast
Choose eggs up to two or three times weekly
Take recommended nutritional supplements with breakfast

DON'T: Eat sausage, ham, or bacon more than twice weekly
Opt for eggs every day
Choose sugary children's cereals
Use too much margarine or butter
Eat doughnuts or pastries daily
Skip breakfast

Lunch

DO: Pack a lunch and Thermos when possible
Choose whole-grain breads
Choose lean meats like turkey over salami or bologna
Use mustard and ketchup as condiments
Choose a hamburger over hot dogs
Choose a baked potato over french fries
Eat pasta as much as you like
Try pizzas without fatty meat toppings
Eat hearty soups and stews

DON'T: Eat fast-food meals if avoidable

Eat fried foods like fish and chips more than twice weekly

Overuse condiments like mayonnaise or salad dressings

Eat fatty and salty luncheon meats too often

Eat pizza or pasta with sausage or other cured meats

Skip lunch

Dinner

DO: Eat pasta with or without meat

Choose pizza with vegetable and lean-meat toppings

Try Chinese food with rice and fresh vegetables

Select fish often. Broiled or poached is best

Trim visible fat from meats and remove skin from poultry

Have soups, salads, and plenty of vegetables

Eat as much bread as you like

Include potatoes, rice, and beans when available

Choose fresh fruit, yogurt, and Jell-O for dessert

DON'T: Choose deep-fried meals more than twice a week

Eat high-fat meats like hot dogs or sausages in excess

Choose meals with heavy cream sauces or gravies

Fill up on alcoholic beverages instead of food

Ruin a baked potato or bread with too much butter

Have heavy cakes, ice cream, and pies every night

Snacks and Beverages

DO: Pack nutritious snacks like fruit, raisins, and nuts

Have rolls, muffins, and breads when you get a break

Snack on popcorn, pretzels, and breadsticks

Drink eight to ten glasses of fluids each day

Drink nonfat or lowfat milk

Drink fruit juices, sparkling waters, and plain water

Drink hot ciders, soups, and hot chocolate

DON'T: Count on potato chips and tortilla chips as good snacks

Eat cupcakes and cream-filled pastries to satisfy hunger

Eat ice cream, cakes, or candies in excess

Drink alcoholic beverages in excess

Drink too many soft drinks, especially cola drinks

Drink too much coffee or tea

More than fifty years ago Otto Schniebs, a legendary Dartmouth ski coach, said, "Skiing is not just a sport; skiing is a way of life!" He was not exaggerating. For most of us, if we are determined to improve our racing results, it will mean a significant change in what we eat. This will take as much willpower and determination as it does to work out daily, rain or shine. The good news is that these nutritional changes will not only help us race faster, they will help us live longer as well!

Hydration

There are a couple of issues related to nutrition that deserve attention. The first is hydration. It is commonly known that the human body contains about 60 percent water by weight. In a strenuous workout or race an athlete loses a lot of water — as much as three liters per hour, which translates to seven pounds of body weight! It may be easy to visualize that level of fluid loss during a twenty-six-mile marathon under the hot July sun, but the same type of dehydration also occurs while skiing in cold, dry air. On those winter days when your breath is visible or your chest is covered with rime frost after a workout, you are looking at body moisture you have exhaled. When dehydration sets in, the quality of your performance drops. In hot weather sweating keeps the body cool and operating at peak efficiency. As an athlete becomes dehydrated, the body can no longer produce enough sweat, cooling is less effective, the body overheats, and the athlete slows down to compensate for the overheating. In severe cases of dehydration the blood thickens and is less efficient in transporting oxygen from the lungs to the muscles.

A doctor advising the U.S. Biathlon Team once said, "You simply can't drink too much water when you are engaged in serious training and racing." The inconveniences of a stomach full of water or the need to urinate more frequently are relatively minor, considering the peak physical efficiency that proper hydration ensures. My observation of competitive skiers over the years suggests that another benefit of adequate hydration is the prevention of illness. We are constantly inhaling bacteria and viruses, which can gain a foothold in the dry, cracked mucous membranes of dehydrated nasal passages. When the mucous membranes in the sinuses are moist, however, the infection is less likely to become established. Adequate hydration not only contributes to strong race results, it improves general health throughout the season.

One indicator that you are properly hydrated is the color of your urine. If your urine is clear and virtually colorless, you are hydrated. If it is cloudy or dark yellow, you are not drinking enough water. (One notable exception: high concentrations of some vitamins, such as C or B complex, create a bright greenish yellow urine.)

How much water should you drink each day? It's like eating carbohydrates: more than you think. Adequate hydration varies with the individual, the intensity of the training program, and the weather conditions, but a good starting point is three quarts a day. Remember, water is usually free, and you can't do any damage by drinking too much of it. A Biathlon Team doctor told our elite athletes that it would do no harm to begin a distance event literally sloshing.

Plan to drink something during any racing event lasting more than an hour. Electrolyte-replacement drinks may provide salts and some glucose, but you never can go wrong with water. Drink before you feel thirsty. During a competition, by the time you become thirsty, your performance has already been affected and it will take some time to return to peak efficiency. It's good to take a drink at every feed station, even if only one mouthful. Several small drinks early in a race will do more good than a two- or three-cup binge late in a race, when it's too late anyway. On a cold winter day I've found that warm water (or Max or Exceed) gives a great psychological boost, although I don't know whether it has any physiological advantage.

Carbohydrate Loading

Carbohydrate loading is an attempt to trick the body into storing more glycogen that it normally would. It has been known for some time that the well-trained human body can store enough glycogen to fuel high-output endurance activities for 60 to 120 minutes. The highly trained athlete is able to use this stored glycogen efficiently and, when it runs out, even convert fat to energy, thus enabling performance at top effort for close to two hours. But foot-running marathons and skiing loppets are routinely longer than two hours. Athletes, coaches, and scientists sought ways to extend human endurance. The concept that first emerged was carbohydrate loading, not surprisingly developed by the Swedes.

The classic carbo-loading routine goes like this: About a week before a major event the athlete eliminates carbohydrates from his or her diet and concentrates on protein. This lasts for three days, while normal training continues. Four days before the race the athlete schedules a "depletion workout" — a distance run or ski that lasts for two hours or more. After this workout the athlete switches to a high-carbohydrate diet until the race, at the same time tapering the duration and intensity of training. The complete depletion of glycogen during the distance workout causes the body to overstock glycogen during the high-carbo meals before the race.

Recently studies suggest that the first phase of the protocol is unnecessary and perhaps unwarranted. Most athletes now begin with a depletion workout four days before the target event, carbo load up through race day, and compete well.

The body is most receptive to replenishment following a strenuous race or training session when it is dehydrated and depleted of glycogen. Therefore, it is beneficial for athletes to begin refueling immediately rather than waiting until after a shower or rest. A good drink of water, Max, tea, or juice, and a bagel at the finish line will probably help speed recovery.

Nutritional Supplements

For as long as athletes have been competing against one another they have been looking for that extra edge or advantage that ensures victory. When it comes to nutritional supplements, reason seems to go right out the window. At one time, while I was on the U.S. Biathlon Team, I was taking forty-two tablets a day of vitamins, minerals, and nutritional supplements. In fact, the only way I could support my habit was to become a dealer; my basement was stocked with jars of vitamins and protein powder, which I sold to my teammates and friends. Did we win more races or have fewer colds? I doubt it. About the only thing you could say with any assurance is that we probably had the most expensive urine at Fort Richardson.

As an active male in my middle forties, I have settled comfortably into the one-a-day multiple vitamin routine. Nothing exotic, nothing expensive, just a little insurance that I'm not missing something important in my diet.

I'm not saying that all the supplements are bogus; they may fill vital needs in specific cases. I *am* saying that I didn't notice any dramatic improvement in my health or performance when I used a lot of expensive supplements, and that an athlete's time, energy, and money would be spent more effectively in planning a healthful and nutritious diet.

Iron may be one exception. Serious athletes who train full-time are often found to be anemic, or iron deficient. This affects not only competitive performance but general health as well. Treating anemia often requires the supervision of a doctor or nutritionist. If you are training hard and are run down and tired much of the time, you should consider being checked for anemia. Women are more prone to iron deficiency than men, but endurance athletes of both sexes may have a higher incidence of anemia than the general population. A study of elite endurance foot runners found that 29 percent of the men and 80 percent of the women tested were iron deficient.

Alcohol and Drugs

I could just say that drugs and alcohol have no place in sports and be done with it. But it's not that simple. Let's consider alcohol first. I was a superstraight arrow when I was younger. I don't think I had a beer until I was a senior in college! I gradually learned that an occasional beer or glass of wine was not harmful, even for someone involved in a full-time training program. In fact, as Dartmouth ski coach, I advocated moderation rather than total abstinence for those students of legal drinking age. The only difficulties we ever had were when my definition of "moderation" differed from theirs.

Having made my pitch for moderation, I must now point out some pitfalls. Alcohol, like oxygen, readily attaches to the hemoglobin in the blood, thereby cutting down the oxygen-carrying capacity of the circulatory system.

This would probably be a factor only if someone drank too much the night before or the morning of a race. What is more insidious about alcohol is its ability to erode your willpower or resolve. Many times I have seen conscientious athletes attend a party or social event determined to have only one beer. But often that one beer puts them in a relaxed frame of mind where a second beer seems totally appropriate. Chances are an athlete may end up having more alcohol than originally intended — enough to have a negative effect on training. To compound the problem, the athlete stays out too late, oversleeps the following morning, and is in no frame of mind to train.

On my first trip to Europe with the Biathlon Team, we raced in Chamonix, France. The French soldiers were friendly and gracious. After the first race (in which our team performed well), we celebrated with wine before supper, wine with the meal, drinks with the French soldiers after dinner, and a late-night wine fondue in the home of one of the French officers. Four of us, including Sven Johanson, staggered back to the barracks in the wee hours of the cold alpine morning. What seemed like only minutes later, Sven was shaking us awake. "Time to go skiing, boys, We got to sweat out dat poison!"

We were up, in our ski clothes, and back out on the racecourse before breakfast! There would have been a lot of grumbling, perhaps even a mutiny, if we hadn't been so hung over. It had snowed quite a bit, so Sven had us stomp out a loop the size of a football field, which we skied round and round and round. Once I hooked a ski tip in the deep powder on a turn, fell face first in the snow, and just stayed there (it felt so much better to be still). But Sven and a couple of my teammates dragged me to my feet and the workout continued.

This was the toughest, most merciless workout Sven Johanson ever forced me to do (and he had me do many). I learned firsthand just how debilitating overindulgence in alcohol can be. Though painful at the time, it was a wonderful lesson. Very seldom since then have I had too much to drink. It simply wasn't worth the unpleasant side effects I knew would follow.

Over the years I have observed a disturbing pattern. Nordic skiers are famous for training hard. We pride ourselves on being stoic about inclement weather, minor aches and pains, and pushing the limits physically. We also train and often race in almost total obscurity. This selfless determination and adherence to rigorous training regimens sometimes leads to wild celebrations following major championship races, all in the name of blowing off steam. I have seen some of the world's best Nordic skiers passed out on the floor following a National Championship, Olympic, or World Championship series. The attitude among coaches and teammates seems to be "Aw, he's been training so hard for so long, he needs to relax a little."

I don't dispute the need for serious athletes to take a break from training or celebrate once in a while, but I don't believe these events have to involve alcohol abuse. Young skiers see their idols overindulge and assume that it is acceptable or part of the program—train hard, race hard, party hard. Relaxing and changing pace is as important for an elite ski racer as for anyone else in a high-stress, competitive environment, but the successful athlete can relax without abusing alcohol. He or she learns to control its use rather than being controlled by it. In moderation it is probably not harmful; in excess it can destroy what would have been a brilliant athletic career.

The topic of drug abuse is even more confusing. No one drinks alcohol to improve athletic performance, but modern science makes performance enhancement through chemistry possible. It would be convenient if the issue were clear cut, right or wrong. But it isn't.

No one would criticize an athlete for taking aspirin to relieve the soreness and pain from an especially strenuous workout, drinking a couple of cups of coffee in the morning, or using an antihistamine for hay fever or exercise-induced asthma. But if an athlete pops pain killers every day, drinks caffein-laced feeds during a race, or has his nose drops show up in a postrace urine test, we scream "foul play." We tend to applaud innovation, while at the same time demanding a "level playing field." Many of us celebrated Bob Seagren's mastery of the fiberglass vaulting pole and were disgusted when the Olympic Committee would not allow him to use it in the 1972 Summer Olympics. But when muscle growth is stimulated during training by the use of anabolic steroids, we justifiably assume athletes and trainers have gone too far in the pursuit of gold medals.

The Olympic Committee used to approach the drug issue with the general philosophy that any use of an artificial substance to enhance an athlete's performance was contrary to the Olympic ideal of fair play and therefore illegal. Then the Scandinavians discovered "blood doping." In endurance sports performance is limited to a large degree by the blood's ability to transport oxygen to the muscles. It was discovered that, since the human body will gradually replace a pint of blood withdrawn from the circulatory system, if that pint of blood were put on ice and reinfused just before a major event—and after the athlete's body had reestablished a normal blood level—the athlete could compete with an extra pint of oxygen-carrying capacity. And there was no foreign substance involved, simply an additional pint of the athlete's own blood. Conducted under carefully supervised hospital conditions, the procedure seemed perfectly safe. Early estimates indicated that the additional blood supply could translate into a 10 to 15 percent improvement in elapsed time for a typical endurance event. A 50K ski race normally requires 2½ hours for a good skier. Even over such distances major international events are often won by a handful of seconds. A 10 percent advantage because of blood doping, or 15 minutes, would be an insurmountable lead, impossible for those who had not doped to overcome.

Even though ethically questionable, blood doping was not declared illegal until after the 1984 Summer Olympics in Los Angeles, where several medal-winning American cyclists admitted to using the procedure. It remains almost impossible to detect and is probably still being used by a certain number of unethical athletes, overzealous trainers, and mercenary promoters.

I had a very interesting conversation with a Soviet coach during the Calgary Olympic Games. The Soviet Nordic skiers so dominated the events that there was considerable speculation that they had been blood doped. The Soviets adamantly denied the innuendos. During a quiet moment a Soviet coach and I discussed the problem of doping. He assured me the Soviets would not break the rules. But he speculated that simply withdrawing a pint of an athlete's blood at a strategic stage of the training cycle, with no intention of reinfusing it, might create an artificial workload — one to which the body might respond even more dramatically than to normal training. In a way the concept was not unlike training at altitude or even roller skiing with a weighted vest. The idea raises an interesting question, however: If it is illegal for an athlete to be reinfused with his or her own blood prior to a major event, may an athlete donate a pint of blood with no intention of receiving it back? Where and how do you draw the line? There are no easy answers, and we will probably struggle with these questions as long as the Olympic Games continue to command the attention of the world.

Unfortunately, the high visibility of many sports is a central cause of drug and other abuses. Years ago an athlete might have been content to train hard, make the team, and do his best under the flag of his country. Today, with multimillion-dollar contracts for product endorsements, film careers, and public appearances, a lot more than a gold medal is at stake, and athletes as well as coaches, trainers, and managers are willing to take great risks to achieve victory.

Although I doubt blanket rules will ever solve the drug problem in sports, three philosophical principles should go a long way toward keeping us in line. First, a fundamental reason for the participation in sports is for physical and mental well-being. Anything that contributes to that goal is probably okay; anything that detracts from it is not.

Second, any substance that creates an unfair advantage is probably wrong. An extra pint of one's own blood may not be a foreign substance, but racing with a 10 to 15 percent advantage over competitors who have not blood doped is clearly not fair in my book.

Finally, we should focus on the process rather than the result; in other words, "the ends don't justify the means." A victory achieved by unethical means — performance-enhancing drugs or otherwise — is not a victory at all, but a charade.

8: Sun Valley Masters National Championships

THE ALARM WENT off at 4:30 A.M. I dressed quietly in the dark, had a bowl of cereal and a cup of coffee, and threw my gear into the pickup truck. The driveway was like a skating rink from freezing rain. I locked the hubs, grateful to have four-wheel drive. My wife, still groggy with sleep, stumbled downstairs to see me off.

"Will you make it to Burlington in time for your flight?" she asked.

"Sure, no problem." I tried to sound confident.

"Drive carefully, good luck at the races, and have fun," she reminded. "We'll be thinking of you."

I gave her a kiss and asked her to say goodbye to Julie, our twelve-year-old, still asleep upstairs.

"I'll call to let you know how it's going," I promised.

It was a white-knuckle drive to the Burlington airport, where I checked my baggage, parked the truck in the long-term lot, and jogged to the departure gate. As I proceeded through the security check, my flight was announced. I joined the line of boarding passengers, found my seat, and stashed my coat in the overhead bin. Then I sat down and, for the first time in several hours, took a deep breath, closed my eyes, and tried to relax.

The miracles of modern transportation are truly amazing, especially when compared with how our ancestors traveled a hundred years ago. I was setting out on what amounted to an almost coast-to-coast trip—from Vermont to Sun Valley, Idaho—that would take just a few hours.

Anyone who has traveled realizes it can be emotionally and physically exhausting. A common mistake many endurance athletes make is to consider a travel day a rest day (since it's hard to work out while flying across the country). In fact, travel days are usually more stressful, both physically and mentally, than a normal training day and probably should be followed by one or two rest days or very light training days. Another subtle danger of travel is dehydration. I keep my plastic water bottle handy during the flight.

Soon after takeoff we broke through the clouds into sunshine, leaving ice-encrusted Vermont below. I took it as a good omen for the week to come. Here I was, headed for the 1990 Masters National Cross-Country Ski Championships. After fifteen years of coaching I was a genius at the art of positive thinking, but privately I regarded myself as a realist. I mentally listed the pluses and minuses of the upcoming events. On the down side I had trained neither enough nor appropriately. I don't like roller skiing—an integral part of fall training—and had done it only twice all fall. My strength training had been sporadic. During the summer I had constructed a roller board but had used it only once. Although I had been among the top dozen or so Nordic skiers in America when I retired in 1976, the skating revolution of the eighties had drawn in a lot of talented athletes, several in their forties, who might lack Olympic or U.S. Ski Team experience but were every bit as dedicated and committed as I had been back in the wooden-ski days.

Another factor to consider was altitude. At 6,200 feet the elevation at Sun Valley was not crippling for a lowlander from Vermont, but it definitely figured into the equation. All else being equal—conditioning, technique, wax, psychology—the competitor who lived and trained at altitude would have an edge over the lowlanders in these races. And finally, three of the races were skating events and only one was diagonal, and I still felt more comfortable skiing classic technique. One race out of four was not great odds.

But balancing out the picture were some pretty strong pluses. Early-season time trials with the Dartmouth skiers indicated that things were going okay. My mental approach to the season and my motivation also helped. I'd learned a lot about myself and about life in the previous fifteen years. My whole feeling of self-worth was not wrapped in race results, as it often is with younger competitors. I wasn't putting a lot of pressure on myself about performance. I felt fortunate to be able to train and compete again, and I knew I was capable of doing well but that winning would depend upon a myriad of variables, many of which were beyond my control. I was prepared to win but realized there are no sure things in ski racing.

I also had experience going for me. Although there have been dramatic changes and significant technological improvements in Nordic skiing in the last decade, there is still a premium on experience. Even though I didn't feel especially comfortable skating, during my years of coaching at Dartmouth and helping with the U.S. Biathlon Team I had been exposed to more national and world-class skaters than all but a handful of other Americans had. At least I knew what good technique *should* look like. Whether I could translate that knowledge into action on the racecourse remained to be seen. I had raced at altitude before, so I approached that challenge with confidence. Finally, I figured I could hit the wax as well as almost anyone else competing. I had been waxing cross-country skis since about 1962; a lot has changed, and it has become more complex in the last thirty years, but hitting the wax consistently is a sense that's developed over years of experience.

After changing planes in Chicago, I began reviewing my goals for the season. I wanted, first, to complete several events during the winter, racing at a rate of three minutes per kilometer or better; second, to improve my national ranking points from just under 20 to below 15; third, to ski most of my races within 90 percent of the winners; and, finally, to win at the Masters National Championships. Three of the four goals were somewhat theoretical, requiring number crunching or analysis of season-long results. But there was nothing ambiguous about the last objective. I had three chances to win an individual National Championship within the next eight days (the fourth race on the schedule was a relay).

In Denver I was joined by three friends with whom I would share housing for the week. Kathy Farineriz and Alex Kahan had only recently passed the thirty-year mark, thereby qualifying as masters. John Donovan, in the 45–49 age category (one older than mine), had taken up cross-country skiing only a couple of years earlier. He had learned fast and of the four of us was probably the most dedicated to training.

The flight to Boise, Idaho, was smooth and uneventful. Breaks in the clouds afforded us perfect views of the snow-covered wilderness of southwestern Wyoming and southern Idaho, which to an easterner looked more like the moon than part of our own planet. In Boise we picked up a rental car and headed east to Ketchum. Our animated conversation subtly gave way to silence in awe of the stark landscape. For northeasterners accustomed to a town over every hill, the mile after mile of barren sagebrush was almost impossible to fathom. We arrived in Ketchum at dusk and found our motel about a half mile south of town.

Although tired from traveling, I awoke the next morning at four o'clock. My body was still on eastern time. I tossed for hours and finally gave in at six and began to dress for a morning run.

I believe in morning runs, especially during the competitive season. I find that they are great times for visualization and mental rehearsal, especially on race days. I seem to be able to get a jump on the waxing situation simply by listening to the snow under my feet and feeling the air on my face. It's fun to see who else is up at that hour—the town crew plowing parking lots; truckers stopped for coffee, their diesels idling patiently—and smell the rich, delicious aroma of fresh bread from a bakery. The main reason to run is to work the soreness out of muscles, still stiff from the previous day's race or workout. I'm also convinced that morning runs facilitate the adjustment to altitude. I have no scientific evidence for this and believe it only because my own experience has confirmed it as true.

An endurance athlete competing at altitude should ideally arrive at the site two to three weeks in advance of the event, allowing the body to produce the additional red blood cells necessary to compensate for the reduced amount of oxygen in the air. That is a luxury seldom available to Nordic skiers and never to college competitors enrolled in classes. The next best option appears to be arrival at the race site as close to race time as possible, which usually means travel the day before the event, overnight at the site without working out, and racing the next day. This is done in an attempt to trick the body, which theoretically doesn't realize until after the event that it should have slowed down to compensate for the reduced amount of available oxygen. This approach, like the first one, appears to work but has some drawbacks. First of all, it usually means racing the course without having skied it beforehand. In races at altitude I think it is important to know where the hills are, how long they are, and whether the following downhills will offer sufficient recovery. Second, this method requires racing the day after a travel day, which often can be quite stressful. Finally, although the "arrive and race" method might be worth a try for one major event, its merits are significantly reduced with a four-race series spanning six or seven days.

A compromise that seems to work for me is to arrive at the site two or three days before the first race — enough time to recover from travel, adjust to the time change, tour the racecourses, and do some wax testing. The course inspections barely count as workouts; most are skied with warm-ups on, walking up all the hills and skiing the downhills fast enough to gain confidence. Since the third or fourth day at altitude is usually the physiological low point for most lowlanders, you acknowledge in advance that the first race will probably not be your best, but that your performance will improve after the fourth day.

In 1968 we arrived at Steamboat Springs, Colorado, for the NCAA Championships several days early, toured the cross-country course each morning about race time to test wax, and otherwise rested. I was nervous about that lung-burning, almost panicked feeling of not being able to get enough air on a tough uphill, so I foot ran in the mornings, sprinting between alternate telephone poles. The workouts were short, certainly not exhausting, but I got the sensation I was after and learned that I would, in fact, recover, rather than fall gasping to the ground like a fish pulled from the water. I was second in that NCAA Championship race, three seconds out of first, and one of the few Easterners in the top twenty. It made me a believer in morning runs.

Now, as I fumbled for my warm-ups in the darkened room, Donovan mumbled, "What're you doing?"

"Going for a run."

"Now?"

"Yup, I can't sleep anymore," I answered.

A long pause was followed by tossing and turning.

"Aw, wait a minute, I'll go with you."

When we returned, Kathy and Alex were up and working on breakfast. One of the pleasures of a project like ours is getting to know each other better, and there is nothing like mealtime to bring out everyone's peculiarities!

Kathy's specialty was coffee. She traveled with her own beans, coffee grinder, and golden filter. The stuff she made sure cleaned out your pipes! Alex tried to make some one morning before Kathy was awake. It tasted okay to me, but when Kathy got up and tried a cup, she threw the whole pot out in disgust. We left the coffee to her from then on.

Donovan had had years of experience cooking on the ocean. Apparently the Outward Bound approach is to throw anything edible into a pot, boil it up, and eat it. Since John has been a vegetarian for a long time, he was pretty creative with stuff I had never heard of: tofu, bulgur, oat groats, mung beans. We had some pretty interesting soups that were unrecognizable but plenty filling. And we never had plain oatmeal in the mornings. It was always laced with bananas, apples, or raisins. My one concession to my prenutrition-consciousness days was a couple of bags of cookies; we did, after all, have two long races during the week that obviously required carbohydrate loading. As I self-consciously unpacked the grocery bag, I tried to slip the cookies unseen behind the cereal boxes on top of the fridge. No such luck. Both Kathy and Donovan yelled in disgust, "Cookies! Pecan Sandies and Oreos! Morty, you should be ashamed!" Before I could defend myself, Alex sprang in from the living room. "Are the Oreos Double Stuff?" he asked brightly. I knew we'd get along all right.

Later that morning we drove across town to the Sun Valley Nordic Center. It was a perfect day, clear and cold, packed powder snow, and bright blue sky. The Nordic Center was all but abandoned because one of the biggest local races of the season, the Boulder Mountain Tour, was under way twenty-four miles north at Galena Lodge. The Tour was an exciting, well-run event that annually drew hundreds of competitors, including several U.S. Ski Team members. We had talked about participating but figured the four National Championship races were enough. We settled for a low-key tour of the race-courses.

The first person we met at the Nordic Center was Hans Muehlegger, the Austrian-born director. He graciously welcomed us, reluctantly pointing out that our National Championship entry fees didn't apply on Sunday, and it would cost us nine dollars each to inspect the courses. It was a perfect day, the tracks were immaculate, and we were so excited to be there we paid the trail fee and listened intently as Hans explained the course. About all I could translate from his five-minute monologue was, "Gunclup loop, Fairvays, and Trailcreke loop." We all understood his final remark: "You goin' relly like it!"

Hans was right, we really did like it! In fact, it was the best skiing we had seen all year. We wandered where the trails took us, not caring particularly which loop we were following. I gradually became aware, however, that this was all golf-course skiing, relatively flat. I wasn't complaining, mind you, but I've always looked forward to uphills as an advantageous part of the course where a strong racer can really make up time on his competitors. When we headed off to inspect the "Gunclup" loop, however, my fears dissolved. The "Gunclup" loop (actually Gunclub—we skied past a trap-and-skeet range) rolled and twisted through the sage-covered hills across from the Sun Valley Resort. It consisted of three major climbs followed by three challenging downhills, each of which ended with a "hang-on" turn. The descents were nothing to worry about under ideal conditions with perfect tracks, but I wondered what they would be like in the traffic of a wave or mass start. We were certainly going to get our money's worth with these courses, and no one would complain about lack of vertical!

That evening we decided to attend the awards banquet for the Boulder Mountain Tour. We'd be able to rub shoulders with all the top participants, catch up with friends, and most important, ferret out wax secrets.

After a few pleasantries I tactfully began to pump my old friend Peter Hale, who worked for Ski*Go, for wax info. Although I'd rather not know what others are using in the last minutes before the start of a major event, if I've just arrived in a new location, I find it helpful to learn from reliable sources what has been running well. Peter had raced the Boulder Mountain Tour and was only too happy to tell me how fast his skis were. Furthermore, the overall winner, Audun Endestad, had used Ski*Go C-280, a relatively new liquid applied to the ski with the finger, allowed to dry, then ironed, scraped, and polished. Peter was justifiably proud of Audun's victory.

But ski wax is a lot like insurance: the people who really know the ins and outs of the product are salesmen trying to push their own brands. You wouldn't expect a Metropolitan agent to admit that John Hancock really had a better whole-life policy; neither would you be surprised to learn from another source that Audun had actually had Rex blue *under* the Ski*Go C-280, which probably expanded the temperature range dramatically. So you spend a lot of time fishing for information, trying not to be too obvious about it, and then evaluate your sources. It never ceases to amaze me how even experienced, knowledgeable skiers lose their confidence in a last-minute waxing panic. They will hear some guy in a University of Florida sweatsuit with bamboo ski poles and wooden touring skis say with great authority, "This Swix purple is as slow as death!" Then all these experienced racers scurry off to rewax! So you evaluate your sources. It's very helpful to know what Peter Hale of Ski*Go or Rob Kiesel of Swix or Jack Lufkin of Rex recommends; but in the final analysis you have to evaluate and synthesize what you hear and use your own best judgment.

Sunday, February 4. The day before the opening race of the 1990 Masters National Championships, a 30K freestyle event for men, three times around a tough ten-kilometer loop. After the morning run and breakfast the four of us drove to the Nordic Center to inspect the course and test waxes. It was another Rocky Mountain day, cold morning, dry snow, and bright sun. These conditions made for wonderful recreational skiing and outrageous tanning, but gave cross-country racers ulcers trying to hit the wax. With a long race the conditions could change significantly during the event. It was necessary to anticipate what the conditions would be like two or even three hours after the start. You could have the fastest skis on the course when the gun went off, but if the temperature rose out of the range of the wax you selected, the last ten kilometers could be torture with other racers overtaking you. So the day before a race you tour the course, usually walking the uphills to conserve strength but riding the downhills flat out to ensure they could be taken that way in the competition. And you watch the weather, feel the snow, keep checking thermometers, and test wax.

The course was perfect, especially when we skied it in the proper sequence. The three climbs of the "Gunclup" would be challenging but not crippling if skied prudently at least the first two times. The Trail Creek section was basically flat and would put a premium on good, efficient technique. The final, Fairways, section was enjoyable rolling terrain past mind-boggling multimillion-dollar homes.

The temperature hovered around freezing. My Swix purple glider was running pretty well but not as fast as Alex's Ski*Go C-280. John was in between us with Rex blue.

Start lists had been posted with participants categorized by age. I anxiously scanned the 40–44 list. I recognized a few names but didn't see any surprises until the bottom of the list: Alan Watson. "He can't be forty," I blurted out. For the past two years Alan had coached the Nordic skiers of the powerful University of Utah Ski Team. Before that he had been both a racer and manager of the Fischer/Salomon Marathon Team, the strongest "factory team" on the Great American Ski Chase. I knew that Alan was the guy to beat in my age category, and I was no longer confident about winning the Nationals. Anything could happen in ski racing, however, and no one knew better than I how difficult it is to coach and race. Perhaps Alan's coaching was interfering with his racing. We'd find out soon enough.

We had an early spaghetti feed in the motel room that night and returned to the Sun Valley Inn for the opening meeting of the Masters National Championships. All the officials were introduced, and they offered welcoming remarks and last-minute instructions. It was a final chance to rib and tease one another before the "serious business" of racing got under way. There was a discernible tension in the air, and there were no more "candid" discussions about waxing. The psych-out artists went to work.

"Morty, have you skied those three hills on the Gunclub loop at race pace yet? I did this morning and are they tough!"

"Hey, how are you guys doing in this altitude? They say you feel the worst on the third or fourth day, whadaya think?"

"John, you're staying at the Ketchum Korral, aren't you? Are you guys getting any sleep right next to the highway there?"

"Morty, what did you have on your skis this morning? I followed you down the long downhill on the Gunclub loop and I had to stand up and aircheck all the way to keep from running you over!"

"Hey, John, when was the last time you skied a 30K at altitude?"

I was experienced at this psych-out game and seldom let it rattle me. The secret was to play with such understatement and candor that no one realized you were playing. One look at John Donovan, however, told me he was soaking it all in; concern about wax, altitude, rest, and diet was written all over his face.

To add to our stress levels, we returned to our rental car in the parking lot to find the keys locked inside. With four potential drivers and only one set of keys, we had agreed to leave the keys under the floor mat and the car unlocked. But when we arrived for the meeting, as we got out, one of us had bumped the electronic door-lock button. We stood around the parking lot under the star-filled Idaho sky while first the security man then the Ketchum police tried unsuccessfully to disengage the door lock without breaking a window. After more than an hour of valiant efforts we decided to leave the car where it was and pass the problem along to the rental agency in the morning. We would take the local shuttle bus to the race. The moral of this story is that no matter how careful your planning, the unexpected often happens and you can't let it rattle you.

On Monday morning I woke up at five o'clock. Unable to get back to sleep, I got up and dressed for a run. Donovan heard me and jumped into his running gear. We jogged down the deserted back streets of Ketchum, listening to the cold, dry snow squeak underfoot. We had waxed after the meeting last night with the combination Alex liked — Ski*Go antistatic covered with C-280. As I swung my arms to increase the circulation to my numbing fingers, I wondered if it would warm up into C-280's temperature range (18°F–32°F) by the time the race began.

We arrived at the touring center about an hour before the start. Swix representatives had set up a speed trap across the road and competitors were flocking to it to test their wax speeds. I ignored it because, first, the trap was not on the course and was testing wax performance on snow conditions somewhat different from what we would race on; and second, since I didn't have the capability of changing wax before the start, I didn't want to know if my skis were slow. In fact, I was afraid they were. It hadn't warmed up as much as I had hoped (although it certainly would have by the time we finished). I reassured myself that our wax would continue to improve during the race. Although those who had waxed colder would have an edge early on, they would be "dragging a piano" later. That's called positive thinking!

Just before ten we lined up for wave starts by age group. The seventeen men in the 30–34 pack led the charge. These were the hotshots, the guys who could still be very competitive on the national-team level. Thirty is not old for a cross-country skier; in fact, many of the world's best competitors race at World Cups and the Olympics long after reaching thirty. A minute after these "young kids," the 35–39 group charged off. As my group approached the line, I glanced at the twenty or so racers I would be competing against. I spotted Alan Watson in the front row wearing the fluorescent yellow, pink, and purple Lycra of the Fischer marathon team. I knew I had to keep Watson within range if I hoped to do well in this race.

The starter said "Go!" and we were off. There is only one strategy in a mass- or wave-start ski race: stay out of traffic and protect your equipment. Skating in a crowd means straddling ski poles, hooked ski tips, poles yanked from your hands, and even pole tips in your feet or legs. My approach is simple: Stay on one edge of the pack so people are flailing at you from only one side. As the traffic thins out in the first kilometer or so, you can weave your way to a better position with less danger of becoming tangled.

I worked my way up the outside as the pack jostled through the first kilometer of flat approaching the road crossing and the three hills of the Gunclub loop. The trail narrowed and we skated single file across the road. I was in fourth place, skiing easily. As expected, Alan Watson was leading the train, but another fluorescent Fischer suit was right behind him. I didn't know who was in the suit, but it wasn't a good sign if, in fact, the skier was a member of the Fischer marathon team. Following these two, just ahead of me, was Dan Gibson, a tough former Dartmouth skier. A Salt Lake resident, Dan would have no trouble with the altitude. Another concern was Murry Banks, close behind me in fifth place. Murry was an experienced athlete who could easily move up in an endurance event.

As we charged up the first hill, I tried to remain relaxed and poised. Thirty kilometers was a long way (about 18.5 miles) and it would be no fun to go under in the first two kilometers. As we tucked down the first S turn, I noticed the two Fischer suits had opened up a gap on Dan. It was decision time. If I let the two leaders pull away, there was a good chance I would never see them again. On the other hand, a sprint to catch them in these hills could put me under so that I might not recover. As I mentally struggled, Dan, Murry, and I crested the second hill. On the second descent, longer and straighter than the first, I tucked tight and glided past Dan. That put me in third place and also reassured me that my wax couldn't be too bad.

I poured on the power to close the gap on Watson and his Fischer team-mate as we skated up the third and longest climb on the Gunclub loop. I was going hard, pulse pounding in my ears, gasping for deep lungfuls of air as we crested the third hill. Although I had put distance on Dan, Murry had hung in behind me and we hadn't gained much on the Fischer "twins." I knew I couldn't keep up that pace for twenty-seven more kilometers. I decided to adopt a new strategy: I would ski strong, smoothly, and efficiently, with the thought that one or both of the leaders might have gone out too fast and would drop back in the last few kilometers of the race. I had to conserve enough to "pour it on" if the opportunity developed.

As the hills of the Gunclub loop gave way to the long flats of Trail Creek, the leaders were out of sight ahead. I had to concentrate to maximize my stride length. I knew the two leaders would be working together, forcing each other's pace. At the far end of the loop the trail crested a small rise, crossed a bridge, and headed back for the Fairways.

It's hard to race relaxed and smooth with someone tucked in behind you. Occasionally you make contact — a pole hits a ski or a ski comes down on a pole tip. It's easier to follow, to match a skier stride for stride, to try to relax and outglide the leader, to avoid spots where he slips or stumbles, to draft on the downhills. As we completed our first lap, Murry was hanging tough right behind me. I tried to remain calm and concentrate on my own race, but I kept worrying that he would draft me the whole way and outsprint me to the finish. I hadn't given up on the two leaders yet, but in open areas I could see that they continued to put distance on us.

As we headed into the Gunclub hills for the second time, I began to think about where and how to drop Murry. I leaned on the accelerator on the uphills hoping I could subtly open a gap. He hung tough and didn't sound like he was laboring. I rarely look back because even a glance over the shoulder can appear to be a sign of concern or weakness.

We crossed the road and headed for the flats of the Trail Creek loop. The course was groomed wide and smooth with one set of classic tracks on the far right. I hopped into the tracks and began to marathon skate for variety and to give my muscles a break from the repetition of V1. Murry continued to V1 smoothly and drew alongside. We were both working hard. I assumed he was making a move, and although it unnerved me a little, I figured I would let him lead for a while.

"All right, Murry, go for it," I grunted as we drove down the track side by side. But after one hundred yards he hadn't pulled ahead. I was getting bored with marathon skating, so I began V2 skating with long, smooth strides. It was almost a kilometer before I realized Murry wasn't behind me anymore. Without realizing it, I had picked the perfect spot for a break: a long, uninterrupted flat. A relative newcomer to skiing from summer triathlons, Murry was tough and determined; his only handicap might have been the lack of experience and poise it takes to ride a flat, gliding ski. I had broken contact by outstridng and outgliding him on the flat.

As I rounded the turn at the far point of Trail Creek for the second time, I broke my rule and looked back. There was a racer gaining, but it wasn't Murry Banks. The 45–49 wave had started one minute behind ours, and the skier bearing down on me now was Mike Elliott. Along with Bob Gray and Mike Gallagher, Mike Elliott had been one of America's top cross-country racers during the 1960s and 1970s. More than anyone else of that era, Gray, Gallagher, and Elliott had made the Europeans take notice of the fledgling American Nordic program. Elliott was both technically proficient and mentally tough. I vividly remembered a U.S. Team training camp in Putney, sometime in the late sixties, when I was feeling sorry for myself because I had developed blisters on a long run. When I was about to quit, Mike Elliott encouraged me to continue. It was only after we had run several minutes together that I noticed he had blisters so severe that blood was soaking through the white canvas of his new tennis shoes.

Mike followed me for quite a while through the rolling terrain of the Fairways loop before gliding past on a downhill.

"Morty, you're skiing well—hang on for the last loop," he said on the way by.

"OK, Mike. Nice going!" I answered.

We skied together through the start/finish area and onto the Gunclub loop for the final time. I was surprised to see Mike take the uphills very deliberately, using diagonal poling rather than the more aggressive V1 skate. He must know what he's doing, I thought; he's made up a minute on me in the first two-thirds of this race. I followed him through the hills and back across the road. As we glided down the long descent to the creek, Mike stood up to take a drink from the water bottle on his belt. I kept my tuck and coasted past him. Then I saw a fluorescent Fischer suit ahead, which gave me a shot of adrenaline. Watson or his teammate had faded! I forgot about Elliott and started thinking about a silver medal. As I stretched every inch I could out of each stride, I could feel my thighs beginning to cramp. I would have to be careful. Almost twenty-five kilometers into this race, running on full power, I didn't have much in reserve. Like a car at the Indy 500 trying to hold its position, I was desperate to make it across the finish line before running out of gas.

I gained on the Fischer suit in the final few kilometers, but Elliott had tucked close behind me. About a kilometer from the finish we closed in on the fluorescent suit, and I realized with disappointment that this was not Watson or his "twin," but a fellow from one of the earlier groups.

With one uphill out of the creek and a half kilometer of flat to the finish line, the three of us were skating hard. Mike and the other fellow made their moves on the uphill. I tried to go with them but cramps above my knees made me throttle back. They would get me at the line, but Mike had a minute on me already, and I was almost a minute up on the guy in the Fischer suit. Besides, we were in different age categories, and there were three more races before the week was out. I skated in behind the two of them, trying to keep my thighs from locking up.

I believe you should evaluate your races before you look at the results: How did you feel? How was your technique? How was the wax? What parts of the course did you ski well and what sections could have gone better? Going through the mental checklist, I was coming out somewhere in the middle. I had set out to win and that clearly hadn't happened. It looked like the best I could finish was third in my age group. I had hoped to be the top man over forty, but Mike Elliott, for one, had blown holes in that goal. I didn't yet know my percent back from the winners or time per kilometer, but I wasn't overly optimistic. On the other hand, I had skied hard. As I leaned on my poles in the bright sun of the finish area, my legs quivering uncontrollably, I knew I didn't have much left over. I had been able to hold off Dan Gibson and Murry Banks and to hang with Mike Elliott for the final ten-kilometer loop. Without seeing times and results, I gave myself a B + .

After we changed into dry clothes, John Donovan and I skied out to watch Kathy compete in the women's race. Donovan clearly was not happy with his effort, although some food and fluid helped him recover somewhat from his postrace depression. By the time the women finished, the men's results had been posted. The good news was that I had finished third in my category, but that was tempered by sobering information. Alan Watson had been first for our group, more than two and a half minutes ahead of me. The fellow who had placed second was Bob Rosso, owner of one of Ketchum's best ski shops. Rosso had finished more than two minutes ahead of me! I was fairly sure I couldn't have gone two minutes faster and held together. I had also been beaten by two guys in the 45–49 division: Mike Elliott and Del Pletcher. It still had not been a bad race, but my chance of winning a National Championship race was looking more remote.

The 15K classic race consisted of two trips around a 7.5-kilometer course. It was much of the same terrain we had skied in the 30K, but we would cover the trails in the opposite direction, heading out on the rolling hills of the Fairways loop, picking up a short segment of the basically flat Trail Creek section, and finishing with the challenging climbs and downhills of the Gunclub loop. It would take careful pacing to have enough left to hammer those three uphills the second time around, only a couple of kilometers from the finish. I felt it would be an excellent course: technically challenging and tough but not brutal. And there was more good news: The men's 15K would be an interval start, thirty seconds between racers. The start list showed Bob Rosso listed as number forty-five; Alan Watson, forty-seven; and me, forty-nine. This meant I would start one minute after Watson, two minutes after Rosso.

I usually downplay the significance of seeding in a race (although some racers and coaches develop ulcers over starting positions). It can be a factor if snow conditions are changing, if other racers of your ability are seeded differently (and thus out of contact in the race), or if there is an especially large field of competitors. But generally I believe the value of a good seed — or the disadvantage of an unfavorable seed — is blown out of proportion. For the 15K race, however, I couldn't have planned it any better. I had the two guys who had beaten me in the 30K just ahead of me. I could focus on them during the race while, psychologically at least, they would be "running scared," knowing there was a significant threat from behind.

Wednesday morning was clear and cold, 0°F, and we again had waxed the night before. Rex blue covered with Ski*Go C-280 seemed to be working well, so we went with that combination for glide. I figured the cold snow might be abrasive, so I torched in a layer of binder underfoot. This is always good insurance and seldom slow unless you get it too thick. I covered it with Rode blue hard wax using a trick Sven Johanson had demonstrated years ago on the Biathlon Team. Hard wax normally is rubbed on and corked smooth. For better kick or longer races you apply several coats, corking each one glassy smooth. At some point, however, corking a thick wax job causes the wax to ripple, which will slow you down. Sven's method was to heat the end of the wax on a torch, then rub it on the kick zone thick, almost in globs. Then he would take the torch and a small piece of cloth, heat the wax till it melted and, using the cloth like a paintbrush, deftly paint it smooth. The process took a very delicate touch and impressive coordination. It was frightfully easy to burn the ski bottoms or your fingers. But a successful application put on more wax — and thus better kick — smoother than was possible with corking. This technique would be perfect for Sun Valley conditions. I could go with a smooth, thick coat, which would be fast early in the race while the snow was still cold but would give good kick late in the race when the sun might have caused some glazing of the tracks.

As we tested our skis in the rock-hard tracks, still cold in the mountains' shadow, I knew we were not going to be far off on the wax. I was charged up and ready for a good race. The announcer began calling the early starters to the line. I wished Bob and Alan good luck, resisting a strong temptation to remind them that I would be chasing them. Understatement is always more effective anyway. They knew where I'd be!

I exploded from the start like a shot. The tracks were perfect — hard and fast — and my Rode blue was giving "magnum kick" on the uphills. Fifteen kilometers (9.3 miles) is relatively short by cross-country skiing standards, normally taking about forty-five minutes to complete. It would be a challenging course, but there would be no time for elaborate strategy or race tactics. My plan was to hammer till I caught Watson, then reel in Rosso. But a minute is deceptive in cross-country. As we charged up the gradual climbs of the Fairways, Alan seemed only a few yards ahead; moments later, when I crested the hill, he was far in the distance. I kept driving, trying to be quick and strong on the uphills and long, smooth, and powerful on the flats. As I gradually overtook earlier starters, I would look past them for Watson and Rosso. After several kilometers it became obvious that I was not gaining on them, at least not significantly, but they weren't pulling away either. This was really going to be a "barn burner"!

The accordion effect kept playing tricks on me as we came through the start area, ending the first loop. Watson and Rosso would appear to be within range on the uphills and I would think confidently, "I've got this one in the bag, just keep the pressure on for one more loop!" Then I would top a hill and Alan would be far beyond, Bob out of sight. I thought, "You're going to be third again, if you're lucky! Gibson or Murry Banks could uncork one today and you'd never know till it was over!"

I settled down and simply tried to ski the best I could. I wanted to hit the hills on the Gunclub loop hard the second time but have enough left for a strong sprint across the flats to the finish. The uphills went well, and I was optimistic until I caught a glimpse of Alan pushing for the line hundreds of yards ahead of me. I was vaguely aware of the spectators shouting as I double poled to the finish, out of breath and light-headed. I knew it would be close, but I couldn't have gone any faster. I hadn't fallen or stumbled and my skis had been fast. You couldn't ask for much more than that! The three of us — Rosso, Watson, and I — hung on our poles, still winded, smiling at each other. No matter how it came out, this had been a great race. We shook hands and

Former U.S. Ski Team member and American Birkebeiner champion Muffy Ritz exhibits excellent poise, control, and assertiveness on a fast downhill turn on the Gunclub Loop in Sun Valley.

slapped backs in the sunshine, feeling the happy fatigue of having done our best.

Alex Kahan and John Donovan added to the festive atmosphere. Alex, who had only planned to race in two skating events, had borrowed a beat-up pair of classic skis, and with his skating boots laced up halfway, he had raced well, passing many competitors who had started ahead of him. Donovan was also excited, feeling like he had skied a good race. We were all rewarded that evening at the awards ceremonies. Donovan had improved from eighteenth in the 30K to tenth in his age group for the 15K. Alex, in skating boots and borrowed skis, had finished sixth in the 30–34 age category. I had finished second—nine seconds behind Alan Watson and one second ahead of Bob Rosso! Bob and I shook hands on the awards platform as the announcer told the crowd Alan Watson had already headed back to Salt Lake to his coaching job. My mind raced ahead to the relay—which had just become a different contest without Watson!

We didn't have a designated team leader for our contingent from the East, but it didn't take long to determine that John Broadhead, Murry Banks, and I would have a decent chance for the gold medal in the over-40 category, especially if Intermountain did not have the services of Alan Watson.

Stacking your relay team takes some strategy. A good scramble man can keep you "in the hunt" even if you are not favored to win. The second leg is generally the most benign, since the race has usually opened up to some degree by then. The anchor, or final, leg can be tough, often a gut-busting sprint to the finish. Sometimes an anchor man takes the rap for a tough loss, which often is not entirely his fault.

Murry preferred to ski second leg, Broadhead was willing to scramble, and I agreed to anchor. One of the exciting aspects of a relay is that, theoretically, you don't know the order of the opposing team. As the leadoff men lined up for the mass start, we learned that Del Pletcher would scramble for Intermountain's top team, John Wells would ski second, and Bob Rosso would anchor. Broadhead would have his work cut out for him, since Pletcher had beaten him by more than five minutes in the 30K and three seconds in the 15K. We also had to be careful not to overlook Mike Elliott's team from Rocky Mountain, a strong team from the Far West, and a second Intermountain team that included former Dartmouth skiers Jim Speck and Dan Gibson. Anything could happen in a relay, and usually did. We had our sights set on winning, but it was just as feasible that we would be out of the awards entirely. I just hoped John and Murry could keep me in contact with Rosso. With only five kilometers for each competitor, it would be a flat-out "lung burner."

Broadhead got a great start and headed up the Gunclub hills in perfect position, third or fourth in the train. A crowd of spectators scurried to where the incoming trail crossed the road, about halfway through the five-kilometer loop. John was still in the train but looked very pale and was laboring badly. The high-altitude boys from Idaho, Utah, Colorado, and northern California had put him under on the Gunclub hills. In such a short leg John knew he had to stay with the leaders to give Murry and me a chance, but the pace was fast enough to send him anaerobic in the first half of the loop. He struggled in to tag Murry in fifth place, more than a minute behind the leader. John had given it his best shot, but the fast pace out of the start combined with the altitude had crippled him. He staggered across the line of the tag zone, patted Murry on the shoulder, and coasted to a stop, gasping for breath. He hung limply on his poles, unable to move, shaking his head in silent frustration. I skied over to give him a reassuring hug, then left him alone to decompress.

Anxiously waiting near the tag zone for the second-leg skiers, I tried to sort out how we were doing. All the men's relay teams had started together. We have been keying on Rosso's team, the favorite in the 40–49 age group. But as the second-leg skiers began arriving, led by the top skiers in the 30–39 category, it was hard to determine which teams were which. I watched John Wells tag Bob Rosso and knew they had a tremendous lead on us. A couple of other teams tagged off as Murry skated toward me in the exchange zone.

"Go get 'em," he gasped as he slapped my butt, having pulled us into fourth place.

I fired out of the start with one thought in mind: catch Rosso! I could see him more than a minute ahead, charging up the hills of the Gunclub loop, and a debate raged in my head.

"No way; five kilometers is not long enough to make up a minute on a guy like that!"

"Hold on — if he falls or breaks a pole, you've got him!"

"No way! Look at him hammer those uphills; he doesn't even feel the altitude!"

"Remember, *anything* can happen in a relay!"

I passed someone, but my attention was so fixed on Bob it didn't really register. I scrambled to the top of the last hill on the Gunclub loop, straining to see Rosso as he tucked down the other side. Mike Elliott appeared beside me. As I pushed past, I heard him say, "That guy ahead of you has the silver medal!"

For the first time I focused in on the skier twenty yards ahead of me. I had been so intent on catching Rosso that I had forgotten there was still another team between us. I tucked tight and cut down the gap to the second-place skier. We crossed the road with 2.5 kilometers of gently rolling terrain to the finish. I didn't recognize the fellow ahead of me, but I knew I had to pass him and break contact soon. There wasn't time left to be cagey about it; I just let him know I was coming by on his left and poured on the coal. I kept the pressure on for a couple hundred meters and stealthily glanced back. He hadn't come with me. If I didn't fall or get hung up somehow in the final kilometer, we had the silver! I scanned the track ahead for Rosso. No sign of him. Second place would have to be good enough for today. I throttled back slightly; all that really mattered now was preserving second place.

Once again there was a lot of animated conversation, back slapping, joking, and camaraderie at the finish area. Murry Banks was elated. The relay had been his best race of the week. He was happy to have stayed for it and proud to be headed home with a medal. John Donovan, Kathy, and Alex were satisfied as well. Kathy had skied a strong leg on the East's number two relay team, finishing a close fourth; Donovan, in his second skating race of the series, felt positive and had put the discouragement of the 30K behind him; and Alex had skied the fastest relay leg of the day.

That evening the relay awards were presented, followed by age-group awards based on the results of the first two individual events. Alan Watson earned the 40–44 men's award with two first-place finishes. Mike Elliott was the 45–49 group combined champion. Dick Mize, from Anchorage, was unbeatable in the 50–54 category. There was a standing ovation for Intermountain racer Loren Adkins, who had dominated his age group . . . 80+! Here was a guy who was pushing his way up hills and tucking for speed on the descents while many of his contemporaries were in nursing homes. As he hopped onto the podium to receive his medal, everyone in the room was thinking, "I only hope when I'm his age . . ."

The next day brought a welcome break from racing. Unlike many of the skiers, who had taken advantage of the other sporting opportunities in Sun Valley, I had been pretty focused on the competitions. I had studied the courses, tested waxes, and raced. I had been religious about my morning runs and stretching. After a week of this my three roommates were giving me heat about being too serious. I knew they might be right, but the upcoming 50K was my last chance at a National Championship. We would ski three times around a 16.5-kilometer loop much of which we hadn't seen before. Although part of me was ready for a break, I knew I should tour the course so I'd know what was in store for tomorrow. But Kathy, Alex, and John gave me no choice. After a leisurely breakfast, we headed to Galena Summit for some telemark skiing.

Looking at the surrounding peaks and snowfields, I silently questioned the wisdom of this adventure the day before a three-hour National Championship race. Though we had several hours of beautiful powder skiing, the truth of it was that I had never become hooked on telemarking. I love nothing better than flying through the woods and fields over flawlessly groomed tracks with superlight racing skis. Occasionally, I enjoy roaring down a mountain on my Alpine boards, carving wide giant-slalom turns from top to bottom. Telemark skiing seems to me to be a lousy compromise of Alpine and cross-country. Tele-gear is too heavy to allow you to do much more than shuffle along the flats, and the toe bindings don't afford much security on steep downhills. Of course, these thoughts are pure blasphemy, as much of the skiing world rushes out to buy new tele-gear and try the latest craze.

After a few runs down the mountain we headed back to town, stopping at a hot spring on the way. There, someone had laid up a stone wall to create a steaming pool adjacent to a freezing mountain creek. Where the springs bubbled from the ground, the rocks were so hot they couldn't be touched, but next to the stream, where ice water seeped through the wall, the water was tepid. We settled up to our chins as the steam rose above the snow-covered hills. I was close to falling asleep when I decided it was time to crawl over the rock wall for a dip in the icy stream. It felt beautifully invigorating. After a couple more repetitions of hot soak and cold rinse, we dressed and staggered to the car. I was so relaxed that I barely stayed awake during the ride back to the motel.

But there was work to be done and I didn't want to be up all night. I had decided to wax up both pairs of skating skis, one for colder temperatures, the other for warmer. Waxing skating skis should be easy: anticipate the tempera-

Rob Sleamaker, John Morton, and John Donovan training hard for the Masters National Championship 50K in Sun Valley. Kathy Farineriz

ture, iron on the glide wax, scrape off the excess, and brush in a little texture. But somehow it had become complex, technical, and exotic in only a couple of years. Now a super wax job required several steps involving a couple of different waxes or additives. Some of these additives were outrageously expensive powders, which were delicately sprinkled on the ski with great care taken not to spill a grain. My dry-snow choice was Ski*Go C-280 over antistatic graphite. Variations of that combination had worked well for us all week. But a 50K would be close to three hours long, finishing at noon. If it warmed up fast, the Ski*Go might be too cold. I decided to wax the second pair with Solda orange covered with Swix Cera F, the combination that had worked so well for me at the White Mountain Marathon in Waterville Valley. I was looking at two to three hours of waxing!

"That's a lot of work for only one race," Donovan remarked.

"It won't seem like it tomorrow if they're fast!" I answered.

The next morning I wondered if it would warm up enough by 9:00 to make the Cera work. Frightfully expensive and with an almost mystical reputation, Cera F was unbeatable in new snow warming from $-4°C$ to $4°C$. That was a narrow temperature range, and the wax was so expensive you didn't want to waste it. But if the sky stayed clear, the sun would put the temperature right in that range during the three hours of the race.

Since I had two pairs of skis ready to go this time, I broke my boycott of the speed trap. Racers were lined up a hundred yards up the hill. At a word from the Swix man, each would glide down the track past two light-sensitive timing devices. When the skier reached the bottom, a technician would announce his speed.

I rode my Ski*Go C-280 skis through the trap first. "Seven point seven two," came the voice over the speaker. I skated up for another try. "Seven point five six," the voice reported. I asked how that compared with other times through the trap.

"One of the best," was the answer.

I switched to the Cera skis and skated back up the hill. As I coasted to a stop, the speaker produced a long, slow wolf whistle followed by, "What do you have on *those* boards?"

That was all I needed to know! I walked away from the radio and waved casually to the technician stationed halfway up the hill. I tried to ignore the racers who had heard the last announcement; I didn't want to talk to anyone about wax.

Minutes before the start I sought out Donovan to reassure him and offer some last-minute advice.

"Remember, this is a wicked long walk through the park, so don't get sucked into going out of the start too fast and wind up real sorry for it on the third lap. If you have anything left for the last ten kilometers, you're going to knock guys off like crazy because our wax will only improve as the temperature warms up."

"OK, thanks Morty," he responded nervously. "Have a good one."

I knew Watson had headed back to Salt Lake, and I looked in vain for Bob Rosso in the mob of sixty-five starters. The owner of an upbeat, full-service sports shop, Rosso had worn a different wild Lycra suit for each of the previous races. I didn't know what suit to look for. Oh well, I was sure I'd see him as the race developed. I wished Dan Gibson good luck. He had been right behind me in the previous races and would be a tough contender in this one. I saw Mike Elliott and Del Pletcher, both of whom had bested me in the 30K skate race (although they had been in an older age group). And John Broadhead was ready to go. I still remembered the twelve minutes he put on me in the last lap of the Lawrence Loppet in Lake Placid.

With the Lake Placid "death march" still vivid in my mind, I was determined not to run out of fuel this time. I peeled a couple of bananas and placed them in the snow on their peels. I hung my vest on the snow fence to mark their location. My plan was to wolf down sections of bananas as I came through the start area after the first and second laps. As I prepared my private food station, I remembered that by the time you feel hungry or thirsty it's already too late, so I broke a banana in half and ate it as we lined up for the start.

I had tried to talk Donovan into taking a couple of bananas, but he preferred Power Bars and a health-store variety of fig bars. I had tried them back at the motel and thought they might be a little hard to swallow thirty-five kilometers into a 50K race, but John assured me he loved them and they provided instant energy. Kevin Sweeney, a former top collegiate racer for the University of New Hampshire, was spending the winter in Sun Valley and had volunteered to provide a food station for Donovan and me at the far end of the loop. He loaded his backpack with food, water bottles, and Exceed and headed out from the start. I had also given Kevin a bottle of stale cola, which would provide the sugar surge I almost surely would need late in the race.

Moments later the starter shouted his commands, and a kaleidoscope of fluorescent racing suits charged off into the Idaho hills. My goals were simple: I wanted to win my age group; in fact, I wanted to be the top man over forty. I would also try to ski better than three minutes per kilometer and to finish within 90 percent of the winners. Finally, I was shooting to break the top ten overall.

My strategy was also pretty straightforward: Stay out of trouble in the start, ski in control and conserve energy for at least the first lap, and be aware of Rosso, Gibson, or anyone else over forty who was going well. As we crossed the road and funneled down into a train, I was about twentieth behind Dick Hunt, a big, strong guy from Bend, Oregon, who is perpetually second to Dick Mize in the 50–54 age group. As we skated easily up the first long hill of the Gunclub loop, I could see the leading pack of the train pulling away. I didn't want to be stuck behind Hunt, but his size caused him to straddle the entire trail as he skated up the incline. I forced myself to stay relaxed; there was plenty of time left in the race. When we crested the hill, there was already quite a gap ahead of Hunt. I stepped out of the tracks and rocketed past him in a tight tuck. These skis were going to be super!

Within a couple of kilometers I had rejoined the second pack and fell in behind Dick Mize. We were on a section of Trail Creek — long, flat skiing — and Dick appeared effortless as he V2 skated gracefully up the valley. The pace was comfortable, and we even talked a little during the seemingly endless gradual climb. Occasionally I looked ahead to the lead group and could make out Dan Gibson skiing smoothly at the tail end. Dick must have sensed something because he stepped over and said, "You've got to get going, John, and I've got to throttle it back a notch or two."

"Thanks, Dick, see you at the finish."

As we continued up the valley, I gradually worked my way through the second pack until I had a clear view of the lead group several hundred meters ahead. I didn't dare go after them, at least not yet. I skied the remainder of the first loop alone, concentrating on being smooth and conserving energy. Kevin was where he had promised to be and handed me a bottle of Exceed.

Seven or eight kilometers later, going through the start area, I reached down, grabbed half a banana, and stuffed it into my mouth. Then I skated across the stadium to the water, still gagging down chunks of banana.

As I started up the hill on the Gunclub loop for the second time, I looked ahead and got a shot of adrenaline. The lead pack was breaking up! Dan Gibson was dropping behind, skiing on his own. I still couldn't make out Rosso among the leaders, although I assumed he was there, but Gibson at least might be vulnerable. I leaned on the pace a little, concentrating on reeling in Gibson. As we crossed the road from Gunclub to Trail Creek, several bystanders cheered.

"C'mon, pour it on — this is your day!" I recognized that voice. It was Bob Rosso, standing in street clothes with the group of spectators. My bewilderment must have shown, because he shrugged and held out his hands, palms up, in the "What can I say?" gesture. I skated on in confusion. One part of me was thrilled. With Rosso on the sidelines, my chances of winning were significantly improved. But another part of me was disappointed. I felt I had been improving all week, adjusting to the altitude, the time change, and the snow conditions. The 15K had been a great race, and part of me was anticipating another epic battle.

I skied on, trying to sort out my feelings. Then I noticed Dan Gibson far ahead, marathon skating smoothly on the endless gradual climb. Although he had been dropped by the leaders, I didn't seem to be gaining on him. I forced my mind back to the present; Rosso might not be in this race, but Gibson was, and he was leading the 40–44 age group at the moment. Several kilometers later I had gained slightly on Dan. I knew if I succeeded in passing him, I would have to put some distance between us. He could ski these flats as well as or better than I could.

I gained on Dan throughout the remainder of the second loop. This time passing Kevin I shouted, "Coke," and he handed me my bottle. I took one good slug, popped the top back on, and dropped the bottle in the snow, hoping Kevin would retrieve it for the final loop.

I passed Dan as we started the third lap. I offered words of encouragement as I went by, at least partly to show how poised and relaxed I was. It was good psychology even if it was a charade. I knew I had to drop him in the hills or he would wear me down on the long flat of Trail Creek. I crossed the road off Gunclub for the final time, with a couple of hundred meters on Dan. Then I began focusing on a green-and-black Landsem suit far ahead. By the far turn, about seven kilometers from the finish, I had closed enough on the suit to recognize fellow Vermonter Keith Woodward. His skis were slowing down as the tracks warmed in the sun, and I glided by on a downhill.

"Nice going, Morty, you're in eighth place!" Keith forced a smile on his strained face.

"Hook on and we'll kick it in together, buddy" I said over my shoulder.

We still had a couple of serious uphills in the final kilometers, and as I leaned into the biggest one, I realized I was about out of gas. Keith scampered by on sheer mental toughness. In desperation I looked back and saw Gibson approaching the bottom of the hill. "I can't lose it now!" I thought in a panic and tried to focus on Keith, who had already picked up twenty meters. I pushed over the top of the hill heaving and gasping, knees quivering and thigh muscles cramping.

Kevin was waiting with my bottle and I emptied it down my throat. He held out a fist full of Donovan's bran and sawdust fig bars, but I waved them off. Coasting down the rest of the hill trying to collect myself for the final few kilometers home, I smiled to see several fig bars littered across the trail.

The downhill had given me a little breathing room on Gibson, although he appeared to be skiing strong. If I could just hold the pace for the final rolling kilometers to the finish . . . Up the last hill out of the creekbed, my thighs began to cramp again and Keith pulled away. If Dan had been in contact, he surely would have gone by as well. But he was not yet in sight as I skated stiffly to the finish line. I coasted over to Keith and thanked him for the encouragement late in the race. I turned in time to see Dan Gibson cross the line. After he caught his breath, we compared notes on the tactics of the race.

Reaching for water, Exceed, and giant cookies, exhausted racers swapped stories about wax, close calls on the downhills, and the relative merits of different skating techniques. The scuttlebutt seemed to confirm the information Keith had given me during the race: He had finished eighth overall, I was ninth, and it didn't look like anyone over forty had finished ahead of me.

I spotted Donovan skating the final flat stretch and cheered him in. Coasting to a stop, he caught his breath before I got over to him. He was exuberant!

"Morty, this was the best race of my life! The skis were unbelievable! I just kept gliding past guys! I skied my own pace, hung with it the whole way, and never cramped! God, that was great!" He gave me a bear hug as tears filled his eyes.

"Hey John," I blurted out after the moment had passed, "how were those sawdust fig bars?"

His head went back and he roared with laughter.

A couple of hours later we had showered, checked out of the Ketchum Korral, loaded the rental car to the roof, and were back at the Sun Valley Nordic Center for the final awards presentation. I was proud and grateful to receive the gold medal for my age group and to applaud racers I had admired for decades, such as Mike Elliott and Dick Mize.

The printed results showed John Donovan in sixth place in the 45–49 age group, a dramatic improvement over his 30K results. He beamed with satisfaction.

The drive to Boise into a flaming sunset was filled with animated conversation. We were riding a postrace high, Donovan excitedly arguing some point of ski technique from the backseat, me feeling the rosy glow of victory and the weight of the gold medal around my neck under my sweater. Donovan was still going strong several hours later as we waited to order supper in a Boise restaurant. Alex looked at me from across the table, "Morty, you've still got your medal on!"

"Yeah, I know."

Donovan stopped talking and looked at me. His long arm wrapped around my shoulders and he gave me a strong hug. The waiter arrived to find four very suntanned people barely regaining control over their laughter and tears and not quite ready to order.

9: Equipment and Waxing

A S A HIGH school coach in Alaska from 1973 through 1978, I tried hard to deemphasize most of the topics covered in this chapter. It was during the "fiberglass revolution" in cross-country ski technology, and every high school racer was an expert on ski construction: composite laminates, foam cores, and synthetic bases. It sometimes seemed that my athletes spent more time discussing ski construction and waxing techniques than they did training My attitude became, "If it turns up on the end and slides on the snow, you can race on it."

When Thomas Magnusson of Sweden won the World Championship gold medal in the 30K event at Falun in 1974, he plunged the Nordic ski industry into chaos. Until that day the Scandinavians had had the corner on the cross-country racing ski market with amazingly light, lovingly constructed wooden skis by respected companies like Jarvinen, Sundens, Landsem, and Blå Skia. Then Magnusson, a bull of a skier, plowed his way through thirty kilometers of heavy, wet slush on a pair of fiberglass Knessels from Austria. The headlines in Oslo the next day read: "Magnusson takes 30K gold; Norwegian ski industry in jeopardy!"

The complexion of the sport changed overnight. No longer was it the best athlete — primarily a question of conditioning, technique, and psychology — who won on a given day. In certain conditions an average athlete could defeat far stronger rivals if he had the advantage of fiberglass skis. The ski industry scrambled frantically to cash in on the new technology. The fallout was sometimes comical, sometimes tragic. Norwegian ski companies rushed fiberglass prototypes to the consumers. Some of the early attempts were so heavy they were scarcely suitable for touring, let alone racing. But the hunger for fiberglass racing skis was insatiable, and even these early clunkers were snapped up. The Austrians had the advantage of years of experience with fiberglass technology from Alpine ski production, so they were able to make fast, relatively light racing skis. They didn't have much background with kick wax, however, and many of their early skis were fast on the downhills but hopeless on the flats and uphills because the bottoms wouldn't hold the wax.

The sad part was that several strong ski companies, famous for virtually handmade wooden racing skis, were unable to adapt and went out of business.

Wooden skis required more preparation, were far more fragile, and were slower than fiberglass, but a good pair of wooden racing skis was a masterpiece of craftsmanship. The Scandinavian ski builders of prefiberglass days were highly regarded as artists. They would tell with pride of trekking through the forest to select straight, true trees. At the factory logs would be cut longitudinally, the two halves kept parallel on the assembly line. After more than seventy laminations for each ski, a pair of top racing skis would contain strips of wood from the opposite sides of the same tree, resulting in a perfect match. Skis were primarily constructed from hickory and birch, much of the hickory imported from the United States. If you weren't one of the favored hotshots on somebody's national team who got free skis, you could purchase the best racing boards direct from the factory for about thirty-five dollars. An additional advantage of buying from the factory was the vast selection from which to choose.

In 1974, just prior to those fateful Nordic World Championships in Falun, Sweden, the U.S. Biathlon Team was training in Norway before traveling on to Minsk in the USSR for the Biathlon World Championships. At the time, Dennis Donahue and I were competing on Splitkein skis, one of Norway's finest brands. On a slack training day we headed to the Splitkein factory. A company official gave us a quick tour, then we were handed over to a sleepy-looking, red-faced old man in overalls, who led us through a maze of stockrooms, lumber piles, and warehouses. We descended dark, rickety stairs to a padlocked room. He opened the lock, turned on the light, and waved us through the door. This was it! The mythical hoard of handmade racing skis, which we had heard rumored for years, lovingly crafted for Norwegian national heroes like Odd Martinsen, Pal Tyldum, and Harald Groenningen and hidden in the dark recesses of the factory.

The old, red-faced guy indicated that we were to help ourselves. Dennis and I looked at each other. There was a wall full of 210 cm skis, the length we needed. Dennis took a pair off a rack within reach, flexed them, and nodded his satisfaction. The old man watched without changing expression. The understanding had been that we would each have the opportunity to select a pair of skis at the factory. Before I reached toward the rack, I turned to our host and asked, "Did you make these skis?" He nodded and grunted, "Yes."

"Then would you select a pair for me? I weigh about 75 kilos with my rifle."

"Oh no," he responded, "I yust bilt the shees, I not racing. You racer must pick the shu you tink is fast for you!"

"May I look through the racks?" I asked.

"Of course." A trace of a smile appeared on his face and he seemed to settle in for the duration.

I began flexing skis. I took a pair out of the rack, placed them bottom to bottom, and squeezed them together at the point where the bindings would be mounted. After a couple of squeezes I put them aside and took another pair from the rack. After twenty or thirty pairs I was beginning to get a feel for the range of flex, from relatively soft to fairly stiff. I was midway down the wall and Dennis was getting impatient. Our host seemed to be enjoying himself. I had resolved to flex only a couple more pairs when I picked up skis I could tell were different. Although appearing identical to the hundreds of other Splitkeins in the room, the camber and flex of these skis were dramatically different. When I held them bottom to bottom and squeezed them together, their spring and resilience made them feel alive! I looked at the old fellow as I continued to flex the skis. He was watching me closely, but his face showed no expression. I put the magic pair aside and flexed a few more. I went back to the special pair. They were clearly more lively than any other pair I had tested (by now almost fifty). I looked at the old man and said, "I'll take these."

His face broke into a grin as he pulled a small, black notebook from his pocket. As he stepped close to get the serial number of the skis I was holding, I glanced at the open notebook. In neat handwriting was the name Odd Martinsen, followed by a column of serial numbers. The old man flipped to a clean page and asked in halting English, "Please spell for me your name, slowly!" He carefully wrote my name and the serial number of the skis I had selected, closed his book, and put it back in his pocket.

Moments later, as we walked back to the train station, Dennis grabbed my new Splitkeins.

"What's so damned special about these skis?" he mumbled in frustration. But even before I could answer, he flexed the skis and an expression of awareness appeared on his face.

"You know, Morty, that guy probably planted this one pair of handmade racing skis in the whole room and you found 'em!"

"That's why he wrote down my name and the serial number but wasn't interested in yours," I added.

"Right! No excuses now—these are the same boards the hotshots are on!"

And they were great skis: fast, responsive, and full of life. I had several good races on them that winter, including one of my best international biathlon races ever. By the following season, however, the fiberglass revolution had taken over and my wooden Splitkeins were obsolete.

Ski Selection

With my high school skiers I deemphasized the significance of equipment selection; I wanted them to concentrate on aspects of performance over which they had more control, namely, consistency in training and dedication in developing good technique. I do believe, however, that the flex of a ski is crucial to its speed. Here are two time-tested methods for selecting the right flex.

The first is the paper test. Find a floor that is flat, preferably with low pile carpet. Place the skis to be tested on the floor and stand on them, positioning your feet where they will go once the bindings are mounted. Try to distribute your weight evenly over both skis. Have a friend slide a stiff piece of paper down the length of one ski from tip to tail between the ski and the floor. A ski well matched to your weight should offer consistent resistance to the paper throughout its length. If your friend notices significant additional resistance underfoot, the skis are too soft. If the tips and tails offer more resistance than underfoot, the skis are probably too stiff. Next, put most of your weight on one ski, as if you were kicking. Have your friend draw the paper down the length of the ski again. This time there *should* be increased resistance underfoot. If the paper still slides relatively freely, the skis are too stiff and you will not be able to get your kick wax to work. Ideally, with classic skis your weight should be evenly distributed over the entire length of the ski. It's probably good if the camber keeps the kick wax from dragging in the snow while gliding as long as they aren't so stiff that you can't get the wax down on the snow when you kick (even when you are tired).

The second method of ski selection is more subjective. Simply take along your old skis when you shop for new ones. If you loved your old skis and they seemed consistently pretty fast, look for the same flex in a new pair. If your old skis seemed to wear off kick wax prematurely and you often found yourself double poling the last few kilometers of a race or workout, they were probably too soft and you should look for stiffer skis. If your kick wax didn't wear off but you were frequently slipping on uphills, your skis were too stiff and you should consider a softer flex.

Remember, skis don't come off the rack race-ready and superfast. I'll talk about base preparation and maintenance later, but in the meantime you should know that what makes skis really fast is waxing and scraping, waxing and scraping, waxing and scraping . . .

I served as a team leader for the U.S. Biathlon Team to the 1987 World Championships in Lake Placid, New York, and the 1988 Olympics in Calgary. Our top competitor was Josh Thompson, who won a silver medal in the 20K event at the 1987 World Championships. Both years we had access to an electronic speed trap to test glide wax prior to races. The athletes would arrive at the site often with four or five pairs of skis, waxed for the anticipated conditions at race time. By 1987 biathlon was exclusively skating so the athletes were testing only glide wax, ski bottoms (black graphite or clear P-Tex 2000), and ski flex. Josh, like the others, would ride through the trap on three or four different pairs of Landsems (some pairs were special racing stock not available to the general public). But repeatedly I observed him select and race on an old pair of Landsems with clear P-Tex bases that looked like beat-up practice skis. When I asked him about the skis, he answered, "They're always fastest."

"Regardless of snow conditions?"

"Yup."

"In cold snow as well as slush?"

"Yup."

I've noticed that often elite racers who have several pairs of skis begin to favor one pair and thus wax and scrape that pair more frequently than their others. The more these skis are waxed, scraped, and skied on, the faster they become — and the more confidence the athlete develops in them. Assuming those skis are not abused in marginal snow conditions or overheated during waxing, they could continue to be fastest for several seasons. Therefore, if you have a fast pair of racing skis, take care of them, store them properly during the off-season, and don't automatically make them your "rock skis" for the following year. It's entirely possible that those skis could continue to be your fastest.

When selecting skis, you basically have two options in base material: polyethylene (commonly referred to as P-Tex 2000 or clear bases) and graphite, antistatic bases (usually called black bases). The black bases were initially developed to resist dirt, pine needles, and leaves, which contaminate wax and slow down skis in wet-snow conditions well above the freezing point. I have never been completely sure whether the black graphite base actually resists dirt buildup or simply prevents you from seeing it, but they do seem to be faster in warm, wet snow, and an enterprising racer has discovered that the black bottoms also appear to be faster in very cold conditions, 0°F or colder. I can't confirm or deny this from my experience. The companies putting black bottoms on their skis have proclaimed that the graphite bases are as good as P-Tex in all conditions and significantly better in both very cold and very warm conditions. Some companies, such as Fischer, are so enthusiastic about black bottoms that their 1991 line includes only black-bottom skis. I'm naturally skeptical. Black bottoms may be as fast or faster in all conditions, but they are also significantly softer and thus more susceptible to damage than P-Tex. I'm not entirely sure the manufacturers aren't pushing black bottoms because they will have to be replaced more often — thus the companies will sell more skis.

Much of the polyethylene for clear ski bases is manufactured by a chemical company in Switzerland. The P-Tex is formed into large drums, then thin sheets are pared off like the peel of an apple. Rumor has it that the P-Tex at the core cures slightly differently and for some inexplicable reason is faster on snow. The ski manufacturers order sheets of P-Tex and laminate it to the bottoms of their skis. Skis with exactly the same flex pattern, identically constructed, and tested under scientific conditions by experienced racers or technicians may differ significantly in speed. The composition of the P-Tex on the bottoms does seem to be the only explanation. It may be that a consistently fast pair of skis ended up with P-Tex from the core of the drum. My recommendation once again is that if you have a fast pair of skis, hold on to them and take care of them.

What about brands? I believe there are at least a dozen manufacturers that make excellent racing skis. Just as in buying a new automobile, a lot comes down to personal preference. Here are some guidelines to keep in mind when purchasing new skis.

Be aware that the international superstars affiliated with particular brands are being paid to ski on those products. The skis for the superstar will be carefully constructed and individually selected. Those available in your local ski shop might be quite different.

It's worth your time and effort to establish a good rapport with a local ski shop. An innovative shop will have a wide selection of skis, may offer waxing and technique clinics, and may even support a racing team or club.

Watch for preseason and end-of-season sales. If you know what you're looking for in terms of flex and you aren't overly concerned about having the latest paint job on the tops of the skis, it's possible to pick up great bargains. Many times a "new" ski is essentially a new paint job on a previous year's model.

If you are trying to decide between comparable pairs of skis, then the personality of the company itself may become a factor. For some companies, Nordic racing skis are the main focus, their bread and butter, and they devote a lot of attention to that area. For other companies Nordic is just a sideline, something they have to offer to be a full-service company. Also, some manufacturers are very good about standing behind their products in the event of breakage, delamination, or a defect in manufacturing.

Poles

The story of cross-country ski poles is similar to the ski story. Until the 1976 Olympics in Innsbruck, the Norwegian company Lillidahl produced the poles favored by most of the world's top racers. They had strong, lightweight aluminum shafts and leather grips. At the 1976 Olympics the Finnish company Exel presented a new, lighter pole made of wrapped fiberglass, equipped with an equally innovative handle and basket. Within a couple of years Lillidahl was out of business and Exel was used by all the top racers. Recently, Swix of Norway and Leike of West Germany have produced racing poles that rival Exel's technological innovations, but Exel doesn't appear to be resting on its laurels.

Skating was a boon to the pole companies because a racer needs a different pair of poles for each discipline. Although there are individual preferences, the general consensus is that skating poles should reach no higher than the skier's nose and classic poles should be about shoulder height.

A couple of years ago Swix made headlines with their T-handle, or canoe paddle, grip. Designed specifically for skating, the T-handle presumably allows the racer to exert more force through the pole into the snow than the conventional grip. Originally the grip was banned from national and international FIS competitions, but recently that ruling was overturned and the Swix T-handle is now legal. It does seem to be an advantage for skating, and many of the world's biathlon skiers who skate exclusively in competition are using them. Among racers who compete in both classic and skating events, there are mixed reviews. Some athletes and coaches maintain it is only an advantage if the athlete trains with the T-handle, thereby developing the muscles slightly differently than when training with conventional poles.

Exel's Avanti grip seems to be a successful innovation. A small projection from the base of the handle allows the racer to exert force with the heel of the hand in addition to the conventional strap. These poles can be used for either classic or skating.

When shopping for poles, there are really only three concerns aside from length: durability, lightness, and price. Lightweight poles (carbon fiber or graphite) are expensive. Lightweight poles that can withstand the pushing and shoving of a mass start like the Birkebeiner are ferociously expensive. You can probably get by just fine with slightly heavier, more durable poles if you use your roller board regularly during the summer.

Boots and Bindings

The 1976 Olympics in Innsbruck will also be remembered by cross-country skiers as a turning point for ski boots and bindings. Until that year the Scandinavians had dominated the boot and binding scene with a rat-trap, or three-pin, binding. Boots resembled hiking shoes, usually made of leather and distinguished by a relatively long sole that protruded in front of the toe.

At Innsbruck the German athletic-shoe giant Adidas introduced a revolutionary concept in cross-country boots and bindings. The boot was more like a track shoe, low cut and very lightweight, made of synthetics rather than leather. The sole was a hard plastic, providing much more torsional rigidity. And, most interesting, the traditional three pins and bale had been replaced by a small, lightweight housing equipped with a horizontal metal pin that locked the boot in place.

The new Adidas boots and bindings were the rage as the cross-country Olympic events unfolded in the scenic alpine village of Seefeld in the mountains above Innsbruck. The marketing people from Adidas had done their homework, providing their product to a limited number of visible athletes whom they anticipated would win medals. As the competitions wore on, Adidas basked in the glow of success and international exposure for their products.

Then came one of the final cross-country events, the men's relay. In front of a crowd of thousands the leadoff men for each nation thundered out of the stadium for the ten-kilometer loop. As the Soviet Union's Nikolai Beliaev, leading the pack at about eight kilometers, looped within sight of the tag zone, one ski shot like an arrow down the icy tracks. Frantically he hobbled after it as the spectators watched in disbelief. He retrieved the ski and bent to replace it. Instantly he picked up the ski and began yelling in Russian. Soviet coaches appeared with more shouting and gesticulating. Beliaev bent down and, in front of the astonished crowd, began unlacing his ski boot. By the time he found a replacement boot and reattached his ski, he had fallen from first to eleventh place. The culprit, it was later learned, was the new Adidas boot, which had broken off where the plastic sole protrudes from the upper to insert in the binding. The company took pains to warn athletes that the boots should not be modified, suggesting that Beliaev had created his own problem by filing down the plastic sole and binding attachment to reduce the weight of the boot even more. Adidas survived the incident and continued to produce innovative, comfortable racing boots and bindings; but any athlete who had witnessed Beliaev's disaster in Seefeld would never forget it.

The Scandinavians responded with minor revisions to their three-pin system, and nothing much changed until the French Alpine binding company Salomon introduced a totally new cross-country boot/binding concept in the early 1980s. Salomon replaced the extended sole of the existing boots—the source of constant wear and the cause of many blackened toenails—with a strong metal loop that locked tightly in the binding and acted as a pivot. It was a dramatic improvement, and Salomon became an overnight success. Ever conservative, the Norwegians took a long time to respond to Salomon's innovations, but they eventually used Salomon's advances and improved upon them, developing the New Nordic Norm system (NNN). There have been refinements by both Salomon and NNN in recent seasons, and those two systems continue to dominate the cross-country racing scene.

The advent of skating didn't change bindings much, but it did bring about some innovations in boot construction. Racing boots designed for skating became higher, incorporated more plastic for lateral strength, and had hinged ankle joints.

As with skis, it is hard to go wrong with any of the major manufacturers of cross-country racing boots. The new binding systems eliminate the danger of jammed toes, so boots can be more snug than in previous years. Most athletes probably wear their ski boots as they would a running shoe, with one pair of medium-weight athletic socks. In extreme cold weather, overbooties or old athletic socks are pulled on over the boots rather than extra layers of socks crammed inside.

Another advantage of the Salomon and NNN systems is that their popularity ensures that swapping skis with teammates to test wax or replacing a broken ski in a race is far more likely.

Clothing

It doesn't seem long ago that cross-country clothing was easily identifiable: it was all navy blue poplin. Then, following Alpine skiing's lead, the colors became brighter and the fabric became stretchy. Now the miracle of Lycra makes cross-country one of the most colorful sports. But as racers become more conscious of freedom of movement and wild fluorescent fabrics, it is important to remember some of the basics of cross-country clothing.

Lycra racing suits by themselves are not warm. Worn over polypropylene long underwear, Lycra can provide adequate body warmth for a racer competing in normal winter temperatures. Polypropylene is lightweight, warm, and has the ability to wick moisture away from the skin — an important factor for a hard-working racer. But there are times when a racing suit and polypropylene underwear simply are not warm enough. The perfect addition in those conditions is a lightweight vest, something that offers wind protection and additional warmth to the body core but does not restrict the racer's movement.

What you wear on your head can affect your performance. The trend in racing hats is toward thinner, finer weaves, which often sacrifice warmth. As a result, many racers supplement their hats with the lightweight earmuffs distributed by Swix, Ski*Go, and others. These have saved many earlobes from frostbite when hats ride up, which they often do.

A significant percentage of a person's body heat escapes in cold weather through the head. On an especially cold or windy day a racer who wears earmuffs and an extra-warm hat will conserve body heat, thus making more energy available to get from start to finish. Conversely, if you are racing on a very warm day, you can lower your body temperature by simply discarding your hat.

In the last few years lightweight plastic goggles have become popular in cross-country racing. They serve three significant purposes: they shield the eyes from bright sunlight and snow glare; they protect the eyes from freezing in especially cold or windy conditions; and they are valuable in mass-start races with thousands of skiers scrambling for position, snow flying from their poles. There are two drawbacks to the goggles. If you are racing hard and sweating profusely, they may slip out of place or your vision may become obscured by perspiration on the lenses. Also, a course that switches from wide open fields to dark forests repeatedly can be disconcerting on a bright sunny day, and dark glasses seem to emphasize the contrast. The answer on those days might be clear lenses.

Gloves have been a longtime dilemma for cross-country racers. Once under way, even in relatively cold conditions, most cross-country racers are able to keep their hands warm enough with relatively lightweight gloves. But getting to the start with warm hands is another matter. Big, heavy, well-insulated gloves or mittens that are warm enough to wear while standing around, waxing, or loosening up are usually too bulky for racing. Many competitors solve the problem by wearing warmer mittens over racing gloves before the start, then discarding the mittens to race in the lighter, more flexible racing gloves.

Any clothing that is wet — even damp — cannot be warm. If it's necessary to drive an hour or more in a warm car to the race site, it is safe to assume your socks will be damp when you arrive. If you want warm feet while skiing, change to dry socks before you put on your ski boots. If you go out prior to the race to inspect the course or to get a good warm-up, chances are you will sweat. To stay warm in the race, change to a dry shirt before the start. Always carry along dry clothing to the workout or race — a shirt, socks, and hat — to change into after the event. Even if it is impossible to shower and change into dry clothes immediately, the dry clothing will go a long way toward helping you avoid the chill that can make you more susceptible to a cold or flu. Dressing properly not only improves your results, it also keeps you healthy.

Ski-Base Preparation and Maintenance

This is another topic that elicits lively discussion and disagreement among racers, coaches, and ski companies. I believe some of the divergent viewpoints stem from the wooden-ski days. No matter how carefully a pair of skis was constructed, by the time it reached North America, the grain of the wood in the bottoms had swollen and required hours of patient hand sanding to be restored to mirror smoothness. It was assumed at the time that the smoother the ski, the faster it would be (which we now know is not true in all snow conditions), so these wooden boards were sanded and then impregnated with pine tar to seal the pores and act as a bond for the wax. One of the great tragedies of the fiberglass revolution is that wax rooms no longer emit the pleasantly distinctive aroma of hot pine tar.

Enter the fiberglass racing ski. Company representatives confidently announced "Just wax 'em and race! They're factory tuned; you'll only slow 'em down by sanding or scraping 'em at home." Now there was a whole generation of racers accustomed to spending several hours preparing skis before every major race, and ski companies were in effect challenging those racers to make their race-ready skis faster. To add confusion to the whole debate, there were a wide variety of factory base-finishing methods in the ski industry, some of them indeed race-ready and some of them horrendous. Compounding the variable of the skis themselves was the ability of the racer or ski technician who performed the work. Many perfectly good skis have been ruined by well-intentioned but misinformed racers who thought they were speeding up their boards.

In general, I'm a member of the old school. I believe almost any new skis can be improved by thorough and careful base preparation. But before you roll up your sleeves, get prepared for several hours of tedious work. Set up in a clean, well-lighted corner of the basement or workshop, plug in your cassette player, and have a stack of your favorite tapes at hand.

You'll need some way to hold your ski secure while you "abuse" its running surface. There are several varieties of benches and ski vises available, but if you have access to a band saw you can make an excellent one yourself.

Once your ski is secured and supported along its length, conduct a little test before you commit yourself to hours of sanding and scraping. You'll need a sanding block and a sheet of fine sandpaper, 400 to 600 grit. (Whenever you sand ski bases, use a sanding block to keep the paper flat.) Lightly sand the bottom of the ski, being careful to apply even pressure. After a few minutes a powder will accumulate. Wipe it off with a rag and look at the ski bottom carefully in good light. If the factory base-finishing process is what the manufacturers claim, you should see your tiny sandpaper marks uniformly the entire length and width of the ski. Even with well-made skis, however, there will often be hollows or low spots in the base that your light sanding didn't reach. One of these spots commonly occurs in the shovel area where the groove stops and the curve to the tip begins.

If you're lucky and your bases are relatively flat, you can skip these next steps dealing with sanding and scraping. If the little test revealed some imperfections, however, and you want to start the season with smooth, flat bases, roll up your sleeves, put on a good tape, and settle in for some work. Wipe down the base first with some type of solvent, as several companies coat them for shipment. After the solvent evaporates, begin sanding with relatively rough sandpaper, 80 to 100 grit. The experts would probably cringe, but at this stage I sand back and forth the length of the ski. When you near the end of the process, you'll want to sand from tip to tail only so the microscopic fibers you create will lie down as the ski glides along the snow. But in the early stages you simply want to remove base material. You can extend the life of your sandpaper by removing the clogged base material with a stiff brush. When you believe you have removed the hollows and bumps, wipe the ski down with

Ski Form Bench

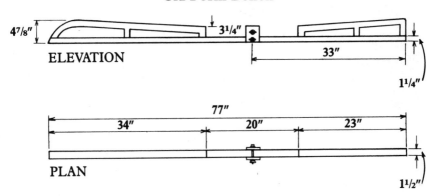

ELEVATION

PLAN

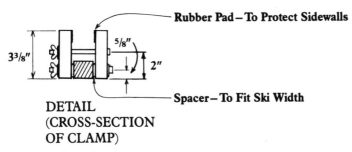

Rubber Pad – To Protect Sidewalls

Spacer – To Fit Ski Width

DETAIL
(CROSS-SECTION
OF CLAMP)

The ski form makes waxing easier and is essential for proper maintenance of skis (sanding, scraping, and repairing base material). The ski form fits easily into a ski bag for travel. You can make your own ski form from an eight-foot 2 x 6. Scribe the curve for the form from the top of your ski.

solvent again and take a careful look. If there are no areas of the base untouched by your sandpaper, you've done a good job.

Many experienced racers and coaches will say that the fastest skis are prepared by sanding and scraping with a metal scraper, but it's very tricky to use one properly, and if you have any self-doubts, stick to sanding. I've used a metal scraper for years, but inevitably at some point every season I'll lose my concentration for a second as I'm scraping away and gouge a series of chatter marks.

If you want to use a metal scraper, get a heavy-duty carpenter's scraper from a hardware store or lumberyard. The steel should be rugged enough that you can't bend it. To sharpen the scraper, clamp a ten- or twelve-inch mill

To smooth a ski with a metal scraper, hold it firmly in a ski form and press down on the scraper at a 45-degree angle from the tip to the tail of the ski.

bastard file horizontally in a vise with the surface of the file facing up. Then hold a long edge of your scraper against the surface of the file. Draw the scraper along the file in a smooth, steady motion. After several passes turn the scraper end for end and draw it along the file several more times. Brush the accumulated metal filings off the surface of the file. If you want to get fancy, you can use a fine whetstone to take the microscopic burr off the edge of the scraper by laying the scraper flat on the stone, first one side, then the other, and moving it in a gentle circular motion. The real pros then use a burnishing tool to put a razor-sharp lip on the edge of the scraper, a touch that requires skill and practice.

Holding your sharpened scraper with two hands, begin at the tip of the ski. Push the scraper along the base with a firm, steady pressure. Use long, smooth strokes from tip to tail. Be very careful if you initiate a stroke midway down the ski. Concentrate! Try to apply equal pressure to both sides of the ski base. A good scraping job at this stage should remove most of the hairy fuzz created by your sandpaper. It should also reveal more clearly any imperfections concealed by your sanding. Some experts suggest dispensing with sanding — because it raises up those fibers — and preparing bottoms by scraping alone. I don't disagree, provided that you are very good with a scraper (I'm not) and the bases are relatively good to begin with. If you have bumps and hollows to get rid of, my contention is that a scraper acts like a snowplow on a typical Vermont dirt road: it bounces over the frozen bumps and gouges out a hollow on the other side. Once you have sanded the base flat, the scraper carefully used can speed and perhaps improve the process.

Once you've sanded, perhaps scraped, cleaned your skis with solvent, and the bases appear to be flat, you need to repeat the process several more times with progressively finer sandpaper. The general consensus is that for wet snow you need more "structure," or texture, in the base to break the suction created by the high water content of the snow. If you intend to use the skis primarily for wet snow, then sanding down to 250 or 300 grit is probably sufficient. If you are from Fairbanks or most of your skiing is going to be on cold, dry snow, you should probably sand to 500 to 600 grit. This sandpaper is available from Swix, sized for your sanding block, but your automotive parts store may have it at a lower price.

Remember in the final few sanding steps to sand only from tip to tail— make a long push stroke toward the tail of the ski, pick the block up, replace it at the tip, push it toward the tail, and so on. With your classic skis there is some logic to keeping the kick zone underfoot relatively rough. The rougher surface will hold your kick wax better, and it won't cut down on your speed since it's covered by kick wax anyway. For example, if you are working on classic skis you intend to use in dry powder and you are going to sand them to 600 grit, leave the kick zone alone after you've finished sanding with 300.

Next, buff the bases vigorously with Fiber Tex, an abrasive pad available from Swix (or under a generic name at the hardware store). Pay special attention to the edges of the ski where the bottom meets the sidewall. Alpine skiers are paranoid about their edges. They file and use fine whetstones until their knuckles are bloody in order to get their edges razor sharp. Then they take emery paper and soften the razor edge to make it faster!

With the advent of skating, some of this fanaticism about edges makes sense for us when you consider how much time you spend on your edges during a skating race. Sometimes a burr or overhang of the base material is created during the manufacture of cross-country skis. In some cases all that's necessary to remove this burr is energetic buffing with Fiber Tex. In more severe cases it might be necessary to carefully run a sharp scraper or knife the length of the sidewall. This procedure should be followed by buffing with Fiber Tex. The final test is to run your thumb and forefinger down the length of the ski, feeling a smooth sharp edge free of fibers, nicks, or imperfections. Considering the excellent mechanical grooming common today, if you have to choose between an especially sharp, hard edge and a smooth, softened edge, I would favor the latter.

Once you have the bases perfectly smooth, flat, and free of imperfections, it's time to start waxing. You need an iron; a nice, old rummage-sale clothes iron with no steam holes works best. To season or condition new bases, pick a soft, warm snow wax — Toko yellow, Swix orange, or something like that. Most wax companies offer Alpine base wax or base prep wax, but I haven't had much experience with either. Set your iron at a temperature that will melt the wax but not cause it to smoke profusely (this varies with the wax). Hold the block of wax against the bottom of the hot iron and drip the melting wax along the ski base. Next, slide the iron along the base of the ski, melting the wax into a thin even film. Keep the iron moving, since even a short hesitation with a moderately hot iron can cause internal damage to the foam cores of many racing skis. Iron for several minutes, heating the melted wax into the base. Use the tip of the iron to melt wax in the groove (or grooves) of the ski. Set the first ski aside and wax the second one. In waxing skating skis, follow the procedure described above, but for classic skis leave the kick-wax zone bare or you will have trouble later getting your kick wax to adhere.

Now go back to your first ski, which has dried and cooled. Clamp it in the vise and scrape tip to tail with a *plastic* scraper. You can (and should) sharpen your plastic scraper the same way as the metal scraper, but the purpose here is to remove excess wax, not scrape off more of the base material. Scrape assertively, however, because the melted wax contains residue from your sanding and other impurities that you want to get rid of. Brush the ski with a nylon- or brass-bristle brush if you like, then follow the same procedure with the second ski.

You can follow this sequence as many times as you have patience for. Three or four repetitions is probably standard, but the more wax you get into the bases, the faster they will be.

In 1977, while teaching and coaching in Anchorage, I was selected as head coach of the Alaskan contingent to the Junior National Cross-Country Championships. The first task was to name a coaching staff for the thirty-six athletes on the Alaska Divisional Team. One of the coaches I selected was Floyd Reishus, a quiet, unassuming man who worked hard and had developed a reputation as a good waxer. In Fairbanks, Alaska, that translates into careful base preparation, since waxing itself is pretty straightforward: the coldest wax you have in your kit! Floyd's Eielson high school team competed on about a dozen pair of Epoke skis that Floyd had bought on a special deal partly because Epokes were not then regarded as being especially fast skis. (In fact, many high school skiers derisively referred to them as "Slowpokes.")

Athletes and coaches congregated in Fairbanks for the Junior Nationals and we went to work. I put Floyd in charge of wax testing but reserved the right to oversee his tests and make the final wax decisions myself. We worked along with several other coaches in the days preceding the races to zero in on the fastest possible combinations for our Alaskan team. An unsettling trend began to emerge. No matter which wax was being tested, no matter which coach rode the skis down the test hill, Floyd's Epokes always took the honors. Among the rest of the coaching staff we had all the major brands represented; my own skis were Fischers I had used in the 1976 Olympics. But Floyd's Epokes kept coming out ahead, sometimes by a lot. Floyd just smiled contentedly and recorded the results.

It became clear that we weren't testing wax as much as we were testing base preparation. We restricted our tests to the several pairs of Epokes Floyd had brought with him. I asked, "Floyd, how did you get those skis so fast?"

He smiled and answered, "Waxing and scraping, waxing and scraping, waxing and scraping . . ."

Word spread to our athletes, and they lined up every evening to have Floyd work on their skis. He probably got less than four hours of sleep a night for the ten days of the Championships. But our team was invincible that year, with several individual champions and the overall team trophy. The most significant victory was probably the boys' relay. The Alaska A Team not only whipped the teams from other regions of the United States, they also beat an impressive team of all-stars from across Canada. Floyd Reishus deserves much of the credit for the success. The lesson I learned from him was that if you want really fast racing skis, there are no shortcuts: You must put in your time waxing and scraping.

At this point skating skis are ready to go, but if you're working on classic skis, you have one more step: binder underfoot. Binder is a hard wax that comes in a tin rather than a tube and is used to help other, colder, kick waxes adhere to your ski. I consider binder (also called gundvalder or gundevax) good insurance in all but very short races in light, fluffy powder snow. It has to be carefully applied, however, or it can be slow.

Heat the business end of the binder in the flame of a torch until it looks shiny, then dab it on your kick zone with a twisting motion. A touch every couple of inches on both sides of the groove should do it. Next, with the torch in one hand and a clean piece of rag in the other, heat and smooth the binder into the base. Keep the torch moving to avoid burning the ski. Work from the rear of your kick zone, below the heel plate, forward. If you inadvertently drag the binder forward out of the kick zone, it's less significant than if you drag it back of the heel plate. Once you've heated a smooth layer of binder throughout the kick zone, take another pass with your torch and rag to wipe off the excess. What should remain on the ski is a tacky film—no globs or lumps—that adheres to your finger about like Scotch tape. Once the binder cools, you can cork hard wax on top of it. A binder job like this could last one race or several weeks depending upon snow conditions. As long as your kick wax hasn't worn off, you can keep adding to it, but if your bases are bare after a long workout or race, you probably need more binder.

Keeping your skis strapped together bottom to bottom helps protect the bases from scratches and gouges in transit. The most common method of holding skis together in this position used to be with an elastic or Velcro ski strap at the binding. Recently, straps have become available for the tips and tails with a pad to keep the ski bases from scraping against each other. Holding the skis together tip and tail helps to preserve their camber.

Those who are really conscientious about their skis "travel wax" them between races. This means simply ironing in a coat of glide wax to protect the bottoms from dirt, dust, scratches, and drying out between races. It is important to travel wax your skis before you put them away for the summer.

Make sure your name is plainly written on your skis, as well as all your other equipment. Indelible Magic Marker works fine. It will help you find them in a crowd, such as the one at the finish line of the Birkie, or will help a coach who is waxing skis while you are out warming up.

Waxing

Now that you have selected the best equipment your budget will allow and have spent hours preparing the fastest bases in skiing history, it's time for the most mystifying and perhaps the most terrifying aspect of Nordic skiing—waxing! After years of careful observation and experimentation, I have determined that expertise in waxing consists of 25 percent technology, 25 percent experience, 25 percent psychology, and 25 percent luck! I can contribute a couple of paragraphs on the technology and the psychology, but as for the other two components, you're on your own.

Like many other aspects of cross-country, waxing used to be relatively straightforward. There were one or two well-known Scandinavian companies that produced ski wax. Each company made a relatively hard wax for dry snow that was rubbed on the ski bottom and smoothed with a cork. For wet snow or ice there was klister, a very sticky, gooey concoction that came in tubes. It was designed to provide grip for kick, yet release for glide. Klister was smoothed onto the ski base from tip to tail with the help of a wooden spreader (or a thumb) and a torch. That was it!

Then things began to get complicated. With the advent of fiberglass racing skis, coaches and competitors realized that the skis' gliding speed could be an overwhelming advantage. Previously, racers had focused on finding a wax that provided enough kick but wouldn't drag or ice up. By 1976 racers had learned to restrict kick wax to an eighteen-inch pocket underfoot and to wax the tips and tails with Alpine wax to increase speed. At one point racers were herringboning even the slightest uphill rather than slow down their glide with too much kick wax.

Marty Hall, head coach of the U.S. Nordic Ski Team during the 1970s, deserves much of the credit (or blame) for the increased complexity of cross-country waxing. Prior to the 1976 Olympics in Innsbruck, while the conservative Scandinavians were still waxing with the time-tested methods used on wooden skis, Marty hired Rob Kiesel as an assistant coach. Rob was from Sun Valley, Idaho, had a strong background in Alpine racing, and knew almost nothing about cross-country. But Rob knew Alpine waxing, and at Innsbruck his job was clear-cut: find the fastest glide wax possible before each cross-country competition. Rob didn't even fuss with kick waxes; he left that to Marty or the other more experienced cross-country coaches. Before dawn every race day, Rob would check thermometers and wax dozens of identical test skis with various combinations of glide wax. By plotting temperatures of previous days hour by hour, he could predict with some accuracy the temperature, snow condition, and thus the fastest glide wax for race time several hours away.

Most informed observers would acknowledge that the Americans had consistently fast skis during the 1976 Olympics; perhaps, as a team, the fastest. In fact, to a significant extent, Bill Koch's spectacular silver-medal performance in the 30K event can be credited to Rob Kiesel's skill with glide wax. The course was twice around a fifteen-kilometer loop that climbed up onto a plateau, then roared for almost four kilometers back to the stadium in the valley. It was said that at twenty-five kilometers Bill was slightly behind Ivan Garanin of the USSR, but in the final descent, thanks to his aggressive downhill technique and Kiesel's fast glide wax, he pulled ahead of Garanin by twelve seconds for the silver medal.

Since that time the variety of available waxes and the complexity of their application has become staggering! Even the handful of full-time professional wax technicians employed by the major companies probably can't keep up with the explosion of products. And a troubling element has surfaced: cost. It used to be that a racer or coach might outwax their opponents by innovative selection, skillful application, or wise anticipation of changing weather conditions. Now races are being won on wax so exotic and expensive that it is beyond the means of many competitors. Some of these new waxes are so effective that to be without them in a race where others have them is to admit defeat in advance. It is a concern that will generate debate in the coming years.

Glide Wax

Is it possible to make sense out of the current state of cross-country waxing? Let's give it a shot, beginning with glide, or speed, wax. The first step in determining which glide wax to use is to listen to a reliable weather forecast. A small, battery-operated weather-band radio has been indispensable to me, since the recorded National Weather Service forecast is more detailed than the weather report on most commercial stations.

Many racers anticipate race-day weather and wax the night before. They often have the flexibility of several pairs of skis and can wax one pair on the colder side of the predicted temperature range and another on the warmer side. When they arrive at the race site, they take the snow and air temperatures, warm up a little on both pairs of skis, project what the snow will be like during the race, and pick the pair to race on. If you have only one pair of skis to race on, you could wax the night before if weather and snow conditions have been pretty consistent, but if the weather has been variable, you should probably wait until the morning of the race. One positive note about glide waxes is their relatively wide temperature ranges. With kick wax, if you misjudge the temperature or consistency of the snow by just a little, you may end up slipping hopelessly or icing up so badly you become a permanent terrain feature on the course. In contrast, most Alpine waxes are pretty forgiving, within reasonable ranges.

Once you've selected a wax, you iron it onto the base as described earlier in the chapter. Most of the readily available glide waxes are paraffin-based hydrocarbons, which means they melt at low temperatures and scrape easily with a plastic scraper. In general, for cold snow conditions you should scrape and buff vigorously, removing all superficial traces of the wax. For warm, wet snow conditions, scrape excess wax off but don't be afraid to leave a visible film, which you will be able to texture with brushes or a riller.

Texture is another important aspect of glide waxing. Some time ago it was learned that as the snow temperature rises and the crystals become more rounded, a smooth-bottomed ski creates a suction effect, which is slowing. A rougher-textured base breaks the water suction, hence a faster ski. To produce texture, racers at first just brushed the waxed bottoms with stiff nylon bristles. Then someone got really assertive and scratched the heck out of his skis with a stiff wire brush. The ultimate step (for a while) was holding a mill bastard file on edge, perpendicular to the ski, and dragging it forcefully the length of the base in one smooth motion. This carved scores of tiny, longitudinal grooves in the base of the ski, which added dramatically to the speed in very wet snow. Now, specialized brushes and rillers (tools that make tiny grooves) are available from the wax companies. The consensus appears to be that the warmer and wetter the snow, the more structure is necessary in the base.

A few specific examples might clarify this principle. If I were racing on cold, hard snow at about 0°F, I would select P-Tex-based skis, sanded and scraped very smooth. I would choose a wax like Start green or Rex green (both very good in cold, dry snow) and iron it in well. Both of these waxes are very hard and brittle, so you must scrape each ski immediately while the wax is still warm or it will tend to chip off rather than scrape smoothly. After carefully using a plastic scraper, I would buff the ski vigorously with fine Fiber Tex.

After the skis had been in the snow for a few minutes during my warm-up, I would buff them again to really polish the bottoms. Cold weather equals smooth skis.

If it were 24°F and snowing, I wouldn't have a strong preference in base material, choosing whichever felt faster. I would probably wax with Swix violet, ironing it in well. I would scrape with a plastic scraper, then brush from tip to tail with long, smooth strokes, using stiff nylon bristles. The skis are ready to go after particles of wax cease to appear as a result of the brushing. For these conditions I would want to keep the microscopic grooves created by the brush, so I wouldn't buff with Fiber Tex.

Finally, for spring snow in warm weather — let's say it's warming well above the freezing point, and the snow is wet, old, and dirty — I would choose black-bottom skis. If yours are factory rilled, so much the better; if not, lock them firmly in your vise and rill them. The wetter the snow, the bigger and deeper the rills need to be. Brush the skis well to clean out the rills, then melt on glide wax. I would probably choose Ski*Go C-242 mixed half and half with Ski*Go antistatic graphite. To mix waxes, hold both sticks against the bottom of a hot iron and drip the melting combination onto the ski base. Iron in the wax for a couple of minutes. Scraping in this case should be done somewhat delicately, because you don't want to scrape the peaks off the tiny rills in the base. Finally, brush vigorously from tip to tail with long, smooth strokes to clean excess wax from the valleys of the rills.

There you have the basics of base structuring. Remember, it is not an exact science; these techniques have emerged as a result of trial and error. Don't be afraid to experiment with base texture.

A ski actually rides on a film of water created by the friction of the moving base over the snow surface. It might be logical to assume, then, that as more of the ski passes over the same crystals of snow, the friction and heat would increase, producing more water. In other words, because of the friction the ski generates, the first few inches of the tip would be traveling over relatively dry snow, while the last few inches of the tail would slide over wetter snow. If this is true (and I don't know that it is), it might make sense to structure the leading part of the ski with tiny rills but use large, deep rills from the binding back. I suppose you could take it the final step and wax the tail of the ski warmer. Give it a try!

It would be wonderful if this were all there was to glide waxing — check the snow, select a wax, and create an appropriate base structure. Unfortunately, it has become quite a bit more complex. First of all, there are additives that can significantly change or improve the performance of standard glide wax. Swix currently carries three of them. Speed granulate comes in the form of tiny black pellets, very much like gunpowder, and is designed to expand the temperature range of the glide wax selected, especially in low humidity. It also performs well in dirty snow. Silicone additive improves wax performance in wet snow and can be used alone in *very* wet snow. Since it is soft and has a low melting point, it is a good choice for preparing new skis. Graphite is used as an additive when snow is dirty and can be used alone for wet dirty snow.

Ski*Go, the Swedish company that emerged during the 1988 season and produced some impressive results at the Calgary Olympics, does not market any of its waxes as "additives." It is understood, however, that the antistatic graphite in candle form is intended to be mixed with other waxes to improve durability and repel dirt, although it can be used alone in some conditions.

Scioline Solda is a line of Italian gliders in flake form (much like laundry detergent) that became readily available for the first time during the 1990 season. Solda Cold Weather Additive is intended to be sprinkled and ironed on top of a waxed and scraped ski to improve speed in cold, dry snow.

Also available is a new generation of exotic, very expensive antifriction compounds. I'm not sure that technically they are even waxes. The first to appear several years ago is currently known as Cera F. It is a fluorocarbon powder (not a petroleum product) that was developed in Italy and was simply unbeatable in new snow warming from $-4°C$ through $4°C$. It was so successful that Swix, the world's leading ski-wax manufacturer, bought the rights to produce and market the product. It initially sold for about one hundred dollars an ounce, enough to wax four pairs of skis, if you were careful. The advantage provided by Cera F in that limited temperature range was so dramatic that Swix used the name Cera for their entire 1990 glide-wax line.

Aside from the exorbitant price, there was another concern with Cera F. Fluorocarbon gliders have a much higher melting point than hydrocarbons, so ironing Cera F onto a bare ski bottom would almost certainly bubble the base material or severely damage the foam core of most racing skis. The procedure that emerged was to first use a conventional wax on the bottom (at a moderate setting on the iron) and then iron the Cera F into that wax. This solved two problems at once: it provided a slightly sticky base to which the grains of Cera F could adhere, and it helped dissipate the high heat necessary to melt the Cera F. When the Cera F dries to a chalky powder, it is lightly brushed (the real pros designate a special horsehair brush to be used for Cera F only).

Ski*Go, an innovator from the start, came out with its own fluorocarbon compound called C-44, with the same temperature range as Cera F and the same application procedure. But Ski*Go didn't stop there. It marketed a Teflon-based compound that consists of tiny particles suspended in a quick-drying fluid. The result is a lotion that, after vigorous shaking, is smoothed on the ski like finger painting, allowed to dry, then ironed. Like Cera F, C-280 requires a hot iron and therefore is best applied over a conventional wax.

C-280 has a very impressive temperature range and is especially fast in new fine-grained or packed snow. Another Ski*Go product is New Fluid Silicone, a silicone-based fluid for warm, wet conditions that dries quickly and does not require ironing.

There's more. The U.S. Biathlon Team returned from Central Europe on a 1990 World Cup tour carrying back word of "new stuff" over there! Cera F type stuff, not just for the −4°C to 4°C range, but for all conditions. It's a powder that looks like confectioners sugar and comes in small, nondescript plastic bottles with labels reading MO 50, MU 30, SP6 pur, SP6, or M9-2. It's produced by a chemist in West Germany, and its cost makes Cera F seem cheap! But according to the biathletes returning from the World Cup races, you simply can't win if you don't have it.

By the time you read this, that will probably be old news; things are happening so quickly in the waxing area of Nordic skiing. But the basic principles of selection, application, and structuring should remain valid for a while, at least.

Experience is an important factor in successful waxing that is nebulous and subjective at best, but over the years, under extremely varied conditions, athletes and coaches begin to develop preferences that appear to work well for them time and again. (One caution: Elite athletes may get some waxes for free and therefore have more experience with that brand than with others.) The following are some of my favorites, along with a few others you may want to try.

• For cold, hard snow, cold powder snow, or cold windblown snow, nothing seems better than Start green from Finland. It is very hard, brittle wax requiring a hot iron and scraping while it is still warm (almost fluid). The warmer Start waxes, blue and violet, are also good, but not dramatically better than anything else the way the green is.

• Rex green and Rex blue are fast gliders when the temperature is warming out of Start green range. All the Rex waxes are extremely durable, so for abrasive snow or an especially long race in cold temperatures, Rex is a good choice.

• In the middle temperature ranges up to freezing, Swix is always reliable. Combinations of Swix violet, orange, and speed powder are frequently among the best. If I had to limit my wax selection to one company exclusively, it would probably be Swix.

• I have had limited experience with Solda, but the few times I have used it, I was impressed. The orange is tremendous for conditions around the freezing point and is an excellent base for Cera F.

• Hype and expense aside, in its temperature range Cera F does make a significant difference.

• Ski*Go C-242 plus antistatic graphite is a great combination in old hard-packed, reworked, or even man-made snow that is warming through the freezing point. It has a wide temperature range and is durable.

• Toko wax (from Switzerland) has traditionally been very strong in warm, wet conditions, although I'm not familiar with their latest system. There was a time when nothing would beat Toko red and yellow in spring snow.

• Many coaches and racers include Briko gliders in their wax boxes. I've had very limited experience with them, but it would make sense to try some out.

It's not a complete list, and skiers in various parts of the country may not have the same results that we have here in New England. Asking a racer why he favors a certain wax can sometimes be like asking a motorist why he drives a Ford rather than a Chevy. But my experience might give you a good starting point from which to experiment.

Kick Wax

Once your glide wax is ironed, scraped, and brushed, if you are working on classic skis, its time to go to work on kick wax. In skating all you need to worry about is making your skis go fast, but classic involves both kicking and gliding. This is what used to scare people away from cross-country skiing and was the motivation behind fish-scale and other no-wax bases. But now kick waxing seems pretty straightforward compared with what is going on with gliders.

As I mentioned in the section on base preparation, I'm a big fan of binder, even if there is only a remote chance of the kick wax wearing off. I prefer Rex binder, which, like all Rex waxes, is durable — precisely why you use binder in the first place. It's helpful to mark the kick zone of the ski with an indelible marker, although markings are printed on most P-Tex based bottoms. Heat the binder carefully into the P-Tex, using a rag to smooth it out. If you iron the binder in, you risk contaminating your next glide-wax application with its sticky residue.

Once again, the weather, snow conditions, and temperature dictate your selection. In general, if the snow is new or unthawed, you will be using hard wax in tins. The normal procedure is to select a wax, rub it on the ski, and cork it smooth, either with the traditional block of cork or the modern Styrofoam equivalent. For a typical race in dry snow, three or four thin coats of wax, each polished to a shine with the cork, will probably work fine. If you test the wax and it slips, you have three choices: add more of the same wax to produce a thicker layer; lengthen the kick zone, usually toward the tip of the ski; or move up to a warmer wax. If you are really fine-tuning your kick wax in dry snow, try the first two options before going to the third, since the warmer wax will almost certainly be slower. If your wax is solid on the flats but still a little slippery on the hills, try adding a warmer wax on just the inside half of the ski base, rather than the entire width of the ski. When you climb hills, most of your weight ends up on the inside edges of the skis; thus you will have additional kick precisely where you need it with only minimal drag. You can apply the same principle if you are slipping badly late in a classic race. Stop and switch your skis from one foot to the other. The inside edges, where the wax is probably worn completely off, are now on the outside, and any kick wax that might remain is inside where you can use it.

The concept behind kick wax is basically simple: The wax conforms to the snow crystals when weight is applied down on the ski but slides over them when the ski is driven over the snow. This means hard wax for cold, hard snow crystals and soft, pliable wax for worn, rounded snow crystals. If you want to get really sophisticated with your kick waxing in dry powder snow, try this. Select a wax slightly warmer than you think necessary. For example, if you think the conditions call for Swix green, rub on a couple layers of Swix special blue. Then cover it with a wax you know would be too cold to use on its own, Swix special green, for example. The theory is that the softer wax creates a "cushion" that will provide the necessary kick, but the colder, harder wax on top will be faster. Sometimes this technique works great; sometimes it's better to keep it simple and just go with what you think is the wax of the day.

Anytime you are skiing on snow that has melted or has melted and refrozen, you will probably need to use klister. Klister has a bad reputation because it is frightfully sticky and ends up everywhere: all over your hands, your clothes, door knobs, the steering wheel, and so on. But it is amazing stuff: it enables you to ski, often with "mule kick," in everything from slush to blue ice!

When you anticipate waxing with klister, here are a few hints that will preserve your sanity. Be sure to have an adequate supply of rags—it's easy to go through a lot of them in a prerace wax panic. You'll need a torch or, if electricity is nearby, one of those heat guns designed to strip paint off houses. Hand cleaner and solvent make cleanup a lot easier. Lay out all the klisters you might use where they will be accessible; you don't want to be digging through your wax box later with klister all over your hands, and this also keeps any "wax spies" from knowing which one you are using. Always replace the cap on a tube immediately after use. If a tube is left open, you could return after your race to find it gluing everything in your wax box permanently together. Once you have opened a tube of klister, don't replace it in the cardboard box. Nothing is worse than a last-minute wax panic when you open a klister box thinking you have a full tube, to find instead a twisted, crumpled, almost empty tube. Finally, take the time to carefully roll the tube up from the end as you use it. At five to seven dollars per tube, it's worth it to get every bit you can out of the container.

Selecting the right klister is really where experience comes in and (although it may sound silly) reading the instructions on the box. If you read more than English, you have an advantage since some of the directions lose a lot in translation. The only sure method is to put samples of various waxes on test skis and go try them out. Keep in mind that some skiers require more kick from their wax, while others have the finesse to nurse grippy skis through relatively dry snow without icing up hopelessly. If you are waxing for others, let them do the testing. Once you are in the ballpark, you can fine-tune your selection — longer kick zone to give better grip, thinner coat of klister to speed things up, a little silver mixed in to help repel dirt.

The application of klister isn't difficult if the wax is warm to begin with. Putting the tubes you think you'll need over the defroster vents on the dashboard of your car works great, as does sticking a tube in the exhaust pipe of an idling vehicle. Don't let it get too hot, though, because runny klister is more difficult to handle than cold klister. Dot the klister the length of the kick zone. The size and frequency of the dots determine the thickness of the wax once it's smoothed out. Most klisters come with a plastic spreader, but you will have better control with your thumb. With a torch or heat gun, warm the wax and smooth it into an even layer. Be careful not to drag it back behind the heel plate or too far forward. Place the skis somewhere out of the way to cool. If it's warm weather and you are using red, silver, or the equivalent, lay your skis down to cool or the klister will drip the entire length of the ski. Try to keep your choice simple and concentrate on applying it carefully. When I listen to someone mention after a race that they skied on "Rode red and silver with a little Rex OV underfoot, covered with Swix extra red corked in," it sounds to me like a guy who couldn't make up his mind.

There are times, however, when hard wax over klister is just the answer: an icy track with a dusting of new powder snow, for example. The procedure here is to apply the klister (in this example, blue skare), then let it cool completely. On top of the cold klister, rub and cork the hard wax appropriate for the powder snow. The underlying skare provides the grip on the icy track, while the hard wax on top keeps the skare from sticking. A method that works even better is to "rag on" hard wax. It's tricky and requires practice, coordination, and concentration, but it permits you to apply a thicker layer of hard wax much smoother than is possible by corking.

Once again it was Sven Johanson whom I first saw demonstrate this technique. First he took a small piece of clean rag (an old piece of T-shirt works fine) and taped it around the end of a plastic Swix stick. Then he waved the business end of the hard wax in front of a torch flame until it glazed. He vigorously rubbed the softened wax on the kick zone of the ski, appearing to gob it on much too thick. Then, with the finesse of a surgeon, torch in one hand and rag-covered Swix stick in the other, he heated and painted the melted hard wax into a shiny, smooth layer. His hands were perfectly coordinated in a rhythmic, sweeping motion. There are several advantages to this procedure. You can apply a thicker layer of hard wax than is possible by corking. This is critical for long races or abrasive snow conditions. And since you can apply a thick layer but keep it smooth, you can often go with a colder wax, thereby having faster skis without sacrificing kick. Finally, it is the best way to cover klister with hard wax. It is also the most dangerous method of applying wax, in terms of potential damage to your skis. Practice a few times on some rock skis before you rag hard wax on your favorite racing boards.

If you are waxing a large number of skiers — a club or a team — you can save time and wax and produce a smoother wax job by painting it on. You'll need a small camp stove, pliers, a couple of coffee cans, and some throwaway paint brushes (not more than two inches wide). Untwist the crimped bottom of the klister tube. Using the pliers, hold the tube over the heat until the softened contents slide out into your coffee can. Concoct the mixture you want; it's easy to mix waxes with this method. Holding the coffee can over the stove with the pliers, heat your mixture until it is completely fluid and well blended. Then simply paint the fluid klister on the ski bottoms. Paint from the heel plate

To "rag on" hard wax, the torch must move deliberately to melt the wax but quickly enough to avoid burning the ski. The rag must follow close behind to smooth the molten wax.

forward so that if you have to make any steps in the wax job, they will serve to break the suction, rather than drag. Don't allow the wax to get so hot that it smokes or let the brush touch the bottom of the can (the bristles may burn and become a frizzy mess). Lay the waxed skis flat, bases up, for a few minutes to cool. You get a nice, smooth klister job that can be done by assembly line in record time.

The final klister tip is pretty exotic and may be necessary only once or twice in a racer's career. But on those few occasions when nothing else works, this technique might spell the difference between a smashing victory and a very frustrating slog through the snow. Without question, the most challenging snow conditions for a cross-country racer occur on those days when the temperature is 32°F and it's snowing. Heavy, wet new-fallen snow can be slick and sticky at the same time. A diagonal racetrack becomes glazed after a few skiers have passed, and hard wax offers no grip. But the newly fallen snow crystals stick to klister, causing the icing up that cross-country racers dread. To make these difficult conditions impossible, add a racecourse that climbs significantly in elevation. On a typical winter day a 500-foot increase in elevation can translate into a drop of a few degrees in temperature. Although a klister wax might work well in the glazed tracks on the valley floor at 34°F, the same wax will ice up hopelessly at the high point of the course where the temperature is 28°F and it is snowing steadily.

Here is Sven Johanson's technique for such conditions. Select a klister designed for newly fallen wet snow: Swix or Rode yellow, or Rex OI. Then carefully dot the klister down the kick zone on either side of the groove, a couple of inches between dots. With the ball of your thumb, smudge the dots into flat "islands" on the ski base. Let the wax cool as you normally would. The klister will give you the kick you need on the glazed track, and it *will* tend to ice, especially on uphills where the snow is churned, but rather than icing up in a hopeless block eighteen inches long under your foot, it will ice in small dots. Then a couple of good forward slaps of the ski will usually break off any accumulated snow. It's a delicate application that raises waxing to an art form, but I've seen it work where everything else failed.

Bill Koch also deserves credit for a major breakthrough in these same impossible waxing conditions. He may not have been the inventor, but he was the first one gutsy enough to use this innovation in a major race. The scene was the 1976 Olympics in Innsbruck. Kochie was riding high on the unprecedented success of his silver medal in the 30K and a very strong finish in the 15K. The rest of the American team had caught his enthusiasm, and optimism abounded for the 4 × 10K Olympic relay. The day of the event was ominous, 32°F and snowing. Coaches and athletes scrambled desperately for a wax combination that would give some kick on the glazed tracks in the valley but not ice up hopelessly where the trail climbed the hills. Most athletes preferred to slip on the flats rather than ice up on the climbs.

Bill had been experimenting with an idea for just these conditions. Taking a pair of practice skis with the kick zone carefully marked out, he cut away the P-Tex base and replaced it with strips of mohair fabric. He sprayed this kick zone with silicone and tried the skis out. To his delight, he discovered the mohair strips provided decent grip in wet or glazed snow. The silicone allowed reasonable glide, and since there was nothing sticky on the bottom, the skis didn't ice up. But these skis had never proved their worth in competition. They might kick for only a kilometer or two before wearing out, or they might ice up after the silicone wore off.

American coaches and Nordic skiers not participating in the relay stationed themselves at various strategic points on the course. Along with a couple of biathlon teammates, I stood midway up the most significant climb on the loop. It was clear throughout the first two legs that wax was an issue. Racers struggled up the hill muscling slippery skis with arm power or frantically tried to break ice loose as they crested. Competitors bunched up single file in the tracks, determined not to step out into the softer snow, which would make icing a certainty. As the third-leg skiers approached the base of the hill, Bill Koch was the caboose of the train. When the leaders began to struggle with the climb, Kochie simply stepped into the loose snow beside the track and bounded past. The other racers and spectators gaped in disbelief as he crested the hill and glided back toward the stadium. Bill turned in the fastest lap of the third-leg skiers and moved the American team from eighth to third place in the process. His success was due not only to his world-class technique and conditioning but also to his courage in gambling on an untested waxless ski.

Until recently there were only three major brands of kick wax available in this country: Swix from Norway, Rex from Finland, and Rode from Italy. Ski*Go from Sweden has released a line of hard waxes, but I haven't yet used them enough to develop an opinion. If they reflect the same high quality and innovation as the Ski*Go gliders, however, they should be great.

Swix is probably the common denominator of cross-country skiing. If a ski shop is going to carry only one line of wax, it will probably be Swix. I'm sure they sell more cross-country wax than any other company, perhaps more than all other companies combined. Swix has developed a selection of kick waxes that covers any imaginable snow condition in increments of every few degrees of temperature. If you were to work with one brand of wax exclusively, this should probably be it.

Rex has not invested the time and money in marketing that Swix has, but it is excellent wax. Its most outstanding characteristic is its durability. If you waxed one ski with Swix Skare (for cold, icy tracks) and the other with Rex

Skare, then set out to ski the wax off, the Rex would still be kicking long after the Swix was gone. This seems to be true with most Rex waxes.

I have always felt that Rode wax is generally faster than Swix or Rex. In any given temperature range or snow condition, it might not give the kick that Swix does and it's not as durable as Rex, but it will be faster. If I'm racing fifteen kilometers on cold, new-fallen snow where abrasion is not a problem and Rode green gives adequate kick, I know I will be faster than my opponents who select Swix green.

Earlier in this chapter I mentioned glide waxes that have become my favorites. Keeping in mind that this is purely subjective, here is a similar list of kick waxes I have come to trust over the years.

• Rex binder (or gundevax) in the orange tin is the only thing you'll need for binder.

• Swix Polar is great for those occasional days when it's −10°F or there is windblown snow that feels like sand (or if you ski in Fairbanks or Lake Placid a lot).

• Rode special green and Rode green are great waxes for cold, dry snow.

• Rode blue is absolutely my favorite wax. It seems to have a wide temperature range and it is always fast!

• Rode Multigrade is similar to Swix blue Extra but faster.

• Swix Special red is a great "last step" hard wax for moist snow before going to klister. It resists icing better than the old red.

• Rex Skare (blue) is the only klister you'll ever need for cold, abrasive icy tracks. It will stay on all winter!

• Rex OI and OV klisters are excellent for wet, icy, and changeable conditions.

• Swix yellow klister was the first developed for falling or new-fallen wet snow around 32°F—a major breakthrough in the early 1970s.

• Rode red and silver klisters make one of the best combinations for very wet spring snow. The red gives great kick, while the silver speeds up the skis and helps resist dirt and pine needles in the track.

• Rode Nera is a dark brown klister that is great for *very* wet conditions, such as skiing through puddles.

I opened this discussion of waxing by dividing it into four areas: technology, experience, psychology, and luck. You now have a decent handle on the technology although, as I mentioned, things are changing fast. As far as luck, many psychologists and positive-thinking advocates will tell you that you make your own. I believe that is true to a large degree, but there is always an unpredictable element, especially in waxing. There are simply too many variables for any coach or racer to cover completely. So be prepared for those happy occasions when your educated guesses on temperature, weather, and snow conditions pan out and you really nail the wax. But don't brood too long over mistakes in judgment that caused your wax to be slow, stick, or ice up. Anyone who has raced for a while has "blown the wax." It's one of the bonds that join Nordic racers together.

On the topic of experience, my suggestion is to dig in and try waxing. Don't be afraid to experiment. If you are really organized, keep a waxing notebook and record your impressions of various waxes in different conditions. Before long you will develop favorites and have a sense of when they will work for you. If you are starting from scratch, you might be wise to stick with one brand of wax and really learn it. Swix is probably the most complete in terms of glide and kick waxes, the instructions are clearly translated, and they are readily available anywhere. Ski*Go may be a little more exciting and innovative if you are daring. Once you feel confident with the waxes in one brand, you can begin experimenting with specialty waxes for specific situations and see how they stack up against what you have been using. Accumulating this experience takes time, so be patient.

The final component to successful waxing is psychology. Countless races have been won or lost because competitors *thought* they had great or terrible wax that day. Wax is a very subjective aspect of Nordic skiing. What seems lightning fast at the start may wear off or slow down as the temperature rises. A kick wax that seems hopelessly slow at the start may provide "mule kick" on a critical uphill and thus be the best selection. "Bad wax" seems to be a catchall for a wide variety of disappointing performances.

I believe it is critically important to develop confidence in your waxing ability and a positive attitude toward your wax every time you race. If you get in the starting gate thinking "These skis are slow," you are in for a long, disappointing competition. Be creative in your self-talk. If your skis didn't test out especially fast prior to the race, convince yourself they will improve as the wax wears in, the snow gets churned up, or the temperature changes. Remind yourself that your skis are probably as good as or better than your opponents'. When you talk, think, argue, and brainstorm with friends before and after races, keep waxing in perspective. Sure it's a factor, but does it really deserve all the "air time" we give it? In the final analysis, is waxing more significant to success than mental training, for example? I don't think so.

If you are visibly confident and upbeat about waxing and seldom complain about your skis after a race, you create a psychological advantage. If you appear to enjoy waxing, your opponents assume you are good at it. If you never complain about slow skis, your opponents assume you always have fast skis. It's to your advantage to let them believe that you do, or better still, to confirm their suspicions.

The 1977 Junior National Cross-Country Championships were held in Fairbanks. Waxing in Fairbanks is probably the most straightforward in the nation: just wax the coldest stuff you've got! But coaches are usually more competitive than their athletes, and in the days before the first race, coaches from across the United States and Canada were gliding repeatedly down sections of the track to determine the fastest wax. I had noticed by then that people have loyalties to specific waxes and will try to win glide tests to demonstrate the superiority of their favorites. To eliminate this favoritism among our wax testers, I numbered the test skis rather than labeling them with the wax that was being tested, and gave each skier a wooden tongue depressor numbered to correspond with the skis they rode. We started our tests from precisely the same point on a slight downhill and marked where we stopped with the tongue depressors. (Since ski lengths differ, it is customary to mark these points at the toe of the boot.)

As the races approached, I knew we had a psychological advantage on the other teams. As the hosts we were familiar with the trails and more accustomed to the snow conditions. More than once, after we had finished wax testing, I had noticed other coaches carefully finding our starting mark in the snow beside the track, gliding down the hill, and trying to see how they fared against our test skis. I decided to make it easy for them (sort of). On the final day of training before the first race, I told all the Alaskan coaches to line the tips of their skis rather than the bindings with the starting point. I also asked them to mark their farthest glides by placing their tongue depressors next to the tips. When we finished our tests, I left the markers in the snow. Before long, visiting racers and coaches were testing their skis against our markers, all falling short because they were starting with the bindings rather than the ski tips next to the marker. Our wax during that week was as good as anyone else's, perhaps better than some, but what really mattered was that most of the other coaches and racers honestly believed we had some secret concoction that was giving us a tremendous advantage. The Alaskan team did have a wonderfully successful Championship—its finest for many years. This was not attributable to any secret wax but, mostly, to psychology.

10: The Birkebeiner

F OR THOSE SPORTS fans who are addicted to the smell of high-octane fuel and the deafening roar of powerful engines, the Indianapolis 500 is the ultimate event. If Thoroughbred racing is in your blood, the splendor and excitement of the Kentucky Derby is without equal. But for North American cross-country ski racers, the focal point of the season is the American Birkebeiner the last weekend of February. This race was the brainchild of a visionary midwestern developer named Tony Wise, who needed some type of event to publicize his Telemark Resort, located in remote northern Wisconsin. Over almost twenty years the race has grown to include more than six thousand competitors. That's quite an annual influx of people into the small north woods communities of Cable and Hayward. It's no longer just a big race; it's a week-long cross-country skiing festival involving several races. But the featured event remains the Birkie, a fifty-five-kilometer trek through the rolling moraines left by the last ice age.

The race is modeled after the original Norwegian Birkebeiner, which commemorates the rescue almost eight hundred years ago of Norway's infant king by two soldiers on skis. The Scandinavian race retraces the route taken by the rescuers over a mountain pass and inspired the point-to-point course in northern Wisconsin.

For years I had read about the Birkie and had seen photos of the sea of humanity surging down the main street of Hayward minutes after the start. More recently, as skiers I had coached at Dartmouth went on to jobs or graduate schools across the country, I received cards from Hayward with such messages as "Morty, I just survived the Birkie, unbelievable scene." But the date of the Birkie had always conflicted with the Eastern Intercollegiate Ski Championships, the most important eastern college race of the season. Dartmouth may have given me a leave of absence to help out at the Olympics or the World University Games, but missing the Eastern Intercollegiate Championships to compete in the nation's premier citizens' race would have been pushing my luck.

My departure from Dartmouth provided me with an open calendar, so one of my first steps was to send for an entry form to the Birkebeiner. Like many of the huge foot-running marathons, the Birkie is organized into wave starts according to a competitor's anticipated finish time or speed. Although seeding is not a big deal in most races, it could make a tremendous difference in the Birkie. With more than six thousand competitors skating the same route from Hayward to Cable, being seeded back in the pack of citizen racers and tourists would be comparable to Friday afternoon gridlock on a Los Angeles freeway. At the time the entry information was due, my most recent 50K result was from the 1974 National Championships. I attached a letter to the entry form explaining my situation. In the information they sent me, the organizers listed the pace times for the seven starting waves: wave one, up to 3:45 per kilometer; wave two, up to 4:31 per kilometer; and so on. From the shorter races I had entered over the years, I felt confident that a pace of 3:45 per kilometer was reasonable unless I ran into serious difficulty.

Max Cobb, who had been one of my Development Team skiers at Dartmouth, was in charge of the Domestic Race Series for the U.S. Biathlon Association. When Max offered to pay my expenses to the Birkie if I would help him with a biathlon demonstration and clinic, I jumped at the chance.

February 11 was the deadline for appealing seeding assignments. By that time I had three results, which I figured would help the Birkie officials assign me to the appropriate wave. My first race of the year had been the Lawrence Loppet in Lake Placid. Even though I had hit the wall on the last lap, my total time for the difficult forty-eight-kilometer course was 2:42:54, a pace of 3:24 per kilometer. In the White Mountain Marathon I had finished the rain-shortened twenty-six-kilometer course in 1:11:55, a pace of 2:45 per kilometer. On the day before the deadline I won my age group in the Masters National Championship 50K at Sun Valley, with a pace of 2:58.

When I arrived home from Sun Valley, awaiting me was a card confirming my entry in American Birkebeiner XVIII, starting in wave four! I fired off a letter that day to the organizers, enclosing my Sun Valley results.

On Thursday, February 22, I drove to the airport with Joe and Rob Walsh, two of America's top Nordic disabled skiers. Each has won World Championship medals in the sight-disabled category, and they would be representing the U.S. Disabled Team in the Birkie. I had coached Joe and Rob while they were students at Dartmouth. It was fun to switch roles with them; they were seasoned Birkebeiner veterans and clearly enjoyed filling me in on all the details of the race. One of the greatest joys of coaching is watching your athletes grow and mature.

We would be staying with the other biathletes on the domestic team in a hunting cabin/vacation home Max had rented for the weekend, but when we arrived the place was locked, so we drove on to the Telemark Lodge in Cable. It seemed like a convention of everyone in America who had ever cross-country skied! The main lodge was mobbed with competitors, coaches, race volunteers, officials, and representatives from scores of ski companies. It had the atmosphere of a county fair, with exhibits and booths everywhere and announcements for clinics, panel discussions, and demonstrations every few minutes. I had been to four Winter Olympics and several Biathlon World Championships, but never had I seen so much enthusiasm, excitement, and energy focused exclusively on cross-country. It took us almost an hour (with scores of minireunions) to move from the lobby to the second-floor restaurant. During our meal, three of my old buddies from Alaska came in: Dick Mize, Tom Corbin, and Dave Thomas. I had seen Dick in Sun Valley, where he cleaned house in his age group. Tom Corbin was my contemporary in the 40–44 age group. He was focusing on the Great American Ski Chase and had been training hard. He looked bigger and stronger than ever, and I knew he would be a tough competitor. I had coached Dave Thomas at Dimond High School in Anchorage and then again his senior year at Dartmouth. After starting a family, Dave was making a comeback on the racing scene.

After supper we went through the registration process. My entry verification card indicated I should see Donna in "Special Problems"— a beehive of activity where volunteers patiently listened to scores of "special situations." I showed Donna my registration card, and she broke into a big smile. "Oh, I have good news for you!" she said. "We're going to move you up to the third wave!" I was stunned. With more than one thousand competitors in each of the first two waves, that still put me hopelessly out of the running.

"You got my letter with my results?" I asked calmly.

"Oh yes! That's why we decided to move you up. Normally anyone who hasn't raced a Birkie before starts in the seventh wave."

"But what about your qualifying times?" I asked plaintively. "Wave one is supposed to contain racers capable of skiing three minutes and forty-five seconds per kilometer or better. I sent you results from this season that show I skied 3:24, 2:45, and 2.58 per kilometer!"

"Yes, I know," she responded more seriously, "but we only recognize qualifying times from previous Birkies or other Ski Chase events."

"Well, what about my White Mountain Marathon result?" I shot back.

"We can't accept that. It wasn't even thirty kilometers this year. Look, you're fortunate to be in the third wave; all the other first timers will be in the seventh!"

"I don't believe that!" I was getting frustrated and angry. "If some hotshot Scandinavian or Central European comes over for his first Birkie, I can't believe you'd start them in the seventh wave. Look, I'd never hassle you if I didn't have documented evidence of the pace I can ski. I'm the fifty-kilometer National Champion for my age, for crying out loud!"

Steel jaw, stony gaze, arms folded, and feet firmly planted, Donna had made her decision and nothing was going to change it.

"Is there anywhere I can appeal this seeding decision?" I asked, knowing I was already beaten.

"Nope," was all she said, standing like a rock until I turned and walked away.

Joe and Rob were both seeded in the first wave in deference to their positions on the National Disabled Team. Although both would probably ski faster than the 3:45 per kilometer, I felt confident I would be ahead of them. We walked together down the hall to pick up our entry packets, race instructions, souvenir programs, and competitor bibs. My frustration increased as I compared my start number, 7635, with theirs: 101 and 106.

Then I spotted John Kotar, chairman of the USSA National Masters Committee, who had hung four medals around my neck a couple of weeks earlier in Sun Valley. I cornered John and explained my predicament, asking if he would speak to Donna on my behalf. He agreed, but cautioned me not to be too optimistic. "They are mobbed with people who want to start in the first wave," he said, as he headed to "Special Problems." Not two minutes later he was back shaking his head.

Back at the "biathlon lodge" we reviewed assignments for Friday morning's demonstration and clinic. As we headed to bed, Max Cobb (fresh out of college and twenty years my junior) calmly said, "Don't worry about your start number, Morty; I'll straighten it out tomorrow." What a case of role reversal!

The biathlon demonstration was a big success. Hundreds of Nordic-skiing enthusiasts got a chance to experience firsthand the thrill and challenge of hitting these tiny, black targets as they appeared to dance around on the hillside.

As we finished loading the targets and fencing in the team van, Max approached me with a serious look on his face. "Morty, I talked with Donna about your start number. I'm afraid it doesn't look good. There are more than twelve hundred in the first wave already, and she's holding firm on your third-wave start position. Sorry, I did what I could."

"Thanks for trying, Max. Her mind seemed made up when I talked to her last night."

I had all but given up when I noticed a tent with Salomon banners around it. Like biathlon, several ski companies were capitalizing on the opportunity to reach such a large number of Nordic skiers. Their eastern salesman, Brad Sellew, had taken an interest in my racing comeback and had provided me with new boots and bindings. When I told Brad about the results in Sun Valley and my intentions to race the Birkie, he suggested I look up his midwestern counterpart and friend, Brad Weidt.

The Salomon tent was mobbed with curious racers and spectators. I found Weidt and introduced myself.

"Oh yeah, Sellew told me to keep an eye out for you. How's it going?"

I took the opportunity to give him a brief overview of my seeding dilemma.

"No sweat," he responded casually. "I'm a little busy here at the moment, but if you have the number they issued you, drop it off here. Sometime before two o'clock, I'll go see Linda and exchange it for one in the first wave."

"But, Brad, I've been around on this a couple of times already," I protested.

"Hey, John, no problem. Meet me here at two o'clock and I'll have your new number!"

I retrieved my entry packet including the starting bib from the biathlon van and left it with Brad, who was already surrounded with enthusiastic skiers clamoring to see Salomon's latest advancement in boot and binding technology.

"Now you've really done it, you idiot," I thought to myself. "You've antagonized Donna so much she's apt to disqualify you just for being such a pest, and on top of that you've just given your number away to someone you've never met before who will probably lose the damn thing or sell it to some desperate late entry!"

By the time I returned from a prerace ski tour with Joe Walsh, my attitude had hit rock bottom. It didn't surprise me when I stopped by the Salomon tent and Brad Weidt, looking serious, said, "Hey John, glad you're back. It wasn't as easy as I thought. You've got to come with me!"

"Great," I mused, prepared for the worst. "Maybe they are going to revoke my USSA competitor's card for being such a headache to them."

But I learned that everything was fine. Linda, one of the masterminds behind the whole three-ring circus, wanted to explain the situation to me firsthand. It seems Salomon had been a loyal sponsor of the Birkie for many years and as such was granted a few slots in the first wave for their team members. I wasn't officially one of the Fischer/Salomon Marathon Team, but I *was* skiing on their products, Brad Weidt *did* want me in the first wave, and there *were* a couple of unclaimed numbers remaining. Linda wanted me to know that Donna had only been following orders in not moving me up earlier. All I had to do was go next door and pick up my new first-wave number from Donna.

"Not Donna again," I said in horror. "She's going to kill me!"

Brad and Linda laughed as they escorted me back to "Special Problems." Donna saw us coming, and by the time I reached her table she was holding out an entry packet numbered 874. As I reached for the packet, I recoiled as if from an imaginary punch. Everyone laughed. Resuming her no-nonsense pose, Donna raised her voice as I headed out the door. "All I can say is, you'd damn well better ski fast!"

"I will, I will," I said looking back. "I wouldn't dare not to!"

The spaghetti feed that night was magnificent. The huge colosseum was filled with tables and hundreds of hungry racers feasted on spaghetti, bread, salad, and dessert. We sat wherever we could find a vacant seat and talked with skiers from rank beginners to Olympic veterans. A slightly overweight computer programmer from Chicago had driven all day to get to Telemark, would ski the Birkie, and drive back to the city after the race. He hadn't been on snow yet this year due to demands at work and poor weather, but he was determined to finish the full fifty-five-kilometer race. Since he hadn't missed the event in several years, he knew what he was in for, and I admired his grit.

Back at the "biathlon lodge" that night, the conversation centered around weather and waxing. The forecast was straightforward: cold! In fact, overnight temperatures were predicted at well below 0°F, with a chance that the Saturday temperature would not rise above zero. With almost seven thousand racers from all over the world on the starting line, I couldn't imagine them canceling or even postponing the race. After all, this was northern Wisconsin! These folks were accustomed to weeks on end of subzero temperatures.

The wax was easy, Start green. There were times (especially in warm, wet snow) where it made sense to get fancy, but with the forecast for −30°F overnight, warming to 0°F on Saturday, the message was clear: go with the coldest, most durable glider you've got! For me, that was Start green. It took about twenty minutes to wax and scrape my race skis. There was no sense in waxing a second pair. I went to sleep rehearsing positive self-talk. I had succeeded in securing a first-wave starting position; it was not going to be a wax race; from what I'd heard, it was a rolling, twisty course favoring a technical skier; and I was National 50K Champion for my age group.

The alarm went off at 6:00 A.M. in the pitch dark. I dressed quickly and went outside. The stars were still brilliant in a clear sky, the snow crunched underfoot, and the air bit my nostrils. "Great," I thought, "the wax will be fine. Now all we have to do is get the vans started!"

The start area was a scene from a science-fiction movie. Smoke and flames rose into the crystal-clear, subzero air from half a dozen huge bonfires. There was enough cord wood heaped on each fire to heat my home in Vermont for the entire winter. Hundreds of competitors pushed cheerfully into tight circles around the fires to stay warm. The racers displayed an unbelievable kaleidoscope of colors and fabrics, ranging from fluorescent super high-tech stretch warm-ups to giant olive-drab trash bags that would be torn off and discarded as the stampede began. Sunglasses and eyeshades were in abundance, to both cut down the glare and protect the eyes from snow flying from fourteen thousand ski poles. It gave the impression of a colony of brightly colored insects scurrying busily around. There was a gargantuan American flag, suspended between two telephone poles, being whipped about wildly by the cold north wind. I hoped most of the course would be in the trees, protected from that wind.

I jogged around the start area for twenty minutes in an effort to stay warm and loosen my muscles. Long lines were forming at the portable toilets. With about half an hour to go before the start, I returned to the van. This was the time before every important race when insignificant decisions became monumental. You take off your running shoes and put on your ski boots, snugging the laces good and tight. After thirty seconds you realize the boots are too tight, so you unlace them and retie them looser. You take another healthy slug from your water bottle — you can't be too well hydrated at the start of a race like this. But do you have time to go to the bathroom once more before lining up? Certainly not in the porta-potties. Now those boots feel too loose. You cinch them a little tighter. Should you wear a vest? In a long race like this one, at 0°F and with a strong wind, it could be a real advantage late in the event to have a warm torso, conserve body heat, and use that energy to get to the finish line faster.

Jim Frazier, a member of the domestic Biathlon Team sidelined by sickness, watched as I silently debated whether to wear my Salomon vest. "Morty, wear the vest," came Jim's confident voice, "but put it under your racing suit. It will be warmer and less cumbersome." I looked at him in amazement. It was a great idea that had never occurred to me. After putting on the vest and zipping my suit over it, I began the ritual struggle with my number. If you tie your number too loosely, it flaps and waves all over, a constant irritation during the race; if you tie it on too tightly, the first uphill where you are really hammering, you find your breathing restricted by the number around your chest.

By this time racers were lining up to enter the start area. Each of the seven waves was accessible by its own gate, where volunteers checked competitors' bibs as they entered to ensure that each racer began in the proper wave. With only fifteen minutes to go, there was nervous tension in the air and pushing and shoving toward the gates. The racers' warm-ups were to be placed in labeled plastic bags and transported by truck to the finish line. This presented yet another decision. If the race was delayed for any reason, standing around in the wind and cold in just a racing suit, even for a few minutes, would not be good.

I kept my warm-ups on and, carrying the plastic bag, pushed toward the gate for the first wave. Once in the starting pen, I jogged and stretched as the minutes ticked away. With less than five minutes to go, I slipped out of my warm-ups, stuffed them in the bag, and tossed it over the fence into the truck.

I was grateful to be in the first wave and didn't want to push my luck by fighting to the front row. I lined up about four rows back on the far right side of the starting field. "Hell," I thought, "this is a fifty-five-kilometer race! It's not going to be won or lost in the first kilometer."

Over the years I had competed in several major foot-running marathons, so I thought I would be prepared for the traffic at the start. In foot races, however, you don't have people flailing with skis and poles, taking up three or four times the space a runner does. In those races I had lined up on the edge of the pack and run comfortably down the roadside until everyone spread out. But as the first wave of Birkie competitors surged ahead at the gun, I was forced off the groomed surface into the untracked snow, stumbling and trying to keep up. Though everyone around me seemed polite and considerate, there was a constant clacking of skis against poles and an incessant chatter: "Oh, sorry," "On your left," "Watch your pole," "Hey, pick it up or get out of the way!"

As we swung around the left turn onto Hayward's Main Street, groomed curb to curb and lined with cheering spectators, I realized why fewer people had lined up on the right end of the starting line. With twelve hundred in the first wave, the line must have been almost fifty meters wide. As we turned onto Main Street, those on the left were like the hub of a wheel and scooted easily around the corner, while those of us on the right had to ski a wide arc, which put us well behind the leaders. I glanced down the street and couldn't believe the hundreds headed into the distance.

Betsy Youngman, one of the strongest women on the U.S. Ski Team, appeared beside me. Betsy was the 1989 Birkie Champion, a real spark plug from Cleveland, Ohio, and she was Jim Frazier's older sister. She was matching me stride for stride, with only one pole! As I was about to offer her one of mine, a fellow on the other side yelled, "Here, Betsy, take my pole!" Calmly she answered, "Thanks, but my brother is at the end of Main Street with a couple of spares. I'll get one from him."

"Now, there's poise!" I thought. The defending champion, and clearly one of today's favorites, calmly dealing with an equipment problem that would put other racers into orbit or cause them to drop out. "That woman has spunk," I thought as the crowd of racers separated us.

As we headed across windblown Hayward Lake, things began to spread out a little and I could take stock of my position. The adrenaline that had rocketed hundreds of racers out of the start had dissipated, and folks were settling into their 50K-race paces. The trail across the lake had been groomed wide enough for four or five skiers to skate abreast. I was trying to concentrate on being smooth and conserving energy, but I was constantly being boxed in by slower skiers. It was no use calling "Track." There was really no place for the overtaken skier to get out of the way. Once or twice I tried scampering out of the groomed track into the powder to pick up a few places, but the powder was so much slower it wasn't worth the effort. I thought with some irony how difficult it had been for me to get in the first wave. Unless I was badly mistaken, many of the twelve hundred starters in this wave didn't have a prayer of skiing within the prescribed pace. (In fact, only about one-third of the "exclusive" first wave wound up finishing in 3:45 per kilometer or better.)

As we approached the far end of the lake and the first climb, I looked ahead to see the brightly colored train of racers disappearing into the woods. There had to have been several hundred skiers ahead of me. I decided to concentrate on skiing smoothly, conserving energy, and not getting irritated by the traffic. It was a challenge! I had fast skis—on every downhill I'd ride up behind the guy in front of me, often slipping past when I could. But every gradual uphill brought a virtual pileup as the leaders lost momentum and began skating again.

One saving grace was the beauty and skiability of the trail. Whoever had designed the Birkie trail had been a master. The course rocked and rolled, twisted and bobbed through the hills like a dance. It had rhythm. In spite of the congestion, I began to get the feel of the course. I could power up the hills sensing they would be challenging but skiable, and sure enough, just as my legs began to burn we would get a break. I also knew I could go into the downhills full bore, confidant a corkscrew turn or roll in the trail wouldn't send me into the trees. Even through the "rush hour" stop-and-go traffic, the Birkie trail was a joy to ski.

I had seen the course profile and talked with the Walsh brothers about strategy. My plan was to conserve strength and energy (without being lazy) through the high point of the course at thirty-eight kilometers. They warned me that it was not totally downhill the last seventeen kilometers, but at least it was no longer predominantly climbing. Early on I made certain not to pass up a feed station. I must have sloshed down a quart of water and electrolyte replacement in the first twenty-five kilometers. I stuffed a couple sections of banana in my mouth, expecting to mush them up a bit and gulp them whole. To my surprise they were frozen solid, and I had to gnaw on them for several minutes before I could get them down. I must have looked like a greedy chipmunk!

As we approached twenty-eight kilometers, I could hear the roar of cheering spectators along the trail where the Kortelopet finish chute diverged from the Birkie trail. I risked a wistful glance toward the finish banner and for a second envied Max Cobb, Willie Carow, and the other biathletes who had elected to ski the shorter distance. Just then I was distracted by a voice shouting out numbers. As I skied past, I saw a spectator point to me as he said "eighty-seven." Almost a kilometer later, back in the silence of the woods, I was still trying to process the information. I had hoped to place in my age group, but the eighty-six skiers ahead of me must certainly contain at least a dozen guys over forty! I was headed into the toughest ten kilometers of the course after playing "bumper cars" for thirty kilometers, and I was on schedule to finish within the double digits. I decided to modify my prerace strategy and pour on the coal in the hills. I had always felt uphills were my strength in races, so why waste the chance to capitalize on them? I had pretty much given up on doing well in my age group, but I could certainly move up several places as other racers faded or hit the wall.

I worked hard from the twenty-eight- through thirty-eight-kilometer mark. I was relieved to crest the high point because I had known for the past couple of kilometers that I was "redlining" it. Like an Indianapolis 500 driver who skips a fuel stop late in the race knowing he'll have to nurse his car to the finish line on fumes, I had picked up several places in the hills but was feeling the effects, and I still had seventeen kilometers to go! I remembered only too well the last loop of the Lake Placid Loppet, and I was not interested in a replay of that "death march."

The first clue that I was in trouble was my obsession with spotting the next kilometer marker. I knew I had skied several kilometers past the high point at thirty-eight, but I couldn't remember how many. For the past few kilometers there hadn't been much changing of position among the racers I could see. Those ahead of me weren't getting any closer, and those right behind me weren't overtaking me. Then a good skier roared by on a downhill. "Where has he been?" I thought and tried to stay in contact without going under. He dropped me within a kilometer, and my effort to keep up had been expensive.

By the time I reached the food station at forty-eight kilometers, I was in "survival mode." It was still a race and I was determined to finish in the top one hundred, but rather than picking people off ahead of me, I was desperately trying not to let too many pass. Someone in a fluorescent suit skated steadily by. It was Betsy Youngman, looking strong and smooth with five kilometers to go. Once again I tried to "hook on for a ride," but Betsy gradually skied away. Even though I had no power left, I tried to keep my stride long and smooth. I remembered walking the hills of Lake Placid and kept reminding myself, "I'm not that far gone yet—I'm still skiing the uphills." As we neared the finish line, some of the "old horses" who knew their way back to the "barn" kicked past. I had lost the energy to hold them off, my eyes weren't focusing too well, and I was concentrating on not falling down. Then I heard the loudspeaker through the woods and knew I was going to make it. Soon the back of the Lodge and the huge Conference Center came into view, and I felt a wave of relief. I was vaguely aware of other racers just ahead, just behind, and passing me, but by then they were totally irrelevant. The trail hooked back toward the stadium, then I had one more small hill, one hundred yards of flat . . .

As I coasted through the wooden enclosures of the finish pen, someone looped a participation medal over my head. I nodded a thank-you: I was too tired to speak. When I had shuffled out of the way of the incoming finishers, I stopped and hung on my ski poles, legs quaking uncontrollably.

I reached down painfully and took my skis off. Now that I had stopped, I was aware of the cold. I leaned my skis and poles against the building, found my warm-ups, and sought the nearest door to the Convention Center. I put my stuff at a table and went for a cola and a couple of doughnuts.

Once I had changed out of my wet clothes, my fingers and toes had recovered some semblance of feeling, and the sugar hit my bloodstream, I began to feel better. Racers compared stories with a sense of shared accomplishment, having covered fifty-five kilometers in such cold conditions and pushed to the limits of their ability.

At the awards ceremony that evening the Conference Center was brimming with happy, red-faced skiers. The festive atmosphere was contagious. People shouted to friends across the room, shook hands with old rivals, and swapped lies about wax. I patiently worked my way through a small mob pushing to read the unofficial results posted on a wall. I still had hopes of finishing in the top one hundred, but it would be close. It was. The unofficial results listed me ninety-fifth among the men. "All right!" I thought happily. "I just squeaked it out in spite of the rigor mortis of the last five kilometers!" Almost as an afterthought, I worked my way forward through the list to see how many forty-year-olds had beaten me. My Alaskan friend, Tom Corbin, was ninety-third, but not until number twenty-four, Rudi Kapeller of Austria, did I find another forty-year-old. I'd finished ninety-fifth overall, but possibly third in my age group! I couldn't believe it. I recalled that when I'd heard I was eighty-seventh midway through the race, I'd thought I had lost all hope of placing in my age group. What a good lesson! As Yogi Berra once said, "It ain't over till it's over." I had definitely been exhausted when I'd finished, but I might have skied smarter or with better concentration had I known I was still in the running for an age-group award. The first step to giving up physically is to give up mentally, and I had at least given up on one of my goals. My goal of finishing in the top one hundred had pulled me through, but this was a very good lesson: The winners in this sport simply never give up.

The awards ceremony was terrific. Not only were trophies presented to all the age-group winners of both the Birkie and Kortelopet, but also several citizen racers were selected at random to represent the throngs of skiers whose only reward is being a part of such an extravaganza.

Bjorn Lasserud got a standing ovation from the packed arena. As usual, the Minneapolis resident won his age group, 60–64, but what was truly impressive was that Bjorn's time of 2:59:21 would have put him second in the

50–54 category, against guys ten years younger! I cheered loudly for Betsy Youngman, who finished second by eight seconds. If it hadn't been for that broken pole! But that's ski racing.

It was a tired but animated group of skiers who piled into the Biathlon Team van for the ride back to the house. As we packed our gear in preparation for a 6:00 A.M. departure, I thought back over the action-packed weekend. My attitude toward the race organizers had turned around 180 degrees. They had a tough job managing an event of such magnitude, and they did it beautifully. Could anyone blame the volunteers from Cable and Hayward if they acted as though the Birkebeiner were the only ski race on earth? In fact, it was an unbelievable example of community pride, organization, and resourcefulness. These folks from the north woods of Wisconsin had a good idea, worked hard at it, and made it tremendously successful. Not only are their communities enriched by the competitors who travel from all parts of the world to compete in their event, but they give thousands of folks the chance to be winners. Not just the hotshots who take home the hardware, but average people like the computer programmer from Chicago who goes home a winner simply because he finished. He tested himself against fifty-five kilometers of tough terrain in bitterly cold temperatures, pushed himself well past exhaustion, and endured. That fellow and thousands like him will go back to work Monday morning and stand a little taller in the eyes of their colleagues because they skied the Birkie. I've been to four Winter Olympics, seven World Biathlon Championships, and scores of National Championships, and you know what? The American Birkebeiner *is* a big deal! Get your entry in early and don't hassle Donna about your start number.

11: Psychology

I LIED! AT THE beginning of this book I gave what I believe are the five components for success in Nordic skiing. I also said they were listed in no particular order. That is not true. I began by discussing physical conditioning and technique because they traditionally get most of the attention. I went on to cover nutrition and equipment because recent developments have increased the significance of these two aspects. I purposely saved psychology, or mental approach toward competition, for last because I firmly believe it is the most significant of the five and I hope that by covering it last it will stand a better chance of being retained. In my almost thirty years of intense involvement with skiing, both as a competitor and a coach, the most dramatic victories and the most devastating defeats have been directly related to psychology.

In late February 1966 I was a sophomore at Middlebury College and a member of the Winter Carnival Ski Team. I had earned a regular spot on the cross-country team, occasionally ran "safety valve" in the Alpine events, and I even rode off the jump in a few competitions.

The first day of the Eastern Intercollegiate Ski Association Championships there was a heavy snowstorm. Skiers in New England seldom complain about snowfall, but this was coming down faster than it could be groomed. After the downhill in the morning, Dartmouth led by a couple of points. Then the action moved to Breadloaf for the cross-country. It was tricky waxing: the deep snow required pretty serious kick wax but had a tendency to ice up. It was a fifteen-kilometer course, and we started at one-minute intervals. Visibility was limited because of the snowfall.

Brian Beattie, a senior at Dartmouth, was on the National Nordic Combined Team. He was one of the finest cross-country skiers and jumpers in the East. David Rikert was the captain and leading scorer of the Williams College team. Because Williams lacked team depth, and because David was so talented, he competed in all four events every weekend.

There were also several other strong competitors in the field that day, any of whom had the capability to win. I left the starting gate shortly after Brian. Less than three kilometers into the race I made out a Dartmouth uniform through the falling snow. As I drew closer, I realized it was Brian. I was shocked! Unless he had hopelessly missed the wax, fallen, broken a ski, or been suffering from a serious illness, there was no reason why I should be overtaking him so early in the race. I skied timidly behind him for several strides until I realized that I had been going much faster. As I politely tracked him, Brian calmly said, "Nice going, John, you've got a good race going."

What a shot in the arm! Maybe he wasn't sick or hadn't fallen. Perhaps his wax was okay and I was just uncorking a great race! I charged on through the storm looking for someone else to pass.

About halfway through the race, Tauno Pulkkinen, a Finnish immigrant devoted to cross-country skiing and to Al Merrill, stood beside the track with a stopwatch and a clipboard. He was using the start list to figure the racers' interval times and to determine relative standings at the halfway point. He strained to see my number, then looked at his watch and clipboard. As I passed him, he looked up from his calculations and said in his thick accent, "You leading dis race." I wasn't sure I had heard him correctly, or even if I had, that his calculations had been accurate. But less than a kilometer later one of my teammates, Bobby Nields, was jumping up and down, waving his arms and legs like a marionette gone berserk.

"Sonofabitch, Morty, you're winning this thing, you understand that? YOU'RE WINNING!"

The remaining six or seven kilometers simply flew past. I couldn't seem to go fast enough. I wasn't tired or winded, my legs didn't burn, my skis didn't slip or drag. It was as if I were cruising effortlessly an inch above the snow. I rocketed through the finish line after a flat-out effort through deep, new snow and felt like I could keep right on going for another loop at the same pace or faster! I don't remember much of what happened after the race, but I remember the details of the competition itself as vividly as if it were yesterday.

John Caldwell later explained it to me as an "inspired race." He said that if a competitor trains conscientiously, develops competent technique, and gets lucky with the wax, then occasionally, for no discernible reason, he will "ski out of his socks." There is no way to predict it, and as far as he knew, you couldn't call up an inspired race on demand. In fact, it seems the more a racer wants or needs a great performance — say for the Olympics or the final tryout race of a series — the less the likelihood of "popping" one. Caldwell's recommendation was simply to do your homework, expect the best, and when you sense that you might be flirting with an inspired race, let it happen, celebrate it, and don't interfere with it.

I have raced a lot, on snow and off, since 1966, and I've had my share of satisfying results all the way to the international level. I've enjoyed several races that approached the sense of inspiration that John Caldwell defined for me decades ago. But the euphoric feeling of limitless potential that enveloped me that February day has been an inspiration and a constant reminder that I had one magnificent race in me and therefore probably more if I just let them happen.

My victory that day was due almost entirely to a set of somewhat random conditions that established the mental outlook necessary to win. I have been convinced ever since that the ability to identify and re-create those favorable psychological conditions would result in top performance. The mind holds the key to achievements far beyond the generally accepted level.

The Calgary Olympics provided a graphic example of the negative power of psychology. Josh Thompson is, quite simply, the best biathlete America has ever produced. He is a talented athlete with a self-reliant, no-nonsense approach to getting the job done. By 1987 he had won more than a dozen medals (most of them gold) in national and North American competition and was pointing toward the World Biathlon Championships in Lake Placid. On the clear, frigid morning of the first event, Josh made history by becoming the first American male biathlete to earn an individual medal in a World Championship. It was a monumental personal achievement done in almost complete obscurity. Biathlon is not a high-visibility sport in America. In fact, there was only one American journalist present. But she got a scoop and produced a great article for *Sports Illustrated*.

Josh's performance had a delayed effect. Although few had been there to witness it, word spread fast through the skiing community, and inevitably "experts" began to speculate about a U.S. biathlon medal at the upcoming Olympics in Calgary. The door had been opened and they believed anything was possible. At the Olympic trials Josh looked strong and confident. In Europe at early-season World Cup races, he demonstrated he was right on track with a fifth-place finish at Antholz, Italy (the best U.S. finisher to date in World Cup competition).

The team's arrival in Calgary was marked by cautious optimism. As team leader I saw my mission as one of running interference for the team members and coaches so that they could concentrate on what they had spent the previous years preparing for: winning medals. It is an amazing irony of the Olympic Games that the media and administrators will discuss with unmitigated awe the dedication and sacrifice of Olympic athletes; then during the actual games these same journalists, fund-raisers, and corporate representatives will schedule endless parties, receptions, and press conferences at which the athletes must appear. Nobody seems to recognize the paradox, especially dramatic in an obscure sport like biathlon. A world-class athlete like Josh Thompson can train in total anonymity for more than three and a half years with marginal financial support and none of the valuable motivation that could be derived from a little positive publicity. But once the athletes congregate for the Olympic Games, every sports journalist in the country wants a personal interview at precisely the time when the athlete's attention should be riveted on the goal.

As the 20K biathlon event approached, the pressure on Josh increased dramatically. The first biathlon race was relatively late in the schedule, and by that time the accomplishments of the American team were looking grim; the Alpine skiers had been plagued by falls and injuries; the hockey team had lost two of its first four games; Dan Jansen and Nick Thometz both suffered

Josh Thompson after the 20K Biathlon race at the Calgary Olympics. Josh was in fifth place overall when he entered the range for his final shooting stage. Three close misses dropped him to twenty-fifth and intense disappointment. Associated Press/Wide World Photos

especially cruel disappointments, and failed to earn medals as expected in speed skating; and Debbie Thomas was unable to challenge Katarina Witt for the gold in women's figure skating. As these Americans faltered, the press and commentators looked more desperately for possible medal winners. All within a couple of days, *Sports Illustrated* picked Josh Thompson as a possible gold medalist, his picture appeared in full color on the front page of *USA Today*, and Jim McKay described Josh to millions of TV viewers as "America's last hope for another gold medal."

The weight of the expectations thrust upon him and the media attention were simply too much for Josh. He had prepared for just about any contingency: wind on the firing line, rifle malfunction, slow skis, or glycogen depletion. But there was nothing in the isolation of his training or the obscurity of biathlon racing to prepare him for this avalanche of attention.

Josh was in fifth place overall, only a few seconds away from an Olympic medal, until his final stage of shooting. Then he missed three of his final five targets, errors that totaled only a few millimeters but made the difference between a medal and twenty-fifth place.

When I met him at the finish line, Josh was absolutely crushed. He couldn't believe it was over and that he had done so poorly. He was embarrassed and humiliated, and tears streamed uncontrollably. A true champion must be absolutely convinced he or she is capable of winning, and Josh had been prepared to win. To falter so close to the goal, after so much hard work and dedication, was almost unbearable.

Josh Thompson was in better physical condition going into Calgary than he had been before his silver-medal performance in 1987 at Lake Placid. If anything, his skating technique and procedure on the firing range had improved, and his diet and equipment were the same or better. The significant difference between being second in the World Championships in 1987 and twenty-fifth against virtually the same field of competitors in Calgary was, quite simply, psychology. Although many of us hoped, no one really anticipated Josh's silver medal in 1987. At Calgary, however, the entire nation *expected* a medal.

If psychology is so powerful, responsible for such astounding results, then why don't athletes and coaches spend most of their time studying it? Many of the world's most successful competitors do just that. More than a decade ago the U.S. Biathlon Team hired Marie Alkire as a rifle coach. Marie was a National Champion in the air-rifle event and was a product of the famous Advanced Marksmanship Training Center at Fort Benning, Georgia. One of Marie's accomplishments for the biathlon team was to write and distribute a manual on mental training. The opening sentence of that manual reads,

"Shooting is 90 percent mental, once the technical skills have been mastered." One of the reasons the American shooters trained at Fort Benning are so successful internationally year after year is that they have a very comprehensive mental training program. Why haven't sports teams and individual athletes all over the country picked up on the shooters' dedication to mental training? The answer probably lies in the fact that mental training, unlike physical training, is not concrete and easily quantifiable. We can look at a videotape, determine that a skier's stride is too short, and take steps to lengthen it. A visit to Whit Mitchell's human-performance laboratory can tell an athlete that his or her percentage of body fat is too high or VO_2 max is too low for top international success. We can ski through a speed trap to determine which combination of wax and base material is the fastest. But how can a coach quantify an athlete's feeling of self-worth? How can you evaluate, as you stand among thousands of other racers seconds before the start of the Birkebeiner, whether you are psyched *up* or psyched *out*?

Because the psychological aspects of competition are elusive and difficult to isolate, let alone evaluate, we coaches and athletes tend to ignore them and concentrate on other facets of performance that we can confront more directly. But I believe it is precisely because this area is the least well understood that it is potentially the area of greatest reward.

Perhaps the most basic psychological requirement for success is a positive self-image. To be a winner you must like yourself, be proud of your accomplishments, and be confident that you can achieve the goals you have set for yourself—a subtly difficult task. For one thing, many of us are still influenced by the Puritan ethic of hard work, religious dedication, Spartan lifestyle, self-reliance, and humility. Sometimes this influence can be stifling rather than empowering. For example, I grew up in an era when humility was considered a desirable trait. Great champions, when interviewed after a spectacular performance, would look humbly to the ground, kick their feet aimlessly in the dirt, and mumble, "Aw shucks, it wasn't anything special, it just kinda happened." We celebrated this type of humility in our heroes, and our youngsters mimicked it.

A second source of erosion in athletes' self-image came from coaches. Until quite recently most coaches regarded their primary function as correcting faults in their athletes' training or technique, sending such messages as "You're not going fast enough," "Your weight is too far back," "Your kick is late," "Your stride is too short," or "You are too timid on the downhills." The logic was that if an athlete is doing everything right, there isn't much need for a coach.

Another constant assault on our self-image comes from self-talk. We are constantly carrying on private conversations with ourselves, and very often we are far more critical than anyone else would ever be. This is especially true in the high-stress situations often found in athletics. We have all seen the Alpine skier rocketing through a slalom course, then catching an edge a couple of gates from the finish line and going down in an explosion of snow. Do you suppose that racer is saying to himself, "Gosh, I must have gotten too much weight on my uphill ski"? It is far more likely that he, like most of us when we don't live up to our expectations, indulges in a level of verbal abuse that we would never tolerate if it came from someone else.

Maybe it's a carryover from the Puritan ethic, or maybe it's just human nature, but for most of us it seems easier to imagine the worst-case scenario rather than the best case. We may hope or wish for victory in an important race, but we imagine in detail all the things that can go wrong and keep that victory from us. I have been as guilty of this type of negativity as anyone else. As a lieutenant in the army stationed at Fort Richardson, Alaska, I basically had it made: I was being paid to train for and compete in international biathlon races. We had great early snow, adequate coaching, and state-of-the-art equipment, and yet many of us spent a great deal of time focusing on what was wrong with the Biathlon Training Center, how the Russians had superior sports medical support, or how our remote location made it impossible for us to compete with our European rivals on a regular basis. These were valid concerns, but what I didn't realize at the time is that we were all telling ourselves that we were disadvantaged, poorly coached, and at too much of a handicap to compete successfully against the Europeans.

The messages we send our subconscious are critically important to our self-images, and we have to work hard to make sure they are all positive. As athletes or coaches we can't change our physical environment, but we *can* change our perception of it. Driving my Dartmouth Team to a race through a snowstorm, I may have said to myself, "Dammit! Another klister day and we probably won't have time to test adequately. Why the hell can't it just be cold powder snow and blue hard wax?" You can be sure my skiers would have picked up on my mood, been insecure about the wax, and had miserable races. But with practice and effort you can approach the situation from a dramatically different perspective, with self-talk like this: "All right, heavy, wet snow! A wax race. I'm as experienced and capable waxing klister as any other coach, perhaps more so. This will be a real advantage for my guys. If we really hit the wax today, which is entirely possible, we could do far better than we might have if the waxing were straightforward!" In my excitement and enthusiasm I might even have said to them before we arrived, "Guys, this snow is a real advantage for us. We'll work together to test wax and you guys will have the best skis on the course. We're going to kick butt today!" Is there any question in your mind which type of self-talk would create the stronger competitive results? Which type would motivate my racers?

Successful positive self-talk takes creativity and mental discipline, but it's not lying to yourself. It's a change in your normal perception; you look at things around you from a different angle.

On the biathlon shooting range, a windy day may generate self-talk like this: "Damn, I can't even hold the rifle on the target. I'm going to spray these shots all over the hillside." And I would. A more sophisticated biathlete might say to himself, "Great, the wind really separates the experienced shooters from everyone else, and I'm as good in the wind as anyone in this race!"

It is equally important for a coach or friend to provide positive reinforcement. One of the greatest challenges in coaching is to remain positive in the face of a devastating defeat. Don't fill your memory banks with images of what went wrong; they need to be filled with what went right.

While coaching at Dartmouth I became disturbed by the short, choppy forward arm movement my skiers used in their diagonal technique as a result of skating and longer poles. I pointed out the problem to them and constantly reminded them during workouts, "Don't bring your arms up short in front of your face like this; reach forward." They tried to comply in practice, but in the races I still saw a lot of short, choppy arm motion. Then I bought a videotape of Oddvar Bra, one of Norway's most successful racers, demonstrating classic technique. He didn't show common faults; he just skied for the camera. And there it was for everyone to see: the smooth, natural reach forward down the track. The next day most of my skiers were reaching comfortably down the track like Oddvar! The message is clear: Don't imprint mistakes on their minds, show them excellent technique.

If you want to be a winner, you must act like a winner and you must talk like a winner, especially to yourself. This means if someone congratulates you after a race, look them in the eye, shake their hand, smile, and answer, "Thanks a lot! It did go well today." It means being positive in your outlook and conversations. For example, when you are rehashing the race with friends at the awards ceremony, recount to them what went right, where you picked up time, rather than what went wrong. It also means being kind to yourself, praising yourself when you do well and being tolerant when you don't live up to your own expectations.

Lyle Nelson and I skied together on the Biathlon Team for several years. I was intrigued by his incurable optimism, although somewhat skeptical. He would frequently complete a workout in Europe with a remark like, "Hey Morty, I just skied ten kilometers behind Tichonov [a five-time World Champion] and he isn't so tough! I could stay with him, no problem." Or he would come off the firing line saying, "You guys see that? I came in to shoot even with Svendsberget [a multiple Norwegian and World Championship medal winner]. I cleaned my targets and left before he had fired three shots!" The bottom line is that Lyle Nelson has won more U.S. Biathlon National Championships than anyone else and was a member of four Winter Olympic teams! He was not stronger, faster, or a more accurate shot than the rest of us; Lyle simply talked himself into believing he was, and the results are in the record book. A strong, positive self-image is an essential characteristic of every champion.

Visualization

Visualization, or mental imagery, is a powerful tool to be used in the development of a positive self-image. Your subconscious cannot distinguish between reality and what you imagine. So what do you suppose happens when you visualize yourself skiing beside Gunde Svan, matching him stride for stride? What happens when you envision yourself wearing a U.S. Ski Team jacket or racing uniform? What happens when you picture yourself on the top step of the awards podium, feeling the weight of the gold medal around your neck?

Quite simply, imagery works. Many studies have confirmed its effectiveness. In perhaps the most dramatic, randomly selected participants were tested on their ability to throw basketball foul shots. Each subject was asked to attempt a prescribed number of shots, and a percentage score based upon successful shots was recorded. Three groups were then established, each having an identical cumulative score. Group 1 was sent away with instructions to return in a month. Group 2 was told to practice throwing foul shots an hour a day for the next month. Group 3 was told not to touch a basketball for a month, but to visualize shooting foul shots for an hour a day.

When the groups met a month later, some of the findings were predictable. Group 1 made virtually no improvement over its original test score. Group 2 had significantly improved its score, to no one's great surprise. Group 3 provided the fireworks. Although its members had not touched a basketball during the month, Group 3 achieved a test score only slightly lower than that of Group 2, and far higher than Group 1!

Imagery works best when it is realistic. To add excitement and reality to your mental rehearsals, include all five senses. If you are visualizing an upcoming ski race, be sure to *see* the brilliantly colorful uniforms of the participating racers, *hear* the cheering of the crowd, *smell* the evergreen trees as you glide past, *taste* the cold, crisp air as you inhale, and *feel* the smooth power of your muscles as you charge up the hill.

There are two perspectives from which you can visualize. You can picture yourself skiing past as though you are watching a videotape or, even more productive, you can visualize a scene from within your body, seeing what you expect to actually see and feeling what you think your body will feel during the race. Alpine skiers are experts at visualization. At the start area of a slalom course you will see the racers leaning on their poles, eyes closed, wagging a relaxed hand this way and that. They are running the course in their minds, making the turns and banging the gates.

If you want visualization to produce positive changes in your performance, remember two things: You have to practice visualizing often and with consistency, and you must be sure you are visualizing proper technique. Visualizaton is like physical conditioning in that the more often you do it, the better you will become at it. It's not just standing in the starting gate of a major competition thinking, "I'll just picture myself winning this event," and assuming your victory is assured. But if you have trouble with icy downhills, for example, and you spend a few minutes every day picturing yourself confidently negotiating fast, challenging descents, you will almost certainly notice an improvement when you actually encounter one.

Of course, you have to be sure you are imagining the right thing. Several years ago the captain of the Dartmouth Alpine Team was having real trouble finishing slalom courses. Our Alpine coach astutely observed that the falls always occurred on tight or difficult turns to the left. He watched our captain before a competition: eyes closed, gloved hand tracing the line he was visualizing. On a difficult left turn the hand stopped. The skier was actually anticipating having trouble on that turn! The race went just as he had mentally rehearsed it; he skied well through the top part of the course but leaned into the hill, fell, and slid out at the tight left turn. When our Alpine coach explained to the athlete what he was doing, the skier began to concentrate on visualizing strong, assertive left turns and the remainder of the season was successful for him. Whatever you perceive as your area of weakness, it is important to visualize not how you think you are, but how you want to be.

Another technique I've found to be very helpful with visualization is the use of metaphor. As the old expression says, "One picture is worth a thousand words." At the elite level I see cross-country skiing as a sport of delicate grace, precise balance, and flowing motion. Many competent skiers plod along using correct technique but are unable to achieve the highest level of balletlike, graceful efficiency. All the descriptive phrases I could muster didn't seem to help. But when I asked my skiers to imagine that they were gazelles or cheetahs flying effortlessly over the snow, the improvement was astounding. With a little imagination and innovation, you can develop helpful metaphors for any racing situation. On a long, gradual uphill, you're a powerful locomotive; on a fast downhill, a downhill skier; in the crush of a mass start, a big truck for which the nearby autos make plenty of room.

The use of metaphor can be carried to interesting extremes. I'll give one personal example. At its most basic level, cross-country skiing is a very private, individual sport. Unlike football, basketball, or baseball, where players are clearly in a contest against each other, cross-country skiers really pit themselves against the environment—the weather, the terrain, the snow. The racer who deals most successfully with the challenges presented by the course tops the results sheet. Very often, thinking about, concentrating on, or keying off other competitors in a race only distracts an athlete and makes it impossible to flow into a smooth, relaxed stride that maximizes physical potential. To help avoid the distractions created by other racers, I imagine I am an accomplished artist standing in front of a blank canvas. I have the opportunity, the technical skill, and the experience to paint a masterpiece. What any other artists do is totally irrelevant. The canvas I face is mine alone. I know I'm capable of painting that masterpiece, and with the proper balance of inspiration, discipline, concentration, and dedication, it will happen. The ski race is much the same as the painting. Each stride is like a brush stroke; with the proper balance of inspiration and discipline the individual strides will flow into a magnificent race and I will not be disappointed with the final result.

Arousal and Relaxation

Another psychological aspect that deserves attention is the relationship between relaxation and arousal. In modern society we have the general connotation of stress as being harmful. Stress causes indigestion, high blood pressure, heart attacks, alcohol abuse, and teenage suicide. But what we really mean here is excess stress. Stress in appropriate amounts can motivate us to greatness. For example, would we ever have landed Neil Armstrong on the moon before 1970 if President Kennedy had not provided a little "positive stress" by publicly stating that we would?

The vertical scale on the left of the arousal curve represents physical activity, and the horizontal axis on the bottom represents stress level. At the start of the curve at the lower left corner of the graph, there is no stress and no physical activity. As stress increases, the level of physical activity increases until a peak of efficiency is reached. What is interesting, however, is that as stress continues to increase, the quality of physical efficiency diminishes dramatically until at the maximum stress level there is no physical activity at all. In extreme cases of stress, faced with imminent disaster, people have frozen into physical inactivity, unable to take any steps to save themselves. What makes this concept especially challenging for athletes and coaches is that we all react to stress differently. For example, the confusion, jostling, and kaleidoscope of color at the mass start of a major race like the Birkebeiner might excite one racer to peak physical efficiency but force another right over the top of the arousal curve toward stark terror.

Successful athletes know that it is relatively easy to get psyched up but very difficult, if not impossible, to regain peak efficiency once they have been forced over the top of the curve. The trick is to know yourself well enough to

Performance-Arousal Curve

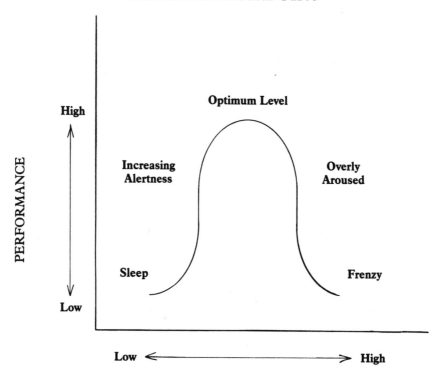

AROUSAL

This diagram of the Arousal Curve shows how performance improves with increased arousal only to a point, then as arousal continues, performance declines.

control your level of arousal. Just as you time your physical warm-up before the start of a race, ensuring that your muscles are loose, supple, and ready for action, it is equally important that you monitor your psychological arousal.

As we drove to the 1990 American Birkebeiner, we got caught in the amazing traffic jam created by seven thousand racers trying to get to the start. As the minutes ticked by, I could feel my level of arousal shoot up, my pulse rate escalate, and my breathing quicken. There was nothing I could do except try to stay calm. When we finally reached the staging area, I was well up on my arousal curve. I bundled into my warm-ups and jogged around the parking lot. This time spent alone enabled me to collect my thoughts, reclarify my goals, and map out my strategy for the final minutes before the start, thus regaining control of my stress level so that when the gun went off, I was positive, eager, and motivated to do my best.

One of the most delicate aspects of coaching is monitoring the level of your athletes' arousal. A stirring pep talk before the race might light a fire under some of your athletes but put others over the edge. In my experience it is far more likely that young skiers will be overly aroused at the start of a race rather than not fired up enough. For this reason I frequently tried to break the tension by making my athletes laugh. Hundreds of spectators at the Calgary Olympics saw me put an arm around one of America's best biathletes and lean my head close to his as he entered the starting gate for the most important race of his life; they probably thought I was imparting the wisdom of experience or some last-minute advice. Actually, I whispered seriously, "Look, I know you're a stud, but are you really going to race twenty kilometers in front of all these people and TV cameras with your fly open?" He shot a frantic glance at the front of his racing suit, which was perfectly zipped up, then looked at me in confusion. My smile confirmed that he had been duped, and when the starter said "Go" seconds later, he was still laughing. He was confident and poised when he entered the range to shoot several minutes later. Ultimately he put together one of the best races of his career under extremely stressful circumstances.

Relaxation may be just as important as arousal. While skiing in competition, a racer must be able to relax for the microsecond between each stride. This is an essential aspect of correct technique since the glide, which follows the power stroke of every stride, will be far more productive if the racer is relaxed. The competitor who can relax instantaneously between power strokes conserves energy, which can be used later for power, and glides farther with each stride than does a tense or nervous competitor who fights or struggles. For athletes who are trying desperately to win an important race, it may seem like a contradiction that to go faster they must actually relax more between strides.

Relaxation is also important off the course, away from racing and training. Top athletes, like successful people in any other field of endeavor, are highly motivated overachievers. Often, winning is so engrained in them that everything becomes a contest. In the late 1960s, the heyday of the Biathlon Training Center in Alaska, there were about twenty of us assigned to the unit, but only six of us were selected each year for the team to the World Biathlon Championships. It was during the height of the Vietnam War, and the unstated assumption was that if you didn't show progress you would be reassigned to a conventional military unit and inevitably draw a "trip to the Garden Spot of Southeast Asia." This led to an environment of intense competition in every facet of life. We competed (openly or covertly) at least three times a day in workouts, and in "free time" between workouts we often competed at cards, hunting, and fishing. Saunas became contests to see who was toughest, and even mealtimes became competitions.

There was an unfortunate side effect to all this spirited rivalry: It became difficult to relax, even away from training. My closest friends, teammates with whom I trained every day, also became constant adversaries. If we had been more skillfull at relaxation techniques, a lot of competitive energy that we squandered on card games and fishing trips might have been redirected toward races.

As a result of my years on the Biathlon Team, I have developed the following theory (although it's probably oversimplified): At any given time we each embody a certain amount of creative energy. It can be replaced or re-charged, but not instantaneously. If we consume this energy worrying whether the car will start, whether we will get caught in traffic, or whether we have selected the correct wax, it won't be available to fuel our physical effort in the race. The same is true on an everyday basis. Energy spent worrying about world politics, the stock market, or a possible career promotion is energy that might have made an average workout a spectacular one; and the more spectac-ular workouts you string together, the greater the likelihood that you will have a spectacular race when you want one. The basic principle here is simple: As the popular song went, "Don't worry, be happy!" A slightly more sophisticated way of saying it is this well-known prayer:

> God grant me the serenity to accept the things I cannot change,
> Courage to change the things I can,
> And wisdom to know the difference.

Another benefit of relaxation involves technique improvement. I spoke earlier about the effectiveness of visualization. Studies have shown visualiza-tion to be far more effective if done in a completely relaxed physical state. This means that if you really want to improve your basketball free-throw average, visualizing the ball swishing through the net as you are locked in bumper-to-bumper traffic is not nearly as effective as when you are lying on your bed with no outside distractions.

Just as it is essential for the serious competitor to learn the proper tech-nique for skating uphills and for fast descents, it is also necessary to learn an effective method of physical relaxation. You want to achieve a state of relaxa-tion just this side of sleep, that physical state where the subconscious is most receptive to visualization and mental imagery. There are many variations, but the following simple approach works. Isolate yourself in a dim, quiet room, free from noise and distractions. (A dimly lit room is probably better than dark because you don't want to fall asleep.) Lie on your back, preferably on a bed or couch, but a comfortable chair or the carpeted floor is okay. Then take several deep breaths: strong, deep inhalations and smooth, controlled exhalations. The next step seems contradictory, but since most of us can't really tell when we are physically tense, it makes sense. Clench your fists. Squeeze them as tightly as you can. Feel the tension, stress, and strength. Then abruptly relax your grip and feel the tension and stress flow out of your fingertips. Concentrate on how different your relaxed hands feel from your clenched fists. If the sensation is not vivid for you, repeat the process. Then work your way through your body, tensing and relaxing one muscle group at a time: arms, shoulders, feet, legs, stomach, chest, neck, and face. In each case tense the muscles for ten or fifteen seconds until you really feel the tension, then release and enjoy the pleasant feeling of relaxation that replaces the tension.

After you have worked step by step through your entire body, tense up all your muscles at once then release. Imagine the tension as water or as electric current that, when released, flows out your fingertips and toes, leaving completely relaxed muscles.

Take another few, slow, deep breaths, and you should now be very relaxed and as receptive as possible to mental imagery. Keep in mind that, as with any technique, your ability to relax will depend upon how often and how well you practice. After a few weeks of consistent sessions of relaxation, you will be much more tuned in to subconscious levels of stress that went unnoticed before. Driving in a car, for example, you might become aware of tension between your shoulder blades or a tight grip on the wheel. By using your newly developed techniques, you can release the tension in your back or hands and make the trip more enjoyable.

Once you are in a completely relaxed state, you are most receptive to mental suggestions and visualization. The night before a big collegiate ski race, when the level of stress and apprehension was pretty high, I would gather my Dartmouth skiers together in a room and talk them through a relaxation session. Once they were completely relaxed (inevitably a couple were snoring), I would calmly and confidently talk them through the racecourse, being as vivid and descriptive as possible, while concentrating on how *strong* they felt on the uphills, how *confident* and *fast* on the downhills, how *long* and *smooth* they were across the flats.

Over the years various skiers responded differently to these mental rehearsals. Those that never really got into visualization at least got calmed down before important races. Those who believed in the process would request a session even on courses they knew well.

If the concepts in this chapter are new to you and you are willing to give them a try, you can count on improving your performance. You might even agree that the potential improvement is more significant than what would be possible with a hundred dollars worth of Cera F or a new, three-hundred-dollar pair of skis! Think how much money I'm saving you! And the best part is that your psychological bag of tricks is only half full.

Goal Setting

I referred earlier to goal setting, an important aspect of the psychological side of competition. Goal setting is based upon a widely accepted observation: We tend to move toward the successful accomplishment of an established goal. Even if we are not sure of the intermediate steps, a clearly defined goal causes us to make decisions (both consciously and subconsciously) that bring us closer to that goal. When President Kennedy publicly stated early in the 1960s that America would put a man on the moon and return him safely to earth by the end of the decade, he set in motion a classic example of the power of goal setting. When he made that statement — in fact, a challenge — the necessary technology, funding, and highly trained personnel didn't even exist. Even so, the goal was so compelling and clearly stated that it motivated the most spectacular technological accomplishment in the history of mankind. Goal setting can be a *very* powerful psychological tool.

There are some guidelines that will help you make your goal setting more effective. First of all, the goals must be appropriate and possible, but not easily within reach. For example, it's unrealistic to set your sights on an Olympic gold medal if you haven't even made the Olympic team yet; on the other hand, year after year some American skiers are limited by setting a goal of making the team instead of doing well against the Europeans.

The nice thing about goals is that they can always be adjusted. A young skier may first strive to make his or her high school team, then to earn a trip to the Junior Nationals. Next he or she might strive to win the state or regional championships, place in the top three at the Junior Nationals, or be named to a national development squad. It's like climbing a ladder: Each time you reach a new step, you celebrate your accomplishment while looking forward to the next step.

This brings up the concept of multiple goals, an approach I strongly support. If our goals are not within appropriate reach, we frequently will fall short in our attempts to realize them. But as I mentioned earlier, success is important for a positive self-image. Multiple goals help to resolve this problem. With my Dartmouth Team I asked each skier to write down three goals: one short-term, one intermediate, and one long-term, or career, goal. The short-term goal should be relatively easy to achieve and a constant source of positive reinforcement. For an incoming freshman it might be to miss no more than one workout each week, while a top skier might decide on an ambitious 600 hours per year of training.

Intermediate goals are a little farther out in the future, often tied to four-year cycles reflecting the Olympic quadrennial and the normal college cycle. An incoming skier with modest success in high school might set his sights on earning a spot on the varsity team by senior year, while one who is more experienced might envision winning the NCAA Championships as a senior. Finally, career goals help athletes keep focused. A college skier who has aspirations for the Olympics will make different choices than the one who plans to attend medical school. Short-term, intermediate, and career goals provide a road map to lead the athlete to success.

I also believe in event goals — mentally determining in advance the purpose or result of each event. This may be nothing more than reminding oneself at the start of a distance workout to keep the pace slow and concentrate on duration, or it may mean establishing specific performance goals for a major competition. I believe in multiple goals for individual events, too. During the past several summers I have run twenty-six-mile marathons to motivate myself to stay in shape. Over the years several mutually reinforcing goals have emerged from my running. My best marathon time to date is 2:43. I would love to break 2:40 and it has become a sort of ultimate goal for me in marathoning. Usually at some point in the race I realize that I'm not able to maintain the pace necessary to break 2:40 so I revert to my second goal, which is to establish a new personal record (PR). Since I turned forty a few years ago, doing well within the masters age category in a race has also become a significant goal. I may finish pretty far back in a strong field of runners, I may not be close to a PR, but if I'm the top master in the race, I'm thrilled.

Finally, there is the goal of beating your number. In big races like New York or Boston, the competitors are seeded according to their previous best results. I entered the New York City Marathon in 1984 and was assigned number 1024 (of more than 18,000 participants). That meant, theoretically, if everyone ran as well as they had run before, I would have finished around 1000. I was well trained and shooting to break 2:40, but it turned out to be very hot that year. At eighteen miles, 2:40 was hopeless; by twenty miles bettering my 2:43:05 PR was unrealistic. I reverted to goal three, just hanging in there to beat my number. Even though my final time was a discouraging 2:49:27, I was number 284 of 18,000, and I was ecstatic. I had failed to meet two of my goals, but that third goal helped me think of the 1984 New York City Marathon as a very rewarding and successful race.

So take a little time and carefully consider some goals. Make sure they are a reach but not unrealistic. They should be quite specific rather than nebulous.

But they don't have to all be competition oriented. Maybe part of your reason for skiing is to keep your weight down and lower your cholesterol level. Maybe you've learned that exercising every day helps you dissipate the emotional stress of your job. There is nothing wrong with creating goals that focus on these benefits of participation in the sport.

A final caution on goal setting. One of the truly wonderful aspects of cross-country skiing is the ability to regard the course, the snow conditions, and the weather as the challenge, and other competitors as fellow adventurers rather than adversaries. I try to wish my fellow racers the best race they can muster, then hope that I can deal with the challenges of the course more efficiently and skillfully than they can. Avoid goals involving other people. You only have control over your own training and racing, not anyone else's. And no matter who you are, there is someone out there who can beat you. Setting a goal of racing at three minutes per kilometer is much more productive than "kicking Walter Langlaugher's butt."

Concentration

The concept of concentration has been much overused and misunderstood. Coaches of every sport, all across our nation, have been pleading with their athletes for generations to concentrate, concentrate, concentrate. The generally accepted definition of concentration is the ability to focus attention exclusively on the task at hand, completely ignoring distractions.

There is another component to concentration, however, that often goes unnoticed. We would all agree that the ability to concentrate suggests ignoring distractions. We might think of Roger Clemens pitching strikes against the Minnesota Twins while the hometown fans frantically wave white handkerchiefs in an effort to distract him.

But equally important is the ability to filter through information that is helpful. Very often skiers become so focused on the track ahead of them that they fail to absorb valuable information that would enhance their performance. In certain snow conditions — especially in warming temperatures as more skiers kick and glide down the trail — the tracks become smoother, exert more suction on the skis, and become slow. Meanwhile, on the corduroy borders of the groomed surface the snow is still relatively dry and slightly rough, thus breaking the suction and therefore significantly faster. Yet skier after skier will slog past, concentration etched on their faces, struggling with the slow, wet tracks while inches to either side the snow is much faster.

While I was a coach at Dartmouth, we would compete at least once every year at the site of the 1980 Winter Olympic cross-country events near Lake Placid. If I anticipated trouble on the most difficult turn, I would position myself above it and yell at my racers to take it wide as they roared past. The experienced skiers would shoot a quick glance in my direction, nod or smile acknowledgment, and sweep smoothly around the outside of the corner. The less-experienced skiers, eyes riveted on the upcoming icy turn, would never even hear me and career into the crusty ruts, often ending up in a heap. When you become *so* focused on an objective that you fail to take in information helpful to your cause, you aren't concentrating effectively.

Motivation

As a young biathlon skier competing against the Europeans and Russians for the first time, I made some interesting observations. In training, our opponents didn't seem invincible, but in the race, the Norwegian you'd been tailing easily in practice would blast by as if he were jet propelled! And it seemed as though they left their sloppy shooting on the practice range.

Mike Devechka, one of America's top Nordic combined skiers, made a similar observation at the 1972 Olympics. In the week before the start of the competitions Mike enthusiastically reported that all the Nordic combined jumpers were landing in the same rut just past seventy meters on the landing hill. "We're right in there with the best of 'em," he remarked enthusiastically. But on opening day of the Sapporo Olympics, while the Americans flew confidently down the hill to the seventy-meter point, many of the Europeans were closer to ninety meters! Mike was despondent that evening. "How the hell can those guys go seventy meters all week in training, then fly twenty meters farther in the competition?" The answer in both cases is motivation.

For many years thereafter motivation for me was some type of mysterious intangible quality that the Russians and Scandinavians had in abundance and we Americans seemed to lack. Then at a sports medicine conference sponsored by the U.S. Ski Team, Dr. Rainer Martins helped demystify motivation. "Motivation," he said, "has two components; a feeling of self-worth and fun." Quite simply, we are motivated to pursue activities that make us feel good about ourselves and are enjoyable.

In *The Psychology of Winning* tapes Dr. Dennis Waitley recognizes two types of motivation: fear and desire. He points out that fear can be as strong an influence as desire. But from the earlier discussion of the arousal curve, remember that fear taken to the extreme inhibits performance. Unfortunately, fear of failure is the primary motivation for far too many athletes. They are afraid of embarrassing themselves, of letting the team down, or of not living up to parents' expectations. These are the athletes who subconsciously expect to fail and soften the landing with a preannounced excuse: "Coach, I'm starting to feel a sore throat coming on. I want to race, but I can't tell how well I'll be able to do." Fear of failure is a crippling form of motivation because it sends constant negative messages to the subconscious.

Desire is the flip side of the coin. Motivation by desire acknowledges all the wonderful aspects of success. It empowers an athlete to reach lofty goals and strive for even higher accomplishments. Athletes motivated by desire focus on the rewards that are important to them: "I'm going to win this tryout today and earn a spot on the Olympic Team." They envision what can go right rather than what might go wrong.

Dr. Waitley also points out that motivation is a private, personal characteristic and seldom can be effectively imposed from outside. Cheerleaders, screaming fans, newspaper clippings, fancy uniforms, and expense money may provide valuable incentive to an athlete, but true motivation comes from within. Why do some athletes hang it up at the peaks of their careers while others continue long after their contemporaries have taken jobs as sports announcers? For the fortunate ones it is because they feel good about themselves and enjoy what they are doing.

In Nordic skiing motivation plays its most important role in the relative monotony of day-to-day training. It's not difficult to get up for an important race, but on a cold, drizzly October day it's all too easy to "bag" a workout because you "just don't feel like it." Truly motivated athletes pull on their training gear even in the crummy weather because they know every workout is like a deposit in their savings account. Real motivation is a very private thing that shines through without newspaper headlines or cheering fans.

Race Strategy

All the aspects of psychology I've talked about thus far are fairly general — they are valuable in career and family relationships as well as ski racing. But there are also some specific applications that translate into great racing strategy.

Always establish an attitude of quiet confidence at the start of a race. If I observe an opponent frantically changing wax, desperately rummaging through the car for a misplaced racing bib, or running wildly to avoid a late start, I know that racer is going to be susceptible psychologically. He will worry that his wax won't work or that he didn't warm up properly. Even if my prerace preparations are not going as smoothly as I would like, I try never to let my opponents see me rattled. I would rather let them think my wax is perfect, I had a great warm-up, and I'm expecting to win — even if I'm not. Some good-natured joking with the starter or other racers helps give the impression that you are relaxed and confident.

On the course, even though I may be concentrating intensely, I try to seem confident and in control. I may give it all I've got to overtake another racer, but as I pass him, I try to control my breathing and perhaps even offer encouragement to give the impression that I'm cruising easily while he is struggling. When you track another racer, it's important to break contact fast. Plan your move in advance and prepare to turn on the jets for a couple of minutes after you've passed him to be sure he won't hang with you. Uphills are the best place to pass. If a skier is working hard, striding up a long hill, it can be very demoralizing to have another competitor come blasting past. It's human nature to think, "Boy, that guy is tough. If he's that strong on this hill, I'll never catch him," although the flip side of this coin is knowing that someone who passes you is going full bore and probably won't be able to keep it up long.

One danger of skiing alone in races, especially long ones, is a tendency to lull yourself into a comfortable pace. If you force yourself to hang with a faster skier for a couple of minutes, especially if you concentrate on relaxing and being smooth, you'll often find it just as easy to go at the faster pace. Also, it is somewhat easier to follow than to lead. Tucked in behind someone, you can watch their steps and try to improve on them. On downhills you benefit slightly from drafting the leader. And most important, the leader usually thinks the follower is just coasting effortlessly while he does all the work. But a smart, confident leader can break a race wide open by pulling away from the rest of the field at a tactically advantageous location. Twisty, turny sections of wooded trail are great for this: Turn on the jets for a couple hundred meters and you are out of sight, which will give you a tremendous psychological advantage.

Ski racing is similar to cycling in that both sports have what amounts to aerobic rests on the downhills, although they are unquestionably endurance sports with competitions often lasting an hour or more. If you look at a long event such as a 30K or 50K race in its entirety, you may be tempted to plod along at a steady pace, especially after you get tired. If, however, you study the course profile and envisage the race as a series of sprints and recoveries, you will have small, manageable segments that are more easily digested. Not only will you be better able to concentrate your effort on the uphills, you will also be able to reap the full rewards of a restful downhill. You may have five kilometers remaining of a difficult race, but psychologically it seems easier if you think of it as only two more sprints and recoveries.

Here is one more mental trick that will pay rich dividends. Imagine that the crest of each hill is about fifty feet over the actual top. If you continue to push well over the summit of each climb until gravity and inertia take over, you will gain seconds on each hill, compared with the average skier who struggles to the top, takes a deep breath in relief (while losing all momentum), then double poles down the other side. Use the same approach for the finish line. If we regard it as the end of the race, most of us will subconsciously begin to let up as we approach it. If you imagine the line twenty-five feet or so beyond the actual finish, you will tend to keep charging at top effort right through the line, saving perhaps a few seconds.

At the finish of the Olympic 50K race in Lake Placid, an exhausted Norwegian coasted across the final few meters of flat and through the finish

Sue Long of the United States in the 1985 World Championships in Seefeld, Austria. This is what ski racing is all about: not just excellent technique and competitive drive, but also the thrill of being part of a world-class event. Eric Evans

line. A moment later the huge electronic scoreboard flashed his name in fourth place, only a couple of seconds out of third. Boy, did he come to life fast, shouting and waving in angry frustration! Had he charged up the last gradual climb and raced for an imaginary spot twenty-five feet beyond the timing light, he surely would have taken home the bronze medal.

Enjoyment

When all is said and done, the single most essential prerequisite for success is that you enjoy ski racing. Far too often, as our commitment increases, the line between avocation and vocation becomes blurred. For many elite-level racers ski competition is a job, with the stresses, disappointments, setbacks, conflicts, and discouragements of any other job. But even at that level the true champions sincerely love what they are doing. They have developed innovative, creative methods of maintaining their interest and motivation. Quite simply, there is nothing they would rather be doing than skiing.

The joy that comes from doing something well does not just happen; it is developed. If you learn to celebrate your skiing, along with the training that supports it, you will be very satisfied with the results. Approach crummy, rainy days and difficult snow conditions as tests of your mental toughness. You can return from a workout sopping wet and physically exhausted but still euphoric because you met the challenge of Mother Nature and persevered. When you come right down to it, life itself is a long string of small daily victories and defeats. With the correct psychological approach, you can make every workout a personal victory. Celebrate your good health, rejoice in a crystal-clear day or a two-foot snowfall, and let your joy of being in the outdoors infuse everything else you do. Remember what Otto Schniebs said: "Skiing is not just a sport, skiing is a way of life!"

12: Östersund

THE TRAIN SWAYED rythmically, heading north through the heart of Sweden. I was in a spotlessly clean, comfortable compartment with only a few other passengers. It was March 9, and I had flown through the previous night from New York to Stockholm, taken a bus to Uppsala, and was finally on the last stage of my journey to the World Masters Ski Championship in Östersund. Even looking into people's backyards from the train, the landscape was impressive: carefully maintained fields and fences; neat barns, sheds, and homes; and coniferous forests that had been cared for like garden plots. There were woodpiles that made me wonder if each piece had been individually fit and numbered, and sitting in driveways were ancient Volvos that should have been in antique museums. I was privately embarrassed over what a Swedish tourist taking the Amtrak Montrealer through Vermont might think of our backyards.

Although the race organizers had assured me by phone that there was no problem with snow in Östersund, the scenery outside the train window was not encouraging. Europe was in the midst of its worst winter in terms of snowfall in modern history. Famous resorts in the Alps had no skiing at all, and several World Cup races had been first relocated and ultimately canceled. I was two hours north of Uppsala, Sweden, farther north than Anchorage, Alaska, and I was looking at bare ground! In fact, the only thing white I'd seen since I'd boarded the train was a flock of snow geese landing in a dark frozen marsh, reminiscent of an Andrew Wyeth scene. But I didn't panic; I'd been to enough race sites when there was no snow to be seen anywhere around only to discover that the race organizers had pulled off the impossible. It was easier to get up for the races psychologically, however, if you drove to the site through two-foot snow banks.

Competing at Östersund hadn't originally been part of my plan. When the idea of racing through the winter had materialized, I had thought that competing at the National Masters Championships would be an appropriate goal, since I hadn't raced seriously for a long time, I had gotten a late start on a regular training schedule, and I wasn't overly optimistic about my skating ability. I had known the 1990 World Masters Championships would be held in Sweden, which was one reason I didn't originally include them in my plan.

Most Scandinavians would be within driving distance, and the Central Europeans would be only a short plane flight away. There would be some very impressive forty-year-old Europeans who had probably been training for a hometown advantage for a couple of years. I didn't need to spend all that money to travel all that distance just to get my clock cleaned!

Then I learned that the races would be hosted in Östersund, where the World Biathlon Championships had been held exactly twenty years earlier. It had been my second European trip with the Biathlon Team, and one of my most memorable. Two of my most vivid recollections of that trip related to extreme temperatures—at opposite ends of the thermometer. I participated in a 20K time trial at $-22°F$. As we returned to the hotel afterward, the van was filled with athletes rocking back and forth in agony, tears streaming down their faces as their extremities began to thaw out.

I also remember experiencing an authentic Scandinavian sauna for the first time. This was not the "warm room and swimming pool" type of sauna bath Americans find at the Holiday Inn. This was the authentic variety: a cedar-lined hot room heated to over $100°C$ $(212°F)$ and a small dipping pool that literally had ice floating in it.

At one point four of us Americans, including our Swedish ski coach, occupied the uppermost (and therefore, hottest) bench. As we sat there, hanging our heads in the intense heat, three young Swedish bucks who had also raced that day entered the sauna. They quickly recognized us as Americans and somewhat dejectedly sat on the bench below us. It was no doubt a great loss of face for them, virtual founders of this form of bathing, to be seated in the lower, relatively cooler position, while the visiting Americans quietly endured the intense heat inches from the ceiling.

It was too hot for any conversation, especially with the language barrier. The four of us on the top had been ready to leave when the Swedes entered, but now national pride demanded that we wait a reasonable interval before calmly descending and exiting for the ice-water pool. We all suffered in silence, not wanting to be the first to give in.

Then the Swedes broke the spell by mumbling among themselves. On the top bench Sven, who understood their every word, stiffened slightly. He casually whispered to us in English, "They goin' force us out, boys, don't nobody move til's I tell you."

Panic set in as the Swede closest to the door casually reached for the wooden water bucket and slowly ladled a couple of pints of water on the red hot rocks. The water droplets danced on the stove for an instant before they billowed toward the ceiling in a cloud of steam. It caught me as I began to inhale and I stopped in midbreath. The hairs in my nostrils curled in the scalding vapor; my arms and back prickled. I was being poached alive!

No one moved. Slowly, mercifully, the steam subsided. But as the cloud dissolved, it revealed the same Swede with the bucket ladling more water on the rocks. The steam billowed, and I braced myself for another onslaught.

I lost track of how many times our Swedish host doused the rocks, but I was drifting into delirium when I again felt Sven stiffen beside me. There was about half a bucket of water remaining when the Swede reached for the ladle again. Sven sprang into action.

With a hand on the shoulder of each of the athletes in front of us, he leaped to the floor like a cat. In a flash he grabbed the bucket from the Swede and, turning toward the stove, shouted, "For Crissakes boys, don't tease us; if you goin' heat dis place up, heat it up good!" And he emptied the bucket on the stove.

I have raced against some fast Swedes, but never have I seen three men move so quickly. In the instant before the cloud of steam engulfed us, all I could see was elbows and buttocks clamoring for the door. As soon as the door slammed closed, Sven ordered us to "hit the deck."

Four grown men lay groveling on the floor, faces pressed to the relatively cool cement like a child's to a toy store window at Christmas. Miraculously, we survived. As the cloud began to dissipate, Sven hauled us back to the top bench. With heads spinning, knees shaking, and nostrils burning we did our very best to act uninterested when, within a minute or so, wide-eyed faces pressed the glass in the door from the outside.

After a polite interval we climbed down on jellied legs and staggered from the hot room. The three young bucks stood naked in the locker room gaping at us. Other men present in various stages of undress simply stared as we did our best to nonchalantly stagger to the ice-water pool, knowing that our knees might buckle with the next step.

Normally the ice plunge is a challenge, even after a hot sauna, but for us it was heaven. We did not pop in and out as is the normal custom but paddled aimlessly around, bobbed repeatedly below the surface, and chatted light-heartedly.

When we finally made our way through the locker room to our clothes, it was as if we had recently arrived from a different planet. Every eye in the place was on us. We were quite a sight, our brilliant red, wrinkled skin sagging on our exhausted, trembling frames. Most noticeable, however, were the ear-to-ear grins on our faces. There is a certain pleasure to beating someone at their own game.

These memories (and others) flooded my mind when I learned the races were to be held in Östersund. A lot had happened in those twenty years: a combat tour in Vietnam, the Sapporo Olympics, high school teaching and coaching in Alaska, the demise of the Biathlon Training Center, Sven's death in a freak accident, the birth of our daughter, a move across the continent to coach at Dartmouth, and finally, racing again. It almost seemed like too much of a coincidence. In late January I phoned the organizing committee in Sweden and learned that the deadline had been extended; I could still enter.

So here I was riding the train toward Östersund and the World Championships, my mind filled with memories of past races and apprehensions about the upcoming ones.

The next morning I was up at seven o'clock in spite of the long hours of traveling, very little sleep the previous night on the plane, and the six-hour time change. I had experimented with the time change. My last-minute travel plans and limited budget had necessitated leaving Vermont on Thursday and arriving in Östersund Friday evening, with the first of four World Championship races scheduled for Sunday afternoon. That didn't provide much flexibility for acclimatization and shaking off jet lag. It is said that our daily routines — waking, eating, exercising, and sleeping — establish a sort of subconscious body clock that helps us regulate energy output and demand for rest. One problem confronted by Americans racing in Europe is asking their bodies to perform at peak output when the established routine calls for sleep. My 1:00 P.M. start in the 30K skating event two days after my arrival in Sweden would seem like 7:00 A.M. to my body clock. The remaining three races would be worse. The 9:00 A.M. starts translated into 3:00 A.M. for my body, ordinarily the time of deepest sleep.

My experiment was to try to adjust to Sweden time before I left Vermont. I mapped out a schedule, back-planning from the six-hour change I needed. It amounted to getting up an hour earlier every day for the week preceding departure and, presumably, going to bed an hour earlier. Like many training schedules, my plan looked good on paper but was less effective in practice. I enjoy getting up early (within reason) so that wasn't difficult at first. But the other end of the plan — going to bed early — presented problems. Family and other obligations, and I suppose my body clock, made it difficult to fall asleep at 9:00 P.M., 8:00 P.M., and then 7:00 P.M., even though I had forced myself awake at 6:00 A.M., 5:00 A.M., and 4:00 A.M. On the day I left Vermont, the alarm rang at 2:00 A.M. (I was fudging the schedule a little at that point.) I'm sure by then my wife and daughter were delighted to have me out of their hair for ten days.

Even though my time-zone adjustment plan was somewhat slipshod in practice, I believe it worked. I awoke easily by 7:00 A.M. each morning in Sweden in spite of the time change and a pretty heavy racing schedule. I'm confident it would have worked even better if I had adjusted my mealtimes to the new time zones as well.

I used my morning run to get reoriented to Östersund, to enjoy the early-morning scenes of the town coming to life, and to locate the cross-country start/finish stadium. The town was much as I remembered it, charming old buildings nestled on the shore of beautiful Lake Storsjön looking across to the

Charming architecture, like this historic Viking church, makes Östersund a popular four-season tourist destination.

island of Frösö. Östersund was joined to Frösö by two bridges, one for motor vehicles and one for pedestrians and bicycles. Under the bridges the thick lake ice gave way to cold, black water. Even with the lakeside park blanketed in snow, townspeople would sit on benches and toss bread crumbs to the hundreds of ducks and geese converged on the open water. I could see automobile headlights and taillights far out on the frozen lake. Every winter a road was plowed across the ice from Östersund to Sandviken, saving motorists a forty-kilometer trip around a long finger of Storsjön. I chuckled to myself, thinking that this ice road seemed a little too risky and frivolous for the serious, prudent, and traditional Swedes. But there they were, cars and trucks of every description headed across the snow-covered expanse of the lake.

The ski trails were about two kilometers from my hotel in the center of town. I figured that the more exercise I got (without putting myself under), the sooner I'd adjust to my new surroundings. I decided to walk to and from the race site. Although Sweden, like the rest of Europe, had suffered from the unprecedented snow drought, the trails in Östersund were flawless. I skated the fifteen-kilometer loop that we would ski twice in the 30K and found it hard to hold back. Not only was the snow well groomed, but the trail had the rhythm of a symphony. There were rocketing downhills followed by winding climbs through evergreen forests; quick, roller-coaster bumps and turns; and sections of straight, flat cruising terrain. The longest and toughest climb, more than a kilometer and a half, was strategically located less than two kilometers from the finish. I was looking forward to some great skiing in the week ahead.

That evening all competitors assembled in the park next to the lake for a torchlight parade through downtown Östersund and the opening ceremonies in front of the picturesque town hall. More than six hundred men and women from age thirty to past eighty assembled behind the sixteen flags of the nations represented. Lining up behind the Stars and Stripes, I greeted the handful of other Americans who had made the pilgrimage to Sweden, where this sport is reputed to have its origins centuries ago. In spite of a relatively small delegation, the American contingent had some horsepower, pretty well spread out over the age categories. Dick Hedenstrom, Bjorn Lasserud, and Arvo Ayranto had each earned a spot on the 1990 U.S. National Masters Team for compiling the best results in their age groups at the Sun Valley Nationals in February; Toini Kanninen had earned a similar distinction in the women's 60–64 age group; Dan Bukley, John Bland, and I had each come away from Sun Valley with at least one gold medal; and both Veli Kanninen (Toini's husband), and Corky Carl had impressive national results.

Bjorn Lasserud was the acknowledged leader of a strong midwestern contingent and was the most widely recognized American in the competitions. Bjorn had just turned sixty and was not adjusting very well to the shorter competitive distances skied by the older age groups. A Minneapolis painting contractor who had emigrated from Oslo as a teenager, Bjorn claims to have started skiing only after he arrived in America. He certainly has made up for lost time. For the past couple of decades he has been virtually untouchable in his age group in both skating and classic. To put his talent in perspective, consider his results for the 15K classic event at the Sun Valley Masters National Championships. Bjorn easily won the 60–64 age category with a time of 58:11. His time also beat the eight competitors in the 55–59 age group, and would have placed him second of the fifteen competitors in the 50–54 age group!

The patriarch of the American delegation was Dr. John Bland of Burlington, Vermont. After a distinguished career in medicine, John retired in 1989 at age seventy-one to devote all his time to research and . . . ski racing! He has won more national and international medals since age sixty than most skiers accumulate in a lifetime. "Why shouldn't I be successful?" he says. "I have decades of experience, training, and competitive savvy behind me!"

Sunday, March 11, was bright, clear, and cold. On my morning run I headed up to the start stadium and checked the temperature. Since the stadium was somewhat higher and farther from the lake than downtown Östersund, I wanted to see how readings from the two locations compared. At 8:15 A.M. in the stadium the air was 21°F, the snow 17°F. It would certainly warm up by one o'clock, probably right into Cera F's range. I jogged back to the hotel for breakfast.

Only after my arrival in Sweden did I learn the actual format and schedule of the races. For men thirty to fifty-nine years old there were four events: a 30K, a 15K, a 3 x 10K relay, and a 50K. In the first two events each competitor selected classic or freestyle technique. The classic races began at 9:00 A.M., the skating at 1:00 P.M. The final two events were classic. I had elected to skate the 30K, so I had most of the morning to prepare.

I could have waxed in a maintenance shed at the start stadium, but that would be mobbed with classic skiers and I prefer to wax out of public view. I scrounged a large, plastic drop cloth and prepared to wax in the hotel room. Now came the exotic part. Before I left the States, I had talked with Max Cobb. He had several varieties of the "next-generation wax" I described in chapter 9, which the World Championships team had brought back from Europe. It was reputedly as good as Cera F but in several conditions, not just a narrow range. The stuff was largely untested and frightfully expensive. Max had been given a modest selection of the new wax to test in the remaining races of the Domestic Series. Just as I was about to swallow my pride and ask, Max offered: "Morty, would you be willing to take some samples of this stuff to Sweden and give it a try?" Now is that loyalty to your old coach or what? So with five small containers the size of aspirin bottles, sketchy handwritten instructions with vague recommendations about temperature ranges and snow consistency, and confidence that I would have wax as fast as or faster than any of my competitors, I headed to Sweden.

But these exotic new fluorocarbon waxes complicated the process significantly. First it was necessary to apply a base, or cushion. Solda orange had worked well for me at the White Mountain Marathon and the 50K Championship at Sun Valley. I ironed it in, let it dry, and scraped gently. Then I checked the bottles Max had given me. I still anticipated the temperature to be around 32°F by start time, and it looked as though MO 50 was the correct choice. I had a moment of serious doubt. I had won two important races on the Solda orange and Cera F; now, at what might be considered the most important race of all, I was ready to switch to a wax I had never used. In fact, I hadn't even talked to athletes who had used it. All the reports through Max were third- or fourthhand.

In the end I decided to risk it. Max had gone out on a limb to give me some of the stuff to test; the least I could do was use it. After all, most of these masters would have access to Cera F; perhaps MO 50 would give me a slight advantage over them. I ironed, lightly scraped, and brushed my skis before walking up to the racecourse.

After the morning's classic race the trail had been regroomed to perfection. It was a joy to ski. The majority of competitors had elected to race classic, so the organizers had lumped the first three age groups of skaters into the same mass start. This made for an impressive crowd at the starting line: eleven in the 30–34 group, seventeen in the 35–39 group, and twenty-four in my 40–44 age group. Not only did it add traffic at the start, but since the bibs did not designate age groups, there was no easy way of knowing how you were doing among your peers (I certainly expected to be well behind several of the guys in their thirties).

The gun went off and we were a herd of knees, elbows, splayed skis, and flailing poles as we scrambled across the stadium toward the opening in the woods. I avoided major mishap but got tangled up enough to be closer to the rear than the front of the herd as we funneled down to single file. No matter how wide or well groomed the trail, it is difficult to pass while skating. I figured with twenty-nine kilometers to go I would take my time and pass on the downhills. Most racers hammered it too hard in a mass start anyway. We rolled through the woods for a couple of kilometers, jockeying for position. There was a constant banter of "Excuse me," "Sorry," "On your right," and "Track" in about eight different languages. Suddenly we burst out of the trees into the sunlight. We were approaching our first major downhill—a long, fast descent under a power line—which had been packed wide and smooth. I could see scores of racers speeding down the slope ahead of me where it made a wide airplane turn back into the woods. I double poled into a tuck, and instantly I seemed to accelerate! The other racers were in two lines on either side of the groomed trail. At what seemed like sixty miles per hour, I "threaded the needle" between them, careful to keep my ski poles from hitting anyone. It was absolutely exhilarating. In the course of just a few seconds I had overtaken at least a dozen other athletes. I held a tight tuck and coasted past where others had already resumed skating.

"Thanks, Max!" I thought with a smile as I finally stood up and poured on the power. This race was still a long way from being over, but it was a tremendous advantage to have such fast skis. What was even more exciting was the mental advantage the excellent wax job created. I attacked the next series of hills knowing I had a chance to do very well in a World Championship race. There was no thought of jet lag, time zones, or inadequate training; I was consumed by the desire to pick off the guy ahead of me, and the next, and the next.

I slowly gained on a tall, strong, young skier who appeared to be Swedish or Finnish. He seemed to be skiing very well, and I surprised myself by staying with him. The reason was more evident on the next downhill when I tucked and glided easily past him. We skied together, sort of, for the remainder of the first fifteen-kilometer loop. I would pull away on the descents; he would gradually gain on me during the climbs. It was a good arrangement. He kept me working on the uphills but without a lot of stress, since I knew he was in a younger category. I did, however, catch a glimpse of three other Scandinavians who were in my age group working together not more than a hundred yards back. Cooperation like that could mean trouble for me, especially late in the race.

At the end of the first lap I was still leading my tall, young friend by a couple of strides, and we seemed to be holding off the Three Musketeers. But as we started the second loop, my euphoria at having fast skis and beautifully groomed trails was replaced by concentration. After all, no matter how perfect the conditions, skiing thirty kilometers fast is hard work. You get tired. And as fatigue sets in, you have to concentrate to maintain your pace, technique, and focus.

With about seven kilometers to go, the young skier passed me—not a crisis, but I knew I was redlining it. We hung together for the next kilometer or so, and I passed him again on a long downhill. But we were approaching the toughest climb on the course, a kilometer and a half of gradual, steady uphill that actually increased in pitch near the top! As we started into the hill, I knew I didn't have much left. The punch was gone from my legs, I was using my upper body weight rather than arm and shoulder muscles to exert force on my poles, and my eyes weren't focusing well.

The young racer stormed by me again, but this time I couldn't stay with him. The Three Musketeers had gained on me, one was pulling ahead of his two partners. If I didn't hang in there for two more kilometers, these three guys would get me—and they *were* in my age group. As we skated toward the stadium I was on the ragged edge. I had no idea of my standing in my age group, but I remembered the lesson I had learned at the Birkebeiner. The Östersund courses have, just at the finish, what amounts to a dirty trick for the racers. You come roaring out of the woods and down a dramatic, sweeping turn toward the finish line. Only a few yards from rest, a warm blanket, and a refreshing drink, and within full view of the finish-line crowd, the sadistic course designer sends you back up a short, steep hill for a final kilometer on the trail. A good skier can cover a kilometer in three minutes, but each time I raced in Östersund, that last kilometer seemed like twenty minutes!

The first Musketeer passed me on the last hill and pulled away as if he were jet-propelled. His two buddies were gaining fast, so, wobbly-legged and bleary-eyed, I double poled for all I was worth across the final flat to the finish line. I held them off—just barely. Yrjo Heinonen of Finland finished less than a second behind me, and Stefan Billstrom of Sweden was only fourteen seconds behind him. We smiled at each other, shook hands, and stumbled toward the refreshment table.

My tall, young racing partner was waiting there for me. He was Tomas Andersson of Sweden and would wind up seventh in the 30–34 category. As we shook hands, he cocked his head and asked in broken English, "You skis, vat vax you haf?" "Solda orange from Italy," I answered. It wasn't actually lying. Besides, waxing is part of the game. Thanks again, Max! When the unofficial results were posted, I learned I had placed sixth in my age group with a time of 1:27:27. I had fantasized a bit about winning a medal at these championships. That was probably out of the picture—the Swede who finished third in my age group was almost six minutes ahead of me. But I had held together and had skied a thirty-kilometer race on a tough course in well under three minutes per kilometer. Let's hear it for multiple goals!

Monday was a training day for those of us who had raced on Sunday but the first competition day for men over sixty. Bjorn Lasserud easily won the 20K freestyle, adding yet another World Championship to his list of victories.

The following morning I was up early, ate a quick breakfast, checked the temperature, waxed, and walked up to the racecourse. My age group started at 9:20 and it promised to be a barn burner, the same fifteen-kilometer loop we had used for the 30K. Once again we lined up for the mass start, this time more than thirty competitors in my category. I thought mass starts in skating events were stressful, but this 15K classic race was no picnic either. There was some pushing and shoving for position as the start lanes narrowed to two parallel tracks. There also was increased urgency, since fifteen kilometers really isn't a lot of distance if you are left hopelessly behind at the start.

As the pack thinned out, it was obvious we were in for a fast race. The guys who led out of the stadium did not slack off or drop back, as often happens with less-experienced skiers. As in the 30K race, I seemed to be skiing about even with another competitor, this time number 129. As we charged up the hills and tucked the descents, we exchanged remarks. He was Stefan Billstrom, the Swede who had finished fifteen seconds behind me in the 30K. Although it wasn't as dramatic as in the previous race, I again had the faster skis on the downhills, so we accordioned our way around the loop. Though we both had been far back in the train out of the stadium, we worked together to pass several other competitors. As the final long climb approached, I knew we were racing well, but I dreaded the hill that had brought me to my knees in the 30K. My hesitation was all Stephan needed, and he surged past. I could tell he was going flat out, but he wasn't pulling away so I tucked in behind him for a ride, thinking I'd collect myself and take him on the final hill above the stadium. Just then, out of nowhere, came a blue-and-red bull, thrashing and snorting past us as if we were weekend tourists. As he passed, he glanced in my direction, and I recognized Magne Mathisen, a Norwegian from our hotel. The hours he had spent waxing and scraping his new skis in the stairwell of the Brittania the previous night were paying off!

I saw my chance and switched tracks to tail Magne the rest of the way up the hill. But Stefan would not be dropped. We roared into the stadium, three tight tucks so close together that if Magne had fallen, we would have piled into him. Up that final frustrating hill out of the stadium, Magne began to pull away and I could feel the Swede right on my tail. We had worked so well together for most of the race that I didn't want to spoil his chance to catch the Norwegian, so I stepped out of the track to let him go by. It was probably a mistake. He was as spent as I was and didn't shoot past as I expected, and I lost my momentum and was a couple of strides behind when I hopped back in the tracks. That's the way it stayed to the finish: Magne the Norwegian, three seconds behind him Stefan the Swede, and six seconds later Morty the American. It's tough to drop a place so close to the finish, but I couldn't complain about the race. I finished thirteenth of thirty-two in my age group with a time of 43:55. Once again I was well under three minutes per kilometer. Interestingly, my sixth place in the 30K had been 92.4 percent of the top three, while my thirteenth place in the 15K was 94.7 percent of the top three: a perfect

Bjorn Lasserud and Dick Hedenstrom, 1990 World Champions and international sports ambassadors for the United States, are role models for young skiers across the nation.

example of better performance being camouflaged by a stronger and larger field of racers.

The real excitement of the day was that Dick Hedenstrom had moved up from silver to gold in the 15K skating event. There were now two World Champions at the Hotel Brittania — and they were both Americans!

Wednesday brought more training for the young bucks and the 15K for the guys over sixty. Brad Peterson and I tested a couple of kick waxes and toured the 10K relay loop before cheering on Bjorn in his event. Once again he was unchallenged: two races, two gold medals!

The next morning the weather had taken an ominous turn. There was a strong, warm wind, the temperature in the stadium was 34°F at 8:00 A.M., and the snow was getting wet. Brad and I had joined forces with Californian P. J. Downey so the United States would have a team in the 40–49 age group of the 3 x 10K relay. We agreed that our goal in the relay was to have fun. There would certainly be Scandinavian teams going for broke, so our chances for a medal were remote. Brad and P. J. would be heading to Norway along with Bjorn to compete in the Norwegian Birkebeiner on Saturday, and I was entered in the 50K World Masters Championship, also on Saturday, so we weren't interested in killing ourselves in the relay.

Brad volunteered to lead off, P. J. would go second, and I was to ski anchor. As the start drew near, Brad walked deliberately into the wax building. The temperature was warming so fast it didn't make sense for me to wax until the last minute, so I had set up my ski vises and was helping Brad and P. J. find something that worked.

"What's the story, Brad?" I asked, sensing his frustration.

"This stuff isn't working; it's slow and slips."

"Slap those boards right up here and go take a pee. They'll be ready when you get back." I quickly scraped and torched the klister and pine-needle mess off Brad's skis. All waxing involves a certain amount of risk. Rummaging through my wax box, I pulled out a tube of Rex OI, hoping it would be fast but still grip on the new, wet snow that was quickly glazing as racers warmed up. The skis were waxed when Brad returned, and he shouted over his shoulder as he jogged toward the starting line, "What'd ya put on 'em?"

"Special secret concoction just for these conditions—it'll be great!" A touch of exotic mystery wouldn't do any harm. In just over half an hour Brad was back, raving about the wax. It was a good thing, since we'd put the same stuff on P. J.'s skis.

As I had been working on my teammates' skis, the Soviets had gathered around for a closer look. It took me a few minutes to register what was different. I had competed against the Russians since 1969. The Soviet Biathlon Team was well supported: new equipment, fashionable uniforms, ample wax. These athletes, however, were not part of the Soviet National Sport machine. They were destitute. Their skis wouldn't have sold for ten dollars in any yard sale, their uniforms were threadbare and out of style, and their meager supply of wax was carried in old, plastic shopping bags. I didn't see one of them open a new tube of klister the whole time we were there. They would arduously squeeze the last molecule of wax out of tubes any of my Dartmouth skiers would have long since discarded.

When I showed some interest in them and demonstrated my flawless six-word Russian vocabulary, I was an instant celebrity. It wasn't long before I was helping them wax, or at least supplying the klister. Our relay team finished a mediocre sixth that day, in spite of excellent wax. The Soviets—with antique boards, three-pin bindings, and knicker socks—took the bronze medal. I figure I provided most of the klister for that third-place finish. *Perestroika* at its best!

As I walked to the ski stadium Friday morning for the next to the last time, it was almost anticlimactic. Several of the friends I had made during the week had left, either to go back to the States or on to the Norwegian Birkie. The warm winds persisted, making streets, sidewalks, and ski trails like skating rinks under two inches of water. The stadium looked forlorn and empty. The melting snow revealed several months' accumulation of dirt and pine needles. What was worse, the forecast called for even warmer temperatures on Saturday. As I began struggling with klisters, I realized it had been a tough week of racing after a long winter. I was tired and ready to go home.

I half-heartedly waxed an exotic combination of Rode red and silver klister on my right ski and Rode Nera klister on the left. Both seemed to kick and slide in the stadium, so I headed out to tour the twenty-five kilometer loop we would ski twice in Saturday's 50K. It turned out to be a good ski. I was in no rush, the weather was beautiful (though too warm), and it was largely a new loop not used in the previous races. I began to work on my mental attitude, remembering what I had often told my Dartmouth skiers on those days when conditions were so terrible no one wanted to compete. "Look guys," I would say, "there's going to be a race today, and somebody's going to win. Might as well be you! A week or a year from now no one will remember what the conditions were like, but you will never forget it if you win!" The same was true of my situation now. Saturday might turn out to be one hell of a tough day to ski fifty kilometers on kick wax, and many of the racers may have already headed home, but there would be a World Championship race and someone was going to win. By the time I returned to the stadium, I had regained a little competitive drive. Winning the 50K was not especially realistic, but I might be able to improve on my earlier results.

A glance at my skis revealed that they had accumulated dirt and pine needles. Both wax jobs seemed to function adequately, but the red and silver appeared completely saturated with debris. Maybe the dirt just didn't show up as clearly on the pine-tar-colored Nera, but I made my choice right then.

I spent the evening cleaning and waxing skis. The weather remained warm with a gentle drizzle. If it just dropped below freezing, it could be wicked fast in the morning. But it didn't, and it wasn't. As I walked to the stadium, water was flowing in broad sheets across the road. The officials were grim-faced. I knew what was on their minds: "Just pull this last race off, just a few hours more, and bring on springtime!"

For glide wax I had applied MO 50, some of Max's magic for wet snow. But I wasn't expecting miracles. Nothing was going to be fast in these conditions. The 40–44 age group looked wet, bedraggled, and a little forlorn, numbering twenty-eight athletes on the starting line. The gun went off and the odyssey began. I was next to last out of the stadium. I was very much aware that I had been prone to fading at the ends of long events, and that would mean real trouble in these slow conditions.

After a couple of kilometers I began passing people. I was skiing comfortably, concentrating on conserving energy, but one by one I reeled them in. I had no idea where I was among my group, but as long as I kept gaining on the leaders, I couldn't complain. The wax worked well, and in spite of the miserable snow conditions, the skiing was pretty good. There was enough of a glaze in the track to keep it moderately fast, although it was definitely hard work.

The final kilometers were hard, as I knew they would be. The two top finishers of the 45–49 age group charged past me within a couple of kilometers of the finish. They had started ten minutes behind our wave and were fighting it out for the gold. I didn't have much left at the end and was thankful I didn't have to sprint for the finish line. I ended up sandwiched between two of my new Soviet friends, about two minutes behind Anatoli Kalbin and thirty seconds ahead of Boris Efimov. I had finished eighth in my age group, not as good as my sixth-place skating race, but somewhat better than my thirteenth place in the classic 15K. But I was happy; the results were almost irrelevant. I had approached the event tired and discouraged, had even considered sitting it out. But I had started and, in fact, skied into it pretty well, pacing myself for a solid result among the best guys my age in the world. It would have been great to be heading home with a medal, but given the quality of the competitors, the depth of the field, and my own sporadic training, medals were unreasonable this time around. More important, I had enjoyed a wonderful reacquaintance with the beautiful Östersund, Sweden. I had also made many new friends, who were inspiring not only in their training or racing capabilities but also in their perspectives on life.

Perhaps this is best illustrated by a conversation I had with one of my Brittania friends, Alfred Ornot, a gregarious banker from Munich, West Germany. As a young boy in Poland he had been a promising bicycle racer. But he refused to join the appropriate political youth group and thus was never named to the top team, even though he routinely beat members of that team. Eventually he defected through Yugoslavia and Austria to West Germany. A German cycling club welcomed him, helped with equipment, and was a source of friends. Alfred is now a successful computer programmer for a Munich bank, still competes internationally in cycling, and skis in the winter to keep fit.

As we said good-bye in his room, I noticed a Russian samovar on his desk. "Oh, Alfred, you've been trading with the Soviets!" I said.

"Yah, I trade everysing: skis, boots, poles, vax, suit! Say haf nothing! I can get more in Munich, but zem?" He shrugged.

Here was a guy who hadn't been able to pursue an athletic career in his homeland because the USSR had imposed its Communist system on Poland, but years later he gave hundreds of dollars' worth of ski equipment to a group of Soviets he had known for less than a week! That's what these Championships were all about.

Date	Race and Site	Distance/ Technique	Result	Time/ KM	% Back
1/6/90	Lawrence Loppet Lake Placid, NY	48 KM FS	2nd M III	3:24	86.3
1/14/90	Eastern Super Series Putney, VT	8.5 KM FS	36th overall	2:48	87.6
1/20/90	Eastern Super Series Farmington, ME	7.5 KM CL	20th overall	3:18	89.4
1/21/90	Eastern Super Series Farmington, ME	15 KM FS	28th overall	3:37	85.6
1/27/90	White Mountain Marathon Waterville Valley, NH	26 KM FS	1st over 40	2:45	88.2
2/5/90	National Masters Champ. Sun Valley, ID	30 KM FS	3rd M III	2:44	91.6
2/7/90	National Masters Champ. Sun Valley, ID	15 KM CL	2nd M III	3:24	94.5
2/8/90	National Masters Champ. Sun Valley, ID	3 x 5 KM relay FS	2nd team	3:12	93.4 (ind)
2/10/90	National Masters Champ. Sun Valley, ID	50 KM FS	1st over 40	2:58	95.7
2/18/90	Whitaker Woods Qualifier North Conway, NH	10 KM FS	1st Master	3:07	94.5
2/19/90	Washington's Birthday Race Putney, VT	16 KM CL	1st Master	3:55	97.3
2/24/90	American Birkebeiner Hayward, WI	55 KM FS	3rd over 40	3:10	87.6
3/11/90	World Masters Champ. Östersund, Sweden	30 KM FS	6th M III	2:56	88.7
3/13/90	World Masters Champ. Östersund, Sweden	15 KM CL	13 M III	2:54	88.5
3/15/90	World Masters Champ. Östersund, Sweden	3 x 5 KM relay FS	6th team 3rd my leg	3:12	88.5
3/17/90	World Masters Champ. Östersund, Sweden	50 KM CL	8th M III	3:24	88.2

13: Conclusion

A N IMPORTANT, THOUGH often forgotten aspect of any training program is end-of-the-season evaluation — taking a good, long look at a program to determine what went right and what should be done differently. It is the best way to study goals and modify them, discarding the ones that have proved to be irrelevant and replacing them with others that should provide motivation and contribute toward success.

As I mentioned earlier, before I was too far into this project in September 1989, I settled on four mutually supportive goals for the season. I wanted to improve my USSA point ranking by at least 25 percent, from a spring 1989 ranking of 19.81 points to something under 15 points on the spring 1990 list; to be able to race consistently at three minutes per kilometer or better during the 1990 season; to have my percent back from the winners be above 90 every time I raced; and to win at the Masters National Championships in Sun Valley.

As I evaluated the season's results, I was pleasantly surprised. When the USSA National Points ranking list arrived in the late spring, I was happy to see that my national points had improved to 14.56. As an added bonus I was ranked at the top of my age group (Masters III, 40–44 years old); in fact, I finished the season ranked number one in the nation for men over forty!

I'm the first to admit that USSA points don't tell the whole story. Alan Watson was ranked second in the Masters III category, with points of 15.67, yet the two times we competed head to head in Sun Valley he beat me. Bob Rosso, who beat me in the 30K at Sun Valley, was ranked third in our age group with 16.80, and my Alaskan friend Tom Corbin, who nipped me by ten seconds at the Birkebeiner, was ranked seventh with 20.27. But this system is designed to reflect season-long results. And though it's not perfect, it's reasonably accurate in general terms. My point-improvement goal may have been somewhat arbitrary, but I definitely felt a sense of satisfaction in having accomplished it. Ending the season as the top-ranked male over forty in the nation was an exciting and unexpected plus.

To determine how I had fared with my second and third goals — time per kilometer and percent back — I had to dig out my training log and summarize racing results. When considering times per kilometer it is important to remember that courses often vary considerably from their stated distance — a

10K race may actually measure 8.6 kilometers—and inaccurate distances can throw off your calculations considerably. Also, there can be significant variation in rate between freestyle and classic technique and with different snow conditions. My fastest time per kilometer, 2:44, was during the 30K skating race at the Sun Valley Masters National Championships on cold, fast, packed powder. In contrast, my pace was 3:55 per kilometer in the Washington's Birthday race in Putney, a classic event in wet, corn snow on a thick layer of klister. So time per kilometer is somewhat arbitrary and valuable only in the general sense.

During the season I had raced in sixteen events: ten skating and six classic. My average for all sixteen was about 3:10 per kilometer. I averaged 3:23 per kilometer in the classic races and 3:04 in the skating races. Six of the sixteen times I raced I was under my goal of 3:00 per kilometer. What all this means is that I had fallen short of my second goal.

My third goal, to finish within 90 percent of the winners, was also somewhat arbitrary. For my college racers, percent back was helpful because, although sites, techniques, snow conditions, and course lengths varied, the participants remained pretty constant. My race schedule, however, involved several different "casts of characters." So I admitted up front that this goal would have questionable validity, and I adopted the following guidelines.

I figured my percent back from the top three *Americans* in the race, ignoring age groups. The World Masters Championships were an exception; there I figured from the top three men in the entire competition. Of the sixteen races, my worst performance based upon percent back was in the first one, the Lawrence Loppet at Lake Placid, with a score of 86.3 percent. My best was in the Washington's Birthday race, in which I scored 97.3 percent. Interestingly, that same race was my slowest per kilometer of the season; my percent back shows that I still did well relative to the rest of the field in those difficult conditions. My average percent back for all sixteen races turned out to be 90.35. In the classic races my average percent back was 91.06; in the skating races, 89.92. These statistics cannot be taken too seriously since I competed at several different levels throughout the winter, but they do show some trends within the season that I believe are valuable. My racing improved throughout the winter until the Birkebeiner, after which my results began to fade. In retrospect, that is not surprising since I had lacked a strong base of consistent endurance training throughout the off-season. In general terms I had accomplished my third goal.

The most specific goal I had established was to win at the Masters Nationals. In some ways it was the most naive challenge of all—I had very little experience racing at that level and knew almost no one racing in my age group. And yet in some ways it was my most powerful goal. After the 30K at

Sun Valley, in which I was beaten by Watson and Rosso, I knew it would not be easy; but I felt the goal was still achievable. The 15K race, in which I finished ahead of Bob and only nine seconds behind Alan only intensified my motivation. More than any other goal, it was the vision of winning a national Championship that fueled me during the 50K. If carefully selected, clearly stated, and only slightly out of reach, a specific goal like winning a National Championship is probably the most powerful one you can define. I'm quite certain if I had gone to Sun Valley with the intention of just doing my best and seeing what happened, I would not have come home with a gold medal.

So I achieved three of my four goals. That's not bad — I'm thrilled to have hit that many. In fact, that's probably the way it should be; if you always succeed in reaching your goals right on schedule, they probably aren't challenging enough. Would I simply modify my existing four goals for next season? Probably not. For one thing, I may not be able to devote the time, energy, and finances to racing all winter again for a while, if ever. Furthermore, I think I've learned the power of specific goals: win the National Championships, earn a spot on the Olympic Team, or finish the season number one in my age group on the USSA point list.

Beyond looking at race results and reevaluating goals, it is equally important to review the program that produced those results. Remember the Olympic rings in the preface?

With your results in mind, now is a great time to thumb back through your training log, make some notes, and analyze which aspects of the program went well and which need revision. For the purpose of illustration I'll review each of the five areas specific to my own racing.

Again, I was delighted with the overall results of the winter. There is always room for improvement, but considering the uncertainty of this entire project in September 1989, I'm very happy with the outcome. Overall I'd grade the season as an A minus or perhaps even an A.

In two of the five areas of concentration, technique and equipment, I believe I performed about as well as I possibly could have. I've always felt my classic technique was fairly decent. Going into the season, however, I was not confident about my skating technique. I expected to be very competitive with my contemporaries in classic but perhaps quite a bit behind in skating. In fact, though, four of my top five results in terms of percent back were in skating races. There are always refinements to be made — I still have difficulty V1 skating to the power right side — but, all in all, I was quite happy with my technique.

I also felt good about my equipment. Thanks to Fischer and Salomon, I had the latest models of skis, boots, and bindings. I spent quite a bit of time preparing my skis before I raced on them, and throughout the winter I felt that they were usually as fast as, and sometimes faster than, anyone else's. I'm also grateful to Swix, Peter Hale at Ski*Go, and my friend Max Cobb for wax. Not once during the season did I have the feeling I was handicapped because I didn't have a particular wax. On the contrary, at the World Masters I might have had a significant waxing advantage (at least in the 30K) thanks to the exotic stuff Max had asked me to test. That is not to say I never missed the wax, however. The two Farmington Super Series races provided an appropriate lesson in waxing humility. But missing the wax twice out of sixteen tries is not too bad.

In the remaining three Olympic rings — nutrition, conditioning, and psychology — I still have a lot of work to do. In terms of nutrition it's mostly a question of breaking eating habits four decades old. It means really believing that the quality of the fuel put in the engine improves performance. It means conscientiously learning what 70 percent carbohydrates and 10 percent fat mean in terms of cereal, bread, fruit, meat, cheese, yogurt, rice, potatoes, and vegetables — every day! It means consistently making the right choices: a chef's salad instead of a burger, a baked potato instead of french fries, oatmeal instead of fried eggs and bacon, ice water instead of cola, an apple instead of ice cream. I recognize the necessity and value of sound nutrition, and I believe that revisions in my diet can improve performance, but I'm afraid I still have a long way to go before I make all the right choices concerning what goes into my "fuel tank."

Conditioning is the area where I believe I need the most work. In spite of fifteen years of telling others how to do it, I demonstrated several typical failings. First of all, I lacked commitment, that trait that keeps you training on a daily basis through the summer and fall. This shortcoming led to inconsistency — periods of several days where I did little or nothing for workouts. I also tended to do what I enjoy (hiking, running, working in the woods) and avoid those activities that I find less pleasurable (roller skiing, roller board, lifting weights). Looking back on my least-successful races of the season, I recognize immediately that I had faded badly before the finish in three of the four. Fading, or "running out of gas," before the end of a race is due primarily to inadequate endurance training. The same shortcoming is responsible for my inability to maintain a competitive peak from the Masters Nationals in Sun Valley through the World Championships in Sweden. Probably the two simplest ways for me to improve performance in the future are to develop consistency in my day-to-day training and devote more hours to those forms of training I know are valuable but tend to avoid.

And what about psychology? Well, as they say, there's good news and bad news. The good news is that after almost fifteen years of semiretirement, I still love to race! Only once of the sixteen times I was in the starting gate — at the

50K in Östersund—was I not really fired up, ready to give 100 percent of what I had to see where I stacked up against the rest of the field. I also learned a lot about goal setting and the special value of specific goals. More than anything, it was a great psychological victory to win the 50K in Sun Valley.

The down side of the psychology area reveals two closely associated challenges that will require significant work: self-image and self-talk. Any time I failed to reach a goal or fell short of my expectations, it was directly related to a shaky self-image fueled by negative self-talk. My least-successful race of the season in terms of percent back was the Farmington skate race. As the temperature plummeted before the start and a light, fine snow began to fall, I started abusing myself for waxing too warm and with a wax I hadn't tested. As fatigue set in during the race (compounded by the classic race the previous day), I ridiculed myself for not having trained properly. I could have reminded myself that many other competitors would also have waxed too warm and that everyone else who had raced the day before would be feeling fatigued too, but I didn't.

In contrast, on days when I raced well, if I flirted with negative self-talk at all, I switched it right off and focused on the positive. The key to success in this area is perspective—how you see and talk to yourself about the world around you. Am I a middle-aged, overweight, has-been ski racer who doesn't really know how to skate, or am I an experienced, knowledgeable former Olympian and current National Champion with an eye toward becoming a World Champion in 1992? The correct answer is both, but which perspective do you suppose is more inclined to produce favorable results?

So where does all this talk of equipment, nutrition, technique, conditioning, and psychology lead us? What about the graphing of race results, recording of daily workouts, and planning of competitive schedules—what's really the bottom line? The answer came from Otto Schniebs almost sixty years ago when he said, "Skiing is not just a sport; skiing is a way of life." And what he should have added was, "It's not just a way of life, skiing is a *wonderful* way of life!" Skiing teaches us to celebrate winter. It shows us the beauty and splendor of a season that nonskiers often dread. Skiing opens to us magnificent vistas of a silent world blanketed in white that the nonskier will never experience.

Cross-country skiing kindles a deeper awareness in us of the mysteries of the human body. We marvel at how effortlessly we glide through the woods and fields. We learn to think differently about distance and time: almost ten miles in forty-five minutes, more than thirty miles in less than three hours! We are amazed by our adaptability: hill running with poles when it's 90°F in July and ski racing in January at −4°F.

Finally, we learn to see our fellow competitors in a different light. Young or old, male or female, National Champion or weekend tourist, this love of winter and willingness to push beyond our comfort zone bonds us together. An age-group champion at the American Birkebeiner can sit in animated conversation with a weekend racer from Chicago who finished hours later while they share impressions of the trail and the weather and respect each other's achievement.

Skiing is not an end in itself; it is a means, a process by which we can add vitality, challenge, and excitement to our lives. As Baron Pierre de Coubertin, founder of the modern Olympic Games, stated almost a century ago:

> The most important thing in the Olympic Games
> is not to win but to take part,
> just as the most important thing in life
> is not the triumph but the struggle.

I would modify de Coubertin's words to the extent that it is not enough just to take part: We need to do our best. For a cross-country skier that means not just in the race, but year-round — in diet, in mental and physical training, and so on. If you can honestly look not just at a particular competition but also at a year of training and say, "I did my best," you can't ask for much more, whether you finished first or somewhere on the third page of the results. In most cross-country ski races, one person is declared the overall winner. But that does *not* make all the rest of us losers.

A quote that I feel captures the true essence of sport comes courtesy of a determined, hard-working young man who ran a popular, upscale hamburger joint in Anchorage, Alaska. On the restaurant's counter was a stack of printed sheets with the following message:

> To win is important.
> To win honestly and fairly is more important.
> Give the game your all,
> But remember how you win is more important than to win.

Certainly winning is important; if it were not, we would have no races, no contests, no games. But the message here is that the process is more significant than the result. It is the same message de Coubertin expressed almost a century earlier and Otto Schneibs verbalized more than fifty years ago. Cross-

As former Dartmouth racer Kathy Maddock clearly shows, the primary objective of racing is to have fun. Dartmouth College Archives

country skiing exerts a strong influence on how we view the natural world around us, how we interact with the people we meet, what we eat and drink, how we approach physical exertion, and how we confront mental challenges. Cross-country skiing is a wonderful way of life! See you on the trails!

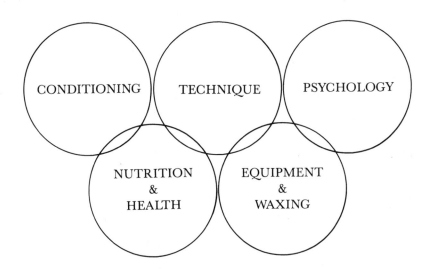

Appendix: Suggested Reading on Cross-Country Ski Racing*

Anikin, Nikolai and Anikina, Antonina. *The Soviet Method of Training for Cross-Country Ski Racing.* Park City, UT: U.S. Ski Team, 1990.

Bergh, Ulf. *Physiology of Cross-Country Ski Racing.* Champaign, IL: Human Kinetics Publishers, 1982.

Borowski, Lee. *Ski Faster, Easier.* Champaign, IL: Leisure Press, 1986.

Brady, Michael. *Cross-Country Ski Gear.* 2nd ed. Seattle: The Mountaineers, 1987.

Caldwell, John. *Caldwell on Cross-Country.* Brattleboro, VT: The Stephen Greene Press, 1975.

————. *The New Cross-Country Ski Book.* Lexington, MA: The Stephen Greene Press/Pelham Books, 1988.

Clark, Nancy. *Nancy Clark's Sports Nutrition Guide Book.* Champaign, IL: Leisure Press, 1990.

Endestad, Audun, and John Teaford. *Skating for Cross-Country Skiers.* Champaign, IL: Leisure Press, 1987.

Evans, Eric. *Mental Toughness Training for Cross-Country Skiing.* Lexington, MA: The Stephen Greene Press/Pelham Books, 1990.

Londis, Leonard, W. Charles Lobitz, and Kenneth Singer. *Skiing Out of Your Mind.* Champaign, IL: Leisure Press, 1986.

Orlick, Terry. *In Pursuit of Excellence.* Champaign, IL: Human Kinetics Publishers, 1980.

Sharkey, Brian. *Training for Cross-Country Ski Racing.* Champaign, IL: Human Kinetics Publishers, 1984.

Sleamaker, Rob. *Serious Training for Serious Athletes.* Champaign, IL: Leisure Press, 1989.

Stegen, Arthur. *Biathlon.* Washington: NRA Books, 1979.

Torgersen, Leif. *Good Glide.* Champaign, IL: Human Kinetics Publishers, 1983.

Woodward, Bob. *Cross-Country Ski Conditioning.* Chicago: Contemporary Books, 1981.

*By no means a complete list, but a good start.

Index

Note: Italicized page numbers indicate illustrations.